# NEW LIFE
# FOR THE
# COLLEGE
# CURRICULUM

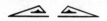

*JERRY G. GAFF*

# NEW LIFE
# FOR THE
# COLLEGE
# CURRICULUM

Assessing Achievements
and Furthering Progress
in the Reform of
General Education

Jossey-Bass Publishers

San Francisco • Oxford • 1991

NEW LIFE FOR THE COLLEGE CURRICULUM
*Assessing Achievements and Furthering Progress in the Reform of General Education*
by Jerry G. Gaff

**Library of Congress Cataloging-in-Publication Data**

Gaff, Jerry G.
  New Life for the college curriculum : assessing achievements and
furthering progress in the reform of general education / Jerry G. Gaff.
      p.   cm. — (The Jossey-Bass higher and adult education series)
  Includes bibliographical references (p. ) and index.
  ISBN 1-55542-392-2
  1. General education—United States—Curricula.   2. Educational
surveys—United States.   I. Title. II. Series.
LC985.G34   1991
378.1′99—dc20                                                            91-19068
                                                                          CIP

JACKET DESIGN BY WILLI BAUM

FIRST EDITION

*Code 9197*

*The Jossey-Bass*
*Higher and Adult Education Series*

# *Contents*

Preface      xi

The Author      xix

**Part One: Reforming General Education:
The Public Debate and the Campus Response**

1. The Curriculum Under Fire      3

2. Trends and Innovations in General Education Reform      32

**Part Two: Assessing the Impacts of the Reforms**

3. Scope and Nature of Curricular Changes      67

4. Faculty Development Programs and Strategies      100

5. Educational Benefits for Students      121

**Part Three: Sustaining Improvements in General
Education**

6. Supporting Quality General Education Programs      149

7. Focusing on Student Learning and Development      176

8. An Institutional Agenda for Strengthening General
Education      206

Resource: General Education Questionnaire      235

References      247

Index      259

# *Preface*

College-bashing, particularly in the way of attacks on the faculty, has become a national pastime. The mass media and academic press have been filled with criticisms of education and calls for better prepared graduates. The popular critics, such as Allan Bloom, William Bennett, and E. D. Hirsch, Jr., have made valuable analyses and pointed to inadequacies that need to be corrected. But nowhere do they give any hint that many colleges and universities are taking concrete steps to strengthen their curricula. The great secret that we have been keeping from the American people, even from academics themselves, is that the nation's college campuses have revived curriculum reform as a top priority.

One after another, college faculties are discussing the qualities of an educated person and qualities students will most need in order to live and work effectively in the twenty-first century. They are reaching agreement, too, about the importance of a broad range of knowledge of history, culture, science, and society; skills such as critical thinking, effective communication, and mathematics; and personal sensitivities to such matters as cultural diversity and global interconnectedness. Furthermore, many are using these goals to design more purposeful general education curricula—courses required of all students regardless of their majors or intended careers.

Although criticisms of higher education, especially of the curriculum, are well known, little is known about the changes colleges and universities are actually making and their results. After a decade and a half of debate and reform, it is time to assess what has been accomplished. The purposes of this book are to (1) provide a contemporary analysis of the public debate and curriculum reforms, (2) assess some of the early consequences of the curriculum changes taking place on college campuses, and (3) suggest a future agenda that includes shifting organizational priorities and creating structures to better support undergraduate general education.

## Background of the Book

As a starting point for answering these questions, I conducted a research project from 1989 to 1991 at the University of Minnesota. I surveyed over 300 colleges and universities of all types. This was not a random sample; institutions were selected precisely because they had been working on improving their general education curricula. My primary purpose was to discover what kinds of reforms colleges were making and the results they were having. Chief academic officers were asked to complete a questionnaire and to send material about their general education programs. The focus of the study was on the characteristics of the revised programs, variations in the kinds of changes made, and impacts of the new curriculum on students, faculty, and the institution.

My views about general education and its reform come not just from this research but also from my own experiences. I was involved in the earliest stages of the current general education revival, directing the Project on General Education Models (GEM) for the Society for Values in Higher Education from 1978 to 1981. In that project, a dozen diverse colleges and universities collaborated to review and enhance their curricula. Project GEM had impact far beyond those few institutions, as leaders spoke and consulted with colleagues at many other campuses. The project prepared a resource guide and published a newsletter that were widely used, and publications summarized barriers and effective strategies we learned for changing general education. From 1981 to 1983, I served on the staff of the Association of American Colleges, working on the project that culminated in the widely read national report *Integrity in the College Curriculum.* My 1983 book *General Education Today* summarized the state of the art of general education and its reform at that time. It analyzed curricular practices and associated changes taking place in the conception, pedagogy, and administration of general education at colleges and universities around the country.

From 1983 to 1988, I held various senior administrative positions (dean of the college, acting president, and vice president for planning) at Hamline University, where I led the faculty in development of a more coherent and comprehensive general education program. Devising that curriculum was the primary strategy for the renewal of the entire university. As the dean, I found myself in the curious position of trying to put into practice the advice that I had been dispensing to others. During that period, I concentrated largely on campus matters but did participate in the study group that prepared the report *A New Vitality in General Education* (1987).

Since taking leave from campus demands, I have been able to revisit general education from a national perspective. In addition to conducting this research project, I have consulted with scores of campuses, participated in various site visits, reviewed foundation grant proposals, evaluated campus curricula, and spoken at conferences and workshops.

I have come to realize that we need a new analysis of general education, one that focuses on the curriculum reform movement. Both the popular and professional literature have been helpful in putting general education on the national agenda and in stimulating curricular changes on individual campuses. Although it is still useful, much of the work described above is becoming dated. *Missions of the College Curriculum* by the Carnegie Foundation for the Advancement of Teaching (1977) called general education a "disaster area" and suggested many useful concepts for improvement. *A Quest for Common Learning* by Ernest Boyer and Arthur Levine (1981) argued for strengthening social bonds by means of a core curriculum that centered on common needs and experiences of all people. The so-called "national reports" lamented failures and called for strengthening key areas of liberal and general education, including the humanities, the natural sciences, and foreign language and international studies. The reports issued by the Association of American Colleges (*Integrity in the College Curriculum*, 1985), the National Institute of Education (*Involvement in Learning*, 1984), and the National Endowment for the Humanities (*To Reclaim a Legacy*, Bennett, 1984) were particularly influential in shaping the national debate and stimulating campus changes. This book builds on the contributions of these earlier works and makes an analysis for today's context. I hope it informs readers and stimulates further improvements on the nation's college campuses.

## Audience for the Book

The book will be useful for academic administrators and college faculty as well as for others interested in the quality of higher education: students, system leaders, government officials, members of boards of trustees, journalists, and citizens. Accordingly, I have tried to keep it free of jargon and technical discussions.

## Overview of the Contents

The book studies general education reform with the same approach that Project GEM followed in assessing curricular changes; it is *institutional, eclectic, practical, data based,* and *action oriented.* The text has an institutional focus because it centers on actual college curricula, not some individual's views of what the curriculum should be. Furthermore, the primary sources of information are individual institutions, and it contains many examples of good practice as well as specific ideas about how colleges and universities can improve their programs. In addition to survey responses, most information comes from institutional publications, including formal publications such as catalogues and brochures and "fugitive literature" such as committee reports, faculty senate resolutions, funded project proposals and reports, and other unpublished campus materials. The book is eclectic because few examples of philosophically pure curricula can be found; most operational general education programs embrace many different ideas and components. It is practical because most general education curricula represent practical compromises among competing values, which reflects the fact that academic politics — like politics in the larger society — is the art of the possible. Additionally, the recommendations are not "pie in the sky" but ones that can actually be put into practice. This work is data based because it presents the results of my survey and draws from other research studies that have recently been conducted on undergraduate education. Finally, it is action oriented because the analysis derives from concrete actions taken at a large number of colleges and universities, and because it is intended to spark further action to improve educational programs.

Part One of the book summarizes the major accomplishments to date. Chapter One examines the public debate about quality education, discusses the central role general education plays in the curriculum, summarizes the calls for reform, and critiques the debate. Chapter Two focuses on actual changes that have been made in general education programs. It discusses several trends that collectively are changing the nature of the college curriculum and mapping the contours of the reform movement.

Part Two is an assessment of those changes. Chapter Three analyzes the many positive impacts of curriculum change on colleges and universities, highlighting the greater benefits from comprehensive change. Chapter Four focuses on the central role of faculty development in fostering effective general education. It describes a range of effective practices and demonstrates that the greatest benefits derive from the most systematic programs. Chapter Five examines the educational benefits of the reforms for students. Reported gains in educational value are greatest with certain curriculum practices, large-scale curriculum change, and substantial faculty development. They also are associated with a number of student support services and nonclassroom activities that have not figured prominently in the public debate. Collectively, these chapters indicate that a rigorous general education program is in the self-interest of students, faculty members, and institutions of higher learning.

Part Three recommends a number of organizational supports to sustain and maintain changes that are made in the curriculum. Chapter Six asserts that we need to train a new generation of faculty members in the values associated with liberal and general education, take teaching and pedagogy seriously, create community and promote collaborative teaching and learning, make shared authority work in the design and implementation of coherent general education programs, and integrate general education with academic majors and the work of departments.

Chapter Seven argues that we need a fuller conception of students that entails understanding their personal and emotional lives as well as their minds, paying greater attention to students' values, responding to the need for greater sensitivity to cultural diversity, and extending the educational purposes of the formal curriculum into co-curricular life.

The final chapter calls for a future agenda to keep the spirit of reform alive. It argues for creating both organizational structures and an academic culture to provide solid support for general education at the undergraduate, or even graduate, level. The goal should be not only a coherent curriculum but an entire campus culture devoted to providing students with a broad general education. To adapt the words of the national report, we should aspire not just to a curriculum of integrity but to a college of integrity, where the official rhetoric about general education is carried out in reality.

## Acknowledgments

I want to express my indebtedness to the many individuals who contributed in significant ways to this book. Richard Johnson, program officer at the Exxon Education Foundation, was the first to urge me to conduct this project. He provided a planning grant for that purpose, which was given to the American Association for Higher Education (AAHE). Russell Edgerton, president of AAHE, and his colleagues were most thoughtful and supportive. Theodore Marchese, executive editor of *Change*, edited and published (July/Aug. 1989) a summary of that project.

Jon Fuller, president of the Consortium for the Advancement of Private Higher Education, and Ralph Lundgren, program director of education at the Lilly Endowment, provided valuable encouragement. They were instrumental in securing funding from their organizations to jointly fund the research project. Although the funding agencies have a proclivity toward small private colleges, both encouraged me to take a broader view and address my analysis and writing to all kinds of colleges and universities.

The University of Minnesota provided access to the resources of the university to conduct my research. Shirley Clark, then acting provost, and Darrell Lewis, professor in the Department of Educational Policy and Administration, were instrumental in arranging for my work. Faculty members throughout the College of Education provided welcome colleagueship. Marcia Finke, associate administrator of the department, cheerfully kept the project affairs in good order. Secretaries Pamela Groscost, Sanh Ngo, Priscilla (Dolly) Soule, and Dolores Wasilak were enormously helpful in a host of large and small ways.

Anna Wasescha, a doctoral student in the higher education program, proved to be the world's greatest research assistant. Her unbounded intellectual curiosity, understanding of the workings of higher education, dedication to seeing the project through to its completion, and persistent good spirits were more valuable than she knows. Her assistance was vital in developing and conducting the survey, analyzing the statistical results, and critiquing drafts of the manuscript.

I was fortunate to form a small advisory committee and to persuade three outstanding individuals to assist me: JB Hefferlin, of the California Postsecondary Education Commission; Arthur Levine, professor at Harvard University; and William Nelsen of the Citizens Scholarship Foundation of America. All reacted to portions of the data and reviewed drafts of the manuscript. Each of them kept me from making some missteps and made suggestions that enriched the final product.

Other professional colleagues critiqued drafts, making important suggestions for improvement. They include Zelda Gamson, professor at the University of Massachusetts at Boston;

Richard Johnson; and two anonymous reviewers arranged by the publisher. Each helped make the result better than it would have been otherwise. Gale Erlandson, editor of higher and adult education at Jossey-Bass, provided important support and guidance in preparation of the manuscript. Her suggestions helped to define the final shape of the book.

Of course, none of this would have happened without the many individuals who are committed to undergraduate general education and who provided campus leadership to make improvements, often at some personal and professional risk. They are the ones who are conducting the "trench warfare" of curriculum reform, and they were kind enough to relate their experiences, happy and unhappy. I deeply admire their commitment and appreciate their sharing their experiences with me.

Finally, because all professional achievement is, at bottom, personal, there is Julia, my wife. This book was a labor of love, and it is a truism that one cannot continue to give without replenishing the supply. She has been in some mysterious way my wellspring; perhaps it is not accidental that this project has taken shape and come to fruition during the early years of our new marriage.

Although each of these people has made this work better, and I am deeply grateful to them, none had the power to veto the final content. They are blameless for any shortcomings that may remain.

*Minneapolis, Minnesota*                                                Jerry G. Gaff
*September 1991*

# *The Author*

Jerry G. Gaff joined the senior
staff of the Association of American Colleges (AAC), a national
educational organization devoted to the advancement of liberal
learning, in 1991. He directs a project funded by the Lilly
Endowment that assists colleges and universities in developing
strong foundations for general education. He is also executive
director of a new office established by AAC to provide a range of
services to institutions—conferences, workshops, resource materials, consultation—designed to foster improvements in undergraduate curriculum and instruction. He completed this
book while serving as senior fellow in the Department of Educational Policy and Administration at the University of Minnesota,
Twin Cities.

Gaff received his A.B. degree (1958) from DePauw University with a major in psychology and his Ph.D. degree (1965) from
Syracuse University with a concentration in social psychology.
He has held faculty positions at Hobart and William Smith
colleges, University of the Pacific, University of California,
Berkeley, and Sonoma State University. He has held administrative positions at Hamline University as dean of the college of
liberal arts, acting president, and vice president for planning.

Throughout his career, Gaff has applied the theories,
perspectives, and methods of his academic specialty to understanding the condition of higher education. He has used psychology to analyze the development of students and faculty and
sociology to examine the structure and culture of colleges and
universities.

Gaff's previous books reflect an enduring interest in the

quality of education, focusing on curriculum, teaching, and learning. They include *The Cluster College* (1970, with others), *College Professors and Their Impact on Students* (1975, with others), *Toward Faculty Renewal* (1975), and *General Education Today* (1983).

Gaff's strong interest in linking ideas with action led him to help colleges and universities make three general types of innovations in undergraduate education: experimental colleges during the 1960s, faculty development programs during the 1970s, and general education curricula more recently. Gaff serves as keynote speaker, consultant to colleges and universities, writer and editor, and member of various higher education boards and blue ribbon commissions. Currently, he is involved with the Lilly Endowment Workshop on the Liberal Arts, which brings together teams of twenty-five diverse institutions to work on campus improvement projects; the Asheville Institute on General Education of the Association of American Colleges and the University of North Carolina, Asheville, which brings campus teams to work on curriculum changes; and the editorial board of the *Journal of General Education*. He reviews proposals and conducts site visits on faculty and curriculum development grants for several private foundations and public funding agencies.

# NEW LIFE
# FOR THE
# COLLEGE
# CURRICULUM

# PART ONE

# Reforming General Education: The Public Debate and the Campus Response

# Chapter One

# The Curriculum Under Fire

Burton Hall at the University of Minnesota was the site of my office while I wrote this manuscript. The names of twenty-four famous personages in the history of arts, letters, and sciences adorn the front of the building; in 1895 when the building was erected this was somebody's idea of a permanent testament to the enduring contributions of these individuals to learning. How did they choose, from all previous scholars, who should have this honor? The question is curiously contemporary, as colleges and their critics publicly debate what is most important for students to learn and which fields of study, ideas, and texts are so profound and fundamental that they should be required of all students.

The chiseled names are these: Bacon, Beethoven, Confucius, Copernicus, Dante, Darwin, Descartes, Emerson, Franklin, Galileo, Goethe, Herodotus, Homer, Humboldt, Ictinus, Isaiah, Milton, Newton, Phidias, Plato, Raphael, Shakespeare, Socrates, and Voltaire. At first blush, this is a wonderful list, but, on further reflection, it is not at all serviceable by contemporary standards nearly a century later. For one thing, the light of some of the stars such as Ictinus and Phidias, has faded. For another, new intellectual figures like Freud and Einstein have transformed our understanding of the world, and the ideas of others, such as Marx, have led to revolutionary changes around the world; they would almost have to be included today. Also, a world in the throes of the nuclear age, the information-communication revolution, and biotechnological break-throughs would include modern scientists. Additionally, America has emerged as an intellectual and educational leader of the world as well as a superpower; it might have a claim to more than two individuals, and, from my point of view, Emerson and Franklin would be long shots for the top twenty-four in world history. Further, the list is Eurocentric; it includes six Greeks, five English, and nine other European figures, with only Confucius from all the non-Western civilizations (if Isaiah from the Hebraic is excluded). No women or American minorities are included—perhaps acceptable for those times, but unthinkable today.

Further, only five fields of study were permanently engraved above the front doors of Burton Hall: literature, science, painting, sculpture, and architecture. The academic disciplines as we know them today were only then being shaped as separate intellectual endeavors, but even so this is a curiously narrow list. Which of these five would you guess was given the most prominent position over the middle door? Architecture. Of course! The decision must have been made by the exterior architect. (A different interior architect featured different fields of the arts and sciences in the lobby.) It is obvious that judgments about the most significant fields and figures are influenced by personal experiences, preferences, occupations, and political views. Answers may be engraved into concrete, but that does not settle the matter—not for different times, different people, or different circumstances.

The point is not that lists like these are good or bad, or that it is foolhardy to try to immortalize individuals and ideas, even in concrete structures. It is that the question of what knowledge is most valuable and enduring is a timeless one; answers change as times and circumstances change, and thus it is a terribly complex issue. Reaching agreements about these matters is especially difficult among college faculties—the bodies responsible for deciding on college curricula—in part because individuals have widely diverse ideas and values, champion different intellectual and cultural heroes, and are trained "to think otherwise." Each morning as I walk into Burton Hall, I am reminded by the engravings that large numbers of colleges and universities are trying to reach agreement about the most important knowledge, skills, and personal qualities their students should acquire to prepare them to live in yet another century. I am aware of the need to design a curriculum to best assure that they acquire that education.

The fact of the matter is that a revival of interest in undergraduate education is sweeping the nation. The 1980s witnessed the emergence of a spirited public debate about the curriculum, especially general education. The mass media and academic press alike have been filled with criticisms of current practices and with calls for improvement. The debate is confusing, because there are many speakers, the diagnoses and prescriptions are various, the voices are strident, and the issues often are not joined. Fingers are pointed everywhere: at students for their lack of knowledge and weak skills in thought and expression, at faculty members for neglecting teaching responsibilities and the needs of students, and at colleges and universities for failing to set high standards and operate purposeful curricula.

The place to start understanding this debate and considering what might be done is with a careful analysis of the current situation. Once the issues are clarified, then we can decide on several specific steps to improve college education.

## Approaching the Debate

The first thing to recognize is that education is high on the national agenda. This is the first time since the late 1950s that the American people have been so aroused about the quality of education. Then the impetus was the threat to our national security posed by the launching of the Soviet satellite Sputnik. Feeling vulnerable to Soviet military sophistication and expansionism, we became aware of the need for more highly educated scientists and engineers, and also for humanists and social scientists competent in foreign language and knowledgeable about far-flung geographical areas of the world. And we fashioned national programs to produce them.

Today the concern throughout society is competition. Fear of superpower military conflict has lessened with the prospect for more peaceful relations with the Soviet Union, the demise of the Warsaw Pact, and the movement throughout Eastern Europe toward democracy and open markets. To be sure, the world is racked by a number of regional disputes. As I am writing this, the United States and its allies are seeking a transition from their victory in Iraq to postwar peace in the Middle East. Other hot spots exist in Central America, Southeast Asia, and Northern and Southern Africa, and as the Middle East war illustrated, modern warfare can produce enormous devastation. Although open warfare of any kind is brutal, these regional disputes no longer seem likely to escalate into world-wide conflagration between the superpowers. The United States must maintain military strength, to be sure, but economic competition has become a much more important threat to our security and to the stability of both the nation and the world order.

This circumstance has many implications, one of which is a concern that our goods and services be competitive in the international marketplace. The fastest growing economies in the world today are reported to be the countries in Southeast Asia, including China, South Korea, Taiwan, Singapore, and Hong Kong. They are fast on the heels of Japan and followed closely by the new growth areas of Malaysia, Thailand, and Indonesia. In 1992 we will see the United States of Western Europe, at least economically, and the European Economic Community will be buttressed by the emergence of the new democracies and open economies of Eastern Europe. That new trading block, largely free of age-old nationalistic restrictions and driven by market economies, will pose new challenges to the United States. Although the United States remains the premier economic power in the world, despite its budget deficit, trade imbalance, and indebtedness to other countries, both East and West are gaining on us. In many respects, the United States is lagging both economically and educationally. Mortimer Zuckerman (1988, p. 68), editor of *U.S. News and World Report*, prescribes several oft-mentioned solutions, including better education, to meet the competition: "America has been lulled by an oratory of blind optimism, as if God were an American. No longer can we lean on our national heritage in resources, geography, and population. America's success today turns more on human creative powers, highly educated and motivated workers, organizational talent, and capital investment, and these can be achieved by public policies and leadership."

Competition operates at the state level, too. States compete with each other for economic development, and leaders have discovered that education is central to this task. Rudy Perpich, a Democrat, was elected governor in 1986 with the slogan of "making Minnesota the Brain Power State," and he was succeeded by Republican Arne Carlson, who in 1990 pledged to make education his top priority. Governors of both political parties in many other states have stressed the importance of high-quality education. This is not simply campaign rhetoric, as many have worked with legislatures to establish policies to strengthen education through such devices as mandated assessment of student outcomes; programs for staff and academic program improvement; budgeting on the basis of demonstrated improvement in student outcomes; substantial financial rewards for academic programs meeting criteria of educational excellence; and other means.

Individual colleges and universities, too, are facing more intense competitive pressures. Part of the pressure is to maintain enrollment during a time when most parts of the country are seeing a demographic downturn in the number of college-bound high school graduates. This pressure is heightened among those institutions where attracting high-ability students is a priority. Furthermore, colleges constantly press for additional state and federal funding, and competition for those dollars is heating up amid needs for environmental protection, drug interdiction and rehabilitation, repair of crumbling bridges and highways, child care, reform of the public schools, health care, and hundreds of other urgent purposes.

A special aspect of the financial picture of colleges and universities is the spiraling cost of college education. Tuition has increased faster than inflation for several years, at public and private institutions alike. The rising costs threaten to deny access to some students, and they force many others to spend long hours in gainful employment rather than in study. Another aspect is the escalation of capital campaign drives. Many colleges and universities, both public and private, have conducted successful fund drives amounting to hundreds of millions of dollars; large numbers of smaller colleges are raising record amounts. Why the need for all of this money? To improve the quality of programs and make institutions more attractive and competitive. After studying the rise in college costs, Michael O'Keefe (1987, p. 33) concluded, "many increases in expenditures. . . can be traced to efforts to improve the quality of instruction, or research, or to provide additional services to students. . . . What we have learned from these six case studies suggests that an important underlying cause of such increases in college costs is that good old-fashioned American phenomenon: competition."

If money is needed to raise quality to be competitive, it works the other way, too. High-quality education attracts money, which allows the rich institutions to get richer. As one fund-raising consultant put it, "Quality sells; mediocrity doesn't." As long as competition exists among colleges and universities, among states, and among nations, and as long as sophisticated knowledge and the ability to manipulate information is central to success in the modern world, quality education will be a top priority.

In fact, education has been transformed in a subtle but fundamental way from a "soft" subject that "would be nice to have" to a "hard" subject that is essential. A cadre of well-educated workers is no longer a frill but a central part of realpolitik in both business and the military. In terms of business strategy, human capital is now as important as financial capital. Consider the following examples.

- Elizabeth Dole, while secretary of labor, declared on the receipt of the report by the Commission on Workforce Quality and Labor Market Efficiency: "The skills of our labor force have not kept pace with the more complex jobs of today" ("Report Says Skills Not Keeping Pace with Job Demands," 1989, p. A6).

- The *Wall Street Journal* (1990) was more blunt, as its headline for a special education supplement read, "Smarter jobs, dumber workers."
- The *Economist* ("Education: Bossy Businessmen," 1989, p. 21) reported that businesses find it difficult to find suitable employees. "In 1987 New York Telephone got 117,000 applications for 3,000 jobs. Only 57,000 were able to take the company's pre-job test, and only 21,000 passed it. Chemical Bank of New York has to interview 40 people to find one it can train as a teller. That is why United States businesses are spending about $25 billion on remedial education."
- In order to find constructive solutions to these problems, the New Jersey Department of Higher Education appointed the Advisory Council on General Education. This remarkable collection of corporate and academic leaders concluded (1990, p. 29) that "a substantial convergence has emerged between the academic and economic communities, both in their growing concern about general education and in their definition of those aspects of general education which deserve emphasis at this time. Because this convergence has taken place around goals that have always been highly valued in the academy, we believe it constitutes a major opportunity to reinvigorate general education in accordance with these traditional academic values—but now with the support of the economic community and with a strengthened hand in speaking credibly to even career-oriented students."

Education is also a key element of modern military strength. A leading economist and two former members of the joint chiefs of staff (Rivlin, Jones, and Meyer, 1990) argue for a "broader concept of national security." Military strategy should be directed away from the threat of Soviet expansionism and toward threats arising from localized military conflict; interruption of oil supplies; Third World poverty; proliferation of high-technology weapons; environmental degradation; and tensions arising from ethnic, racial, nationality, and religious groups. Their recommendations include the following: "The United States needs to get its own house in order if it is going to remain a world leader. . . . We should give top priority to moving the federal budget from deficit to surplus, increasing support for research and development, improving the effectiveness of education and training, and bringing the disadvantaged into the American mainstream" (1990, p. 55).

Weapons systems have become increasingly complex, as the Persian Gulf war vividly illustrated. This places added demands on the skills of service men and women, and Jessica Tuchman Matthews (1981, p. A23) pointedly warns us of a danger. "The military, while spending huge sums for more and more sophisticated weaponry, has been forced to rewrite its training manuals from the 11th grade level or higher to the 8th grade level or lower. Many are aimed at the 6th grade level."

Almost without anyone realizing it, high-quality education has become an absolutely essential ingredient of business and military strategy. It is now a cornerstone of our national security. This does not mean that a college education is important only as a means to economic or military advancement. And it certainly does not mean that all students should learn a trade or that all colleges should become either business schools or military academies. A college education, at its best, broadens the mind, expands consciousness, acquaints one with new ideas and knowledge, sensitizes one about other people, elevates taste, stimulates the imagination, and cultivates the capacity to keep on learning throughout life. It also equips a person, either broadly or more particularly, for finding a place in the world of work. The point is that these qualities — the traditional marks of the educated person — are increasingly needed to conduct the sophisticated, complex, high-tech, and people-intensive work of modern life. Given the rapidly changing technology and the turnover in jobs and careers, preparation only for particular jobs is less functional. A broad general education provides individuals with a better preparation for coping with the inevitable changes they will face, and some policy analysts, such as

Mohrman (1983), argue that it is sounder public policy and more efficient use of resources than to prepare students for specific occupations.

But to say that high-quality education is important begs the question: What is meant by quality? Alexander Astin (1985a) has helped clarify this central idea by identifying three very different conceptions, which he calls the resource, reputational, and talent development views of quality. "In the reputational view, excellence is equated with an institution's rank in the prestige pecking order, as revealed, for example, in periodic national surveys. The resource approach equates quality of excellence with such things as the test scores of entering freshmen, the endowment, the physical plant, the scholarly productivity of faculty, and so on. The reputational and resource approaches are, of course, mutually reinforcing, in the sense that enhanced reputation can bring an institution additional resources such as highly capable students, and nationally visible faculty can enhance an institution's reputation" (Astin, 1985a, p. 35).

These two traditional views do not serve well, because they focus attention on public relations and resource acquisition rather than the fundamental purpose of college, which is the education of students. Further, only a handful of colleges and universities can succeed in terms of reputation or resources, but every one can succeed in developing the talents of students. In Astin's (1985a, p. 36) words: "If it is a given that higher education's principal reason for being is to develop the talents of its students — or as economists would say, to develop the 'human capital' of the nation — then 'quality' or 'excellence' should reflect educational effectiveness, rather than mere reputation or resources. Under the talent development view, then, a high quality institution is one that maximizes the intellectual and personal development of students."

Properly understood, a high-quality college is one that uses its reputation and resources, whatever they may be, to further the education of students. Every college and university can be an excellent one if its curriculum and co-curriculum — its faculty, administrators, and staff — all conspire to cultivate the talents of its students. Astin reminds us to keep our eye on the quality of education students receive rather than becoming diverted by the concerns of some for simply building reputation or garnering resources.

## Focus on the Curriculum

The focus of the debate today is the curriculum, where the most pressing questions of the time are directed. What are the qualities of an educated person? How should a college organize the instructional program to produce educated men and women? What standards should be applied, and what should be required for graduation? How can we assess to assure that students are learning?

The college curriculum, as Clark Kerr (1977, p. ix) reminds us, is "the statement a college makes about what, out of the totality of man's [sic] constantly growing knowledge and experience, is considered useful, appropriate, or relevant to the lives of educated men and women at a certain point of time." Rather than being etched in stone for all time, it is rooted in the historical and cultural realities of the time (Rudolph, 1977). The proper content of the formal curriculum is always a judgment, and that means it is a political judgment in the classic sense of that term. That is to say, the answer is determined by the polity of a college and university: primarily by the knowledge experts, the faculty.

Curricula, not surprisingly, reflect social trends. During the 1960s, for example, colleges tended to relax graduation requirements and to give students more freedom of choice, when pressed by student and faculty activists to be allowed to "do their own thing." During the 1970s, afflicted by economic recession, high inflation, and a demographic downturn, students abandoned the "impractical" liberal arts in favor of more "useful" fields; they flocked to business from economics, to journalism from English, and to medical technology from biology, for example. Today there is a sense that colleges are failing students if all they get is preparation for their first job. Driven by a concern for quality, more people today think that students should understand the heritage of Western history, learn about another contrasting culture, be familiar with some of the best literary and artistic productions, master the principles of modern science, and possess abilities to think clearly and express themselves well. Such broader learning should prepare them for their entire lives, including their work lives, which are likely to see further advances in technology, changing social conditions, and several changes in career. The college curriculum is starting to reflect these new conditions, as we will see.

Strictly speaking, there is no single college curriculum. There are as many curricula as there are colleges, since each institution is a corporate entity with authority over its own instructional program. Unlike many European systems, the United States has neither a national curriculum nor a minister of education to enforce conformity to national standards. American colleges are diverse in terms of mission, locus of control, type of academic programs, and other qualities, and often their diversity is expressed through the curriculum. For these reasons it is hazardous to make generalizations about "the college curriculum."

Yet college curricula *are* broadly similar. Most have three components: a specialization or academic major, which has a required set of courses defined by the faculty members with expertise in that field; electives, in which students can take courses of their own choosing; and general education, which represents those courses that the college regards as so important that they are required of all students, regardless of academic major or intended career.

The focus of the current debate is on the third component—general education. The criticism is not that students have failed to master the technical expertise of their fields of specialization, that they are not sufficiently grounded in their specializations of chemistry, literary criticism, or sociology, for example. It is that too many students do not possess the knowledge, skills, and personal qualities generally accepted as marks of an educated person. What are those marks? One report (Task Group on General Education, 1988, p. 3) put it this way: "We define general education as the cultivation of the knowledge, skills, and attitudes that all of us use and live by during most of our lives—whether as parents, citizens, lovers, travelers, participants in the arts, leaders, volunteers, or good samaritans."

Although there is divergence of opinion about the specific qualities needed, so that different colleges settle on somewhat different answers, a list prepared by the Association of American Colleges (1985) is fairly generic: inquiry, abstract logical thinking, critical analysis; literacy, including writing, reading, speaking, listening; understanding numerical data; historical consciousness; science; values; art; international and multicultural experiences; and study in depth. This list has been adopted at several colleges, and many more have developed their own quite similar lists.

The public curriculum debate was launched as long ago as 1977, with the confluence of three events. The Carnegie Foundation for the Advancement of Teaching (1977) published a book that declared general education "a disaster area." The U.S. commissioner of education and his assistant (Boyer and Kaplan, 1977) called for a common core curriculum as a way to focus on critical issues common to all members of the society. And Harvard's Task Force on the Core Curriculum (1977) presented the Harvard College faculty with a proposal to overhaul its general education program. Each of these events was picked up by the media, reinforced the others, and highlighted the need for improvements in the general education portion of the undergraduate curriculum. The three events kicked off what was to become a public debate, a kind of nationwide faculty meeting on the subject. The debate continues to this day with coverage in both the academic press and popular news media.

### The Issues

The issues in the public debate, like those in a faculty meeting, are many and various. That is to say, in addition to discussion of substance and argumentation, many things are said for their theatrical quality, shock value, and, frankly, the partisan political agendas of some participants. But the most important of the substantive issues that have dominated the debate to date can be boiled down to four Cs: content, coherence, commonality, and comprehensiveness. As we shall see, the critics agree readily and nearly universally about the need for high-quality education, but they do not agree about how that can be accomplished.

*Content.* The issue of content is appropriately a central one, and, as philosophers remind us, the way the question is posed goes a long way to determine the answer. The discussion includes such issues as knowledge, skills, personal qualities, and additional controversial issues.

Asking "What should students *know?*" leads naturally to the identification of various kinds of *knowledge*. One answer, widely articulated, is that a common core of knowledge exists that should be possessed by all educated men and women; such knowledge has been called "cultural literacy" by E. D. Hirsch, Jr. (1987). But individuals disagree about the particulars. William Bennett (1984) asserts that this should include the understanding of Western civilization; leading English, American, and European literary works; the history of philosophy; foreign language; a non-Western culture; and history of science and technology. Allan Bloom (1987, p. 344), in a volume filled with diatribes against the university, says many of the ills he identified may be corrected with one stroke: "The only serious solution is the one that is almost universally rejected: the good old Great Books approach, in which a liberal education means reading certain generally recognized classic texts."

Ernest Boyer and Arthur Levine (1981) agree that there should be a common body of knowledge, but they have a different view about what it should be. They think that all students should study six topics that are common to all people: use of symbols, membership in groups and institutions, activities of production and consumption, relationships with nature, sense of time, and values and beliefs.

Lynne Cheney (1989) weighs in with a different proposal. From the roughly 120 semester credit hours typically required for a baccalaureate degree, devote 50 to general education and distribute them across several subjects: one semester on the origins of civilization, one year on Western civilization, one semester on American civilization, two one-semester courses on other civilizations, two years of foreign language, one year of mathematics, one year of a laboratory science, and one year of social science.

As some wag remarked, "We are more sure of the length of a college education than of its content." The problem facing a college faculty is not the lack of individuals' ideas about appropriate curriculum content; it is the difficulty of getting individuals with very different ideas to agree on the single best course of study. Nonetheless, these analyses help to frame the terms of similar debates on college campuses.

Changing the question to ask, "What should students *be able to do?*" calls forth a different kind of answer and points to the realm of *skills*. Much agreement is found in and out of academe that students need to develop such skills as writing and oral communication, logical and critical thinking, computer utilization, mathematical analysis, and formal reasoning. Indeed, as we shall see, recent curriculum changes have emphasized the development of these fundamental skills.

The argument behind a skill-based curriculum has a great deal of force. It rests on the fact that no general education curriculum can cover all of the relevant and useful knowledge; any given curriculum will be limited in content. Not only that, much knowledge is forgotten by even the most retentive of human minds, much of what students learn is destined to be rapidly outdated, and new knowledge is constantly being discovered. No curriculum can provide the knowledge that students will need throughout all of their lives and careers. The most important thing that a college can do, so goes this argument, is to train the mind to sharpen questions, identify basic assumptions, think through complex topics, find evidence pertaining to the relevant issues, assess alternative interpretations and claims, and make reasonable decisions. These habits of thought are likely to sustain students through the seasons of their lives better than a mind crammed full of knowledge, regardless of the fields. Such an education is the basis for fostering a lifetime of learning.

A third question involves *personal qualities*. Given the stridency of the debate and the need to rethink the content of general education, expanding the discussion beyond knowledge and skills is difficult. But a different question is this: What *kind of people* do we want to form? This question recognizes that both knowledge and skills may stagnate and that either can be used for good or ill. An educated person is one who not only possesses knowledge and abilities but personal qualities such as self-consciousness, empathy for others, curiosity, and a sense of civic responsibility. One would hope that knowledge and skills would be integrated into a wholly functional human being. This is what the Task Group on General Education (1988, p. 3) had in mind when it declared that general education should seek: "to foster desire and capacity to keep on learning continuously. . . to develop habits of and tastes for independent thinking by encouraging active learning and independent investigation, and by helping students assume responsibility for their own intellectual development. These programs exist above all to prevent stagnation of perception and to vivify thought and action through continuing reflection." I cannot help wondering how the national debate would have unfolded had we been concentrating on the kind of people we value rather than on the subject matter they should possess.

The content issue generates sharp disagreements on other controversial issues. Harvard University adopted a ten-course required core curriculum that focuses on "approaches to knowledge"; for example, students are expected to study two courses in history, one dealing with some aspect of the modern world and the other dealing with the interpretation of history. The goal is for students to acquire an understanding of history and its writing rather than knowledge of any particular historical period. The rationale is that since students cannot know all of history, they should know some segment of it, as well as understand how historians think. Some such rationale has guided curriculum reforms at other campuses. Similarly, the

University of Chicago has a highly structured core curriculum required of all students. It is based on the idea that since students cannot possibly cover all of the relevant content, the core can help students learn to read carefully, think critically, and discuss intelligently so that they will become independent learners (Wegner, 1978).

In a speech at the Association of American Colleges, Lynne Cheney ("Further Debate on the Core Curriculum," 1990, p. A17) expressed concern that academics are finding an "intellectually respectable" way of avoiding the question of content. She deplored the reliance on methods of inquiry and championed more emphasis on "what a person knows in various fields." The issue was joined by Professor Rudolph Weingartner, who commented from the floor that Cheney was "contributing to the swing of the pendulum from a misguided emphasis on process to a misguided emphasis on content—as if the two were separable at all. I think that the facts you have been retailing are no more learnable by themselves than it is possible to teach ways of thinking without thinking about something."

An intriguing and more extensive discussion of the issue of content appears around the concept of cultural literacy. E. D. Hirsch, Jr. (1987, p. 2) defines cultural literacy as "the network of information that all competent readers possess. It is the background information, stored in their minds, that enables them to take up a newspaper and read it with an adequate level of comprehension, getting the point, grasping the implications, relating what they read to the unstated context which alone gives meaning to what they read."

He argues that individuals become culturally literate by learning a large quantity of information spanning broad domains of activity, from sports to science. He lists the knowledge that he asserts should be shared by literate people and should be taught to students, mostly in the schools. In an open letter, Wayne Booth attacks Hirsch for focusing on only one aspect of the full educational sphere: subject matter content. Equally important, he asserts, are the nature of the students (for example, their family backgrounds, interests, and motivations), the teachers (for example, their training, careers, and lives), and the environment (for example, respect for educational values, resources, and support). Further, Booth criticizes the idea of students passively memorizing isolated bits of information as misguided force-feeding of facts into the minds of students and the neglect of a pedagogy that engages students as active learners: "though you and I both want a democratic education, we part company on what that would be: for you the goal seems to be a nation of *knowers* who can talk with each other about what they know. For me it is a nation of *learners*, a nation in which teachers, students, parents, and the great public would all be engaged in self-education—all eagerly reading and talking together about matters that matter" (Booth, 1988, p. 21).

There is, in fact, wisdom in each of these contrasting positions: The issues are posed as dichotomies, and we are expected to choose between them. But we need not buy into that approach. It is possible to teach both knowledge *and* skills, substance *and* the methods of inquiry. It is possible to emphasize the content *and* the people—students and faculty—involved in education. Indeed, the content goals will not be achieved unless individuals (not simply their minds) are engaged fully. A sophisticated analysis will go beyond a mere list of subjects, books, or isolated facts—however central to the culture they may be—and include an emphasis on intellectual skills and personal qualities.

Another controversial content issue is the traditional knowledge within the academic disciplines, the "canon," and the "new scholarship" that is reshaping them (Kimball, 1988). This issue most often surfaces in the curriculum debates around Western Civilization, that old mainstay of many general education programs. It is a given that students should know the broad outlines of the history and culture of Western civilization, except for those extremists who view it as oppressive. But at that point the consensus tends to break down. The traditionalists expect to feature a sampling of the classic works that have shaped Western culture. Revisionists, on the other hand, cite the need to diversify the study of history, literature, and culture by incorporating new perspectives. The question invariably arises as to whether to expand the topics and readings to include studies of women, ethnic minorities, and non-Western cultures. Some recent scholarship on these frequently excluded groups provides important correctives to the canon, which has been dominated by white males.

The debate is deeper than having a more inclusive curriculum, although that is a significant piece of it. Books, after all, cannot simply be read; they need to be interpreted. Today a variety of theories of textual analysis exists — feminist, psychoanalytic, Marxist, among others. Most of these posit that the gender, race, class, and general orientation of the readers — as well as the text itself — are essential elements of interpretation. They insist that books cannot be properly interpreted apart from understanding interpretative theories. They seek a "transformation of the curriculum" that includes much more emphasis on diversity — of texts, of interpretative theories, and of individuals doing the teaching and learning. Traditionalists see this enterprise as devaluing the classic texts and even fear that the possibility of knowledge itself is being replaced in favor of personal and political agendas (Kimball, 1990). They are concerned that "political correctness" is replacing rigorous and dispassionate study. They want more emphasis on the texts and less on interpretative analysis. The argument continues with many variations and all manner of players: traditionalists, feminists, African Americans, Native Americans, non-Westerners, gays, and others.

Diane Ravitch (1990, p. 353) has provided a pragmatic way of cutting through the arguments about multiculturalism. "As cultural controversies arise, educators must adhere to the principle of 'E Pluribus Unum.' That is, they must maintain a balance between the demands of the one — the nation of which we are common citizens — and the many — the varied histories of the American people. It is not necessary to denigrate either the one or the many." Here again, one can acknowledge the contributions of proponents in each camp and assert that it is important for students to learn about classics *and* how to interpret them, to grasp the main currents of the Western heritage *and* understand the role of women and ethnic minorities, to gain familiarity with the West *and* learn about another culture with a quite different world view. Few people argue against any of these emphases; the argument is over whose perspectives dominate the sense of history. Since the sense of history goes a long way in defining the present and shaping the future of a culture, the stakes in this debate are particularly high.

The practical questions are how to include all of these perspectives in the curriculum and what their balance should be. Often the debate focuses on a single course or sequence, as in the debate about the Western Civilization course at Stanford University, but to satisfy the various needs may require more than a single course, or even more than a single sequence. In fact, the debate on campuses often centers on the primacy of these and other subjects that also have a legitimate claim for inclusion in the curriculum. Examples of alternative ways that all of these topics are actually included in new curricula will be found in Chapter Two.

*Coherence.* The college curriculum, ideally, should not only possess rigorous content but it should also be coherent. The whole should be more than the sum of its parts. Unfortunately, fragmentation, not coherence, characterizes most curricula, especially the general education portion. The core of the curriculum has been likened to a Chinese dinner menu, a smorgasbord, or a spare room filled with a miscellany of castoffs. Fragmentation should not be surprising when one recalls that many colleges relaxed graduation requirements and dismantled curricular structures in the late 1960s and early 1970s and replaced them with a loose distribution in which students were encouraged to select their own courses. (Lest we idealize the period before the student protests, we should recall that students criticized general education requirements as arbitrary, courses as irrelevant, and teachers as uninspired; the protesters merely declared that the emperor wore no clothes, that previously structured general education programs had already lost their effectiveness.)

The authors of *Integrity in the College Curriculum* (Association of American Colleges, 1985, pp. 2–3) expressed it this way: "The curriculum has given way to a marketplace philosophy: it is the supermarket where students are shoppers and professors are merchants of learning. Fads and fashions, the demands of popularity and success, enter where wisdom and experience should prevail. . . . The marketplace philosophy refuses to establish common expectations and norms. Another victim of this posture of irresponsibility is the general education of the American college undergraduate, the institutional course requirements outside the major. They lack a rationale and cohesion or, even worse, are almost lacking altogether. Electives are being used to fatten majors and diminish breadth. It is as if no one cared, so long as the store stays open."

A subsequent analysis of over 25,000 student transcripts led Robert Zemsky (1989, p. 7) to conclude: "We agree with the authors of *Integrity.* In common sense terms, there is a notable absence of structure and coherence in college and university curricula. Our analyses indicate a continued fragmentation of an educational experience that ought to be greater than the sum of its parts."

Zelda Gamson takes the issue of coherence in a very different direction. She declares (1989, p. 10): "Faculty members make a terrible mistake in thinking that setting up new courses or having a core curriculum will solve the problem of fragmentation and incoherence." A better approach, she argues, is to understand the worlds students inhabit, the experiences they have already had. They possess a kind of common culture drawn from the mass media, the world of work, and the family. The task of general education is to draw upon the academic disciplines to help students become more reflective of their experiences and develop the tools, discipline, and analytic frameworks for making more coherence out of their own experiences. Coherence exists in the minds of students, not in the pattern of college requirements, she argues.

Of course there are critics of coherence, however it is conceived. Phyllis Franklin (1988) lists arguments against the *Integrity* report: "It overstated the problem of 'curricular disarray'; romanticized the coherence and integrity of the American college curriculum of the nineteenth century; and attacked specialization, research, and departmental organization. . . ."

Some critics caution that the ideal of coherence may not be appropriate any longer, because the modern colleges and universities are complex organizations, serve multiple purposes, and enroll diverse students, especially large numbers of part-time and adult students. They ask, "What does coherence mean for students who take one course at a time?" They fear that coherence might be used as a justification to impose the same requirements on students with very different needs, that it might become a straitjacket and represent a throwback to earlier times when higher education was more elitist, students more homogeneous, and the curriculum more limited.

The pathway to greater coherence is thus no more clear or certain than the one toward more rigorous content.

*Commonality.* Yet a third issue raised in discussing the curriculum is the matter of commonality versus individuality. Bloom (1987) laments that universities are awash in cultural relativism, where any value, culture, or individual expression is treated as though it were as good as any other. Students — and many of their professors — prize "openness" to such an extent that they are timid about affirming any idea or value scheme. Bloom yearns for a university that stands for something, that produces thoughtful and committed citizens, that teaches students, in Matthew Arnold's phrase, "the best that has been thought and said."

Boyer and Levine (1981) define general education as "common learning." "General education should concern itself with those shared experiences without which human relationships are diminished, common bonds are weakened, and the quality of life is reduced. It should focus on our areas of interdependence, as members of the human family and of a specific society. In short, it should concentrate on those experiences that knit isolated individuals into a community" (1981, p. 35). Boyer continues to develop this line of thought by writing about the development of community on college campuses (Boyer, 1987; Carnegie Foundation for the Advancement of Teaching, 1990). He is explicit in stating that the development of common bonds in a general education curriculum can foster a campus community, thereby contributing to the strengthening of bonds throughout the nation's social fabric.

Contrasting with this approach is the emphasis on the individual, another time-honored touchstone of educational thinkers. Some institutions, such as Brown University and Grinnell College, have reaffirmed their belief in the individual student and strive to preserve student choice in the face of the trend toward common experiences. Arthur Schlesinger, Jr. (1989, p. 1), speaking on "The Opening of the American Mind" at the inauguration of Brown's president Vartan Gregorian, noted: "The fashion of the time is to denounce relativism as the root of all evil. But history suggests that the damage done to humanity by the relativist is far less than the damage done by the absolutist." While sympathizing with Bloom's laments about higher education, he notes that "the American mind is by nature and tradition skeptical, irreverent, pluralistic, and relativistic." Having a healthy regard for individuals, diversity, and relativism, Schlesinger thumbs his nose at Bloom's analysis, saying that "one cannot but regard the very popularity of that murky and pretentious book as the best evidence for Mr. Bloom's argument about the degradation of American culture."

The issue is joined. How to combine the twin values of the community and the individual? How to develop a curriculum that stresses our commonality as well as our diversity? Again, despite the sharp polarization of the debate, it is quite possible to do both. As we will see, we can use creative mechanisms that may make the result acceptable to all but the most extreme partisans of each camp.

*Comprehensiveness.* The Association of American Colleges report (1985, p. 9) not only discussed the curricular problems but also pointed to the way they can be solved. "Presidents and deans must first confront the obstacles to faculty responsibility that are embedded in academic practice and then, with the cooperation of the professors themselves, fashion a range of incentives to revive the responsibility of the faculty *as a whole* for the curriculum *as a whole*."

Given the many and varied criticisms of the college curriculum, a comprehensive rethinking is necessary to determine what students should learn, how they should be taught, and what organizational and administrative support is needed. Because the general education curriculum touches virtually all departments and most, if not all, faculty members, a change in one part unsettles units and individuals involved in other parts. As many reformers have learned, getting the faculty as a whole to take responsibility for the curriculum as a whole is as difficult and controversial as defining essential content, fashioning coherence, and developing commonality in institutions with pluralistic and individualistic leanings.

Despite the presence of a turbulent public debate about education, some college faculties have been amazingly immune from it. On my visits to campuses I often ask whether the faculty has discussed the serious criticisms of undergraduate education in the national reports or by the best-selling authors. Often they have, but to a surprising degree the answer is no. Individual faculty members, of course, have read the books, and often an ad hoc faculty seminar has discussed them. Most often, however, when an institution has dealt with the criticisms, it is through a small committee dealing with curriculum or faculty development.

Even when academics seriously tackle the curriculum as a whole, and many have, changes they produce may be disappointing. Most academic change, in fact, is modest, piecemeal, and painfully slow (Hefferlin, 1969). Faculty members are skeptical of radical, large-scale change, preferring to make incremental changes that are more certain and less disruptive of established patterns. One of the reasons for this situation is the dispersal of authority among many separate departments. Colleges are characterized by "flat" rather than "tall" authority structures, a condition that makes it difficult to think about comprehensive change. Departments have strong veto power but little power to initiate large-scale changes that would impinge on others. Some scholars (Cohen and March, 1974) have referred to this state of affairs as "organized anarchy." Nowhere is this characterization more true than in the curriculum, which JB Hefferlin (1969, p. xx) characterized in his extensive study of academic change as "the battlefield at the heart of the institution."

Even when an institution manages to launch a comprehensive review, with an unusual show of leadership of academic administrators and the concurrence of faculty leaders, the pressure is toward modest change. Bold proposals are often whittled down to tinkerings by the time compromises are made and approved.

Even more problematic is the fact that general education tends to be an organizational orphan. Virginia Smith (1989) observed that whereas the smallest academic department has a chairperson, a faculty, and a budget, similar arrangements are typically absent regarding general education, even though its size and educational significance dwarf even the largest department. Decisions about courses, faculty staffing, and budget are typically made by the relatively autonomous academic departments or schools. This arrangement maintains the power of departments over general education and virtually guarantees that the curriculum will be fragmented and lack coherence. It also makes it more difficult to develop the political will for the comprehensive examination of the whole curriculum or for the faculty to embrace bold, large-scale change.

One more factor is vital to understanding the polity of general education—the lack of *educational* leadership. These days, top-level academic administrators—presidents, vice presidents, and deans—are selected largely because of their skills as managers, fund raisers, or mediators, not because of their educational vision or leadership. And it seems to be in everybody's self-interest that strong central leadership be avoided so that there is more freedom and authority for the departments and individuals. When I asked what he wanted in a dean, one department chair said "a strong dean who doesn't do anything."

For all of these reasons, some people question whether "the priesthood can reform itself," whether the kind of comprehensive thought—and bold action—that is called for is possible in colleges and universities. Yet, as we will see, many colleges and universities *have* brought together faculty leaders with an institution-wide perspective and academic administrators to develop comprehensive revisions of the curriculum. As Mr. Gorbachev saw in a different context, it takes a large dose of "new thinking" to introduce comprehensive change in a dysfunctional system. And, as I like to remind faculty members and administrators, if massive new thinking and restructuring can occur in the Soviet Union, it surely can take place in an undergraduate college. In each case there may be some dislocation in the transition from one system to another, but pain can be minimized, especially if the jobs of individuals are protected and the change has greater long-term promise. To be sure, academics in college after college that have made comprehensive changes, as we will see in Chapters Three through Five, attribute many benefits to their curriculum revisions. And effective strategies have been devised for dealing with academic politics, which like politics everywhere, is the art of the possible.

### Critique of the Debate

After having raged for a decade and a half, the national debate has not culminated in anything that approaches a consensus. Indeed, it has not advanced much beyond where it was at the outset. All critics agree with only one thing: We are not doing well, and we can — and must — do better. But as we have seen, they disagree, often stridently, about the particulars. Important issues have been raised, but they have not been joined, examined, and resolved. Why is that so?

Several reasons account for this lack of progress. First, some individuals poisoned the well by injecting partisan politics into the debate. At an early stage, Bennett used his political offices as chairman of the National Endowment for the Humanities and secretary of education as a bully pulpit to advance his views, and the tradition continues with the publication of *Illiberal Education: The Politics of Race and Sex on Campus* by Dinesh D'Souza (1991), a former domestic analyst in the Reagan White House. These and others sought to advance a neoconservative political agenda by attacking the academy, calling for more traditional subject matter, criticizing newer scholarship dealing with race and gender, and dismissing efforts to teach multiculturalism as politically motivated. Liberals and radicals took the bait, and they tend to reject criticism that is perceived to come from the right. Furthermore, faculty members often dismiss college-bashing by individuals—politicians, journalists, business leaders—who are outside the academy and may not share their sensitivities. Educational debates are difficult enough without inserting the factor of partisan politics.

Second, like any public debate, participants tend to agree most when terms are most abstractly stated. Most agree that the quality of education is not what it should be and that we should raise it. But as the discussion gets down to specifics, disagreements appear. One camp wants to make improvements by diversifying, even transforming, the curriculum and introducing more material on race, class, and gender, for example, and another wants to purge such content in favor of traditional classic texts. By getting specific, it becomes clearer exactly what a curriculum proposal amounts to.

Third, the critics are in some respects like the blind men describing an elephant from the different spots they touch. The American higher education system prizes the diversity of institutions, and few analyses—hence recommendations—can be generalized everywhere. For example, the popular criticism that research distracts faculty members from teaching may be correct at certain research universities, but it certainly does not apply at the many teaching-oriented two- and four-year colleges; in fact, there are many colleges where faculty are teaching too many students or too many courses to keep up with scholarly developments in their fields. Similarly, the lack of basic skills among students may be apparent at open-admissions institutions, but more selective colleges and universities do not have the same problem. One's "feel" for the higher education animal depends on what part one feels.

Fourth, the critics for the most part, are not trying to join issues and fashion broad areas of agreement. They seem more intent on pressing their own points of view as forcefully as possible and getting individuals to side with them than on clarifying the issues and seeking broad areas of agreement. They often create straw men and women, only to knock them down.

Fifth, the issues are often posed as mutually exclusive alternatives: knowledge *versus* skills, Western *versus* non-Western cultures, the traditional canon *versus* new scholarship that challenges traditional assumptions. One need not be a genius to know that it is possible to have both: knowledge *and* skills, understanding of Western *and* non-Western culture, old *and* new ideas. Indeed, a successful strategy to reform the curriculum demands a "both-and" rather than an "either-or" approach. Further, a full education requires some knowledge and appreciation of each of what is posed as polar opposites.

Sixth, the rhetoric has been harsh, blame has been assigned, and fingers have pointed. Consider the titles of some of the important critical works: *The Closing of the American Mind; ProfScam: Professors and the Demise of Higher Education; Killing of the Spirit: Higher Education in America; Tenured Radicals;* and *The Moral Collapse of the University.* Although harsh criticism often leads to corrective action by various other social organizations — safer and more fuel-efficient cars, cleaner air and water, and less discriminatory workplaces, for instance — it has not had the same effect on the college curriculum. Harsh attacks do not lead to change on the campuses; where curriculum change is produced, it is by constructive work of individuals who lower the level of rhetoric, resist assigning blame, and seek to fashion broad agreement for needed changes.

Furthermore, the question that has dominated the debate has been that of content, which is admittedly a central concern. But by concentrating on the "what" to the exclusion of the "who," the question has neglected the reality that education is a process of shaping people — students — their motivations, attitudes, values, and habits, as well as their minds and skills. And it is a process conducted by other people, primarily faculty members and secondarily administrators, who have their own lives, interests, and futures to consider. Some otherwise intelligent people who are insensitive to the people side of education seem to think that they can just stamp out ignorance or weak skills by altering graduation requirements or mandating assessment, for example. A more sophisticated view of who our students and teachers are helps to leaven the debate and make it more productive.

Finally, the focus on the formal curriculum, as important as that is, is too narrow. We know that factors beyond the formal curriculum play a large role in determining whether a student receives a broad general education: the expectations and values that pervade the campus culture; relations with faculty members beyond the classroom; use of learning resources in the library, computer center, and science laboratory; enrichment provided by speakers and visitors; relationships with student peer groups; work experience; and involvement in extracurricular activities. In some fundamental sense, the entire college environment is the effective curriculum presented to a student, and to focus on only the formal instructional program, as the debate has done, misses a great deal.

The debate, for all its faults, can claim several important accomplishments. One is that it has kept education as a high priority among the public. More citizens are more supportive of better education than at any time in decades. Educational excellence is recognized as a prominent strategy for advancing the interests of businesses, states, and the nation. It is often difficult to see support in the criticisms of the educational establishment, but we should remember that criticism, even cynicism, is often the result of failed dreams. Americans have always had a love affair with education, and they would like to believe in it again. The debate has helped generate support for efforts to nurture generally educated students.

A second important accomplishment of the public debate is that it has provided both impetus and direction for a large amount of curriculum change on college campuses. It frames important issues for the campus debates, and the issues tend to be similar to the public debate. The difference is that on the campuses curriculum task forces typically *do* join issues, work to create broad areas of agreement, and culminate in actual changes. Indeed, as we will see in Chapter Two, a good deal of change is taking place, much more than one would infer from the public debate, which, with a few exceptions, seldom includes examples of progress.

Despite the American people's much-cited short attention span, the opportunity for progress still exists. If they have not already done so, leaders of a college or university can find this an ideal time to rethink and strengthen the heart of its instructional program. This is one of those rare times when business and government leaders as well as the public at large join academics in supporting a high-quality educational program for all students. This may well be a limited window of opportunity; it may exist only as long as the public debate continues.

*Chapter Two*

# Trends and Innovations in General Education Reform

Although the national debate has not led to agreement about a specific course of action for improving undergraduate education, it has sparked similar debates on college campuses. This is the most important place for such discussion to take place, because only individual colleges, as legal entities, can determine the nature of their instructional programs. At this level, the debates often are more productive, for two reasons. Although the problems, issues, and themes on campuses resonate to their counterparts in the national debate, the particular local context brings abstractions down to concrete reality. Further, curriculum review committees typically make a serious effort to join the issues, address specific problems, avoid unnecessary conflict, and help their colleagues reach broad areas of agreement.

For this reason, more than a national debate is taking place. Talk is leading to action. Hundreds of individual colleges and universities have overcome the substantial barriers to change and taken concrete steps to strengthen their general education offerings. Some of the changes are large and significant, others are more modest, even trivial. But so many institutions are involved, the changes are so central to a student's academic program, and the changes so affect the education of all students in the institutions that they constitute a curriculum reform movement.

Adding to the movement is the fact that the work on college campuses is aided by a wide range of extrainstitutional activities. Foundations and public funding agencies operate programs to support curriculum, course, and faculty development to improve student learning. Educational associations conduct programs to assist reforms, establish model programs, and disseminate results. All sorts of groups offer conferences and seminars on such topics as the teaching of writing and critical thinking, freshman year programs, and assessment, for example. System offices, boards of trustees, and offices of governors and state legislatures search for ways to stimulate improvements on the campus. Books and articles on general and liberal education have multiplied.

Most improvements on individual campuses are made quietly and out of the spotlight. Unlike attacks on the curriculum, which are flashed in the media, curriculum improvements are not particularly newsworthy: another case where good news is no news. As a result, most citizens, even many academics, are unaware of the extent or significance of the changes taking place in the instructional programs. After studying the sweep and shape of the changes, I can only conclude that the character of the college curriculum is changing in a significant way.

## Curriculum Trends

On the basis of completing my survey, reading descriptions of hundreds of new curricula, and visiting scores of campuses, I have identified a number of trends that point to the directions of change in the college curriculum. As a group, these trends give an overview of the curriculum reform movement. Today's curriculum trends emphasize the following, and each will be discussed in some detail.

1. Liberal arts and sciences subject matter
2. Fundamental skills
3. Higher standards and more requirements
4. Tighter curriculum structure
5. The freshman year

6. The senior year
7. Global studies
8. Cultural diversity
9. Integration of knowledge
10. Moral reflection
11. Active learning
12. Extension through all four years
13. Assessment

Before discussing the individual trends, let us be clear about what they actually are: prominent tendencies that can be observed in large numbers of diverse colleges and universities. Some colleges embrace several of the trends, while others may incorporate only one or two. The trends take different shapes in different institutions; to use the example of writing, one college may require more writing courses in the English department and another may increase the amount of writing courses across the curriculum. Finally, one may cite examples that run counter to these trends. Nonetheless, these appear to me to be the dominant changes taking place in today's curriculum. Collectively, they constitute a general description, a kind of road map, of the changes that are bringing about a new general education curriculum.

*Liberal Arts and Sciences Subject Matter.* Educators are rediscovering the liberal arts and sciences after an infatuation with vocational education during the 1970s and early 1980s. Spurred by the concern for excellence, they are recognizing the importance of understanding history and culture; having a familiarity with science and technology; and knowing principles of human motivation and behavior, logical and critical thinking, clarity of expression, and other aspects of a broad general education. Under the banner of providing this broad general education for all students, the liberal arts are taking a more prominent place in the curriculum, even in professional and preprofessional programs.

The liberal arts were seriously eroded as colleges added a host of new vocationally related programs, and students flocked to them in droves. Colleges that had previously been dominated by a liberal arts ethos found the liberal arts disciplines overtaken by new fields such as business, computing, and communications. Indeed, David Breneman (1990) argues that career-related study has become so pervasive that there are only about 200 private colleges left that can truly be called liberal arts colleges. While there is controversy about some of his assumptions and about his precise list, Breneman's main point about the growth of vocational subjects eclipsing the arts and sciences remains valid. Large numbers of new faculty were hired, often at high, market-driven salaries, which further diminished and demoralized faculty in the arts and sciences. The opportunity to conduct curriculum reviews provided an opportunity to redress the balance.

Leaders in professional programs, too, saw the centrality of the liberal arts to the successful practice of their crafts. Two reports (Holmes Group, 1986; Carnegie Forum on Education and the Economy, 1986) recommended that teacher training programs, for example, abolish the undergraduate major in education and require prospective teachers to earn the baccalaureate degree, including a liberal arts major, before beginning pedagogical training. As the conduct of business changed, business programs, such as the one at the University of Minnesota, gave more emphasis to such subjects as communications, cross-cultural studies, science, ethics, and social science. A report (Task Force on the Future of Journalism and Mass Communication Education, 1989) recommended that future journalists need a broad general education with only about a quarter of their study in professional journalism courses. The Panel on the General Professional Education of the Physician (1984, p. 5) recommended that undergraduate education should be broadened as one way to strike at what it called "the premedical syndrome." "College and university faculties should require every student, regardless of major subject or career objective, to achieve a baccalaureate education that encompasses a broad study in the natural and the social sciences and in the humanities."

These are indications that professionals are seeing greater value in the study of the arts and sciences through general education. Many professionals have concluded that the liberal arts are practical arts. Rather than seeing them as subjects that, in the patronizing language of an earlier time, are "good for students" and make them "better people"—which may be just as true if not so widely believed—more leaders are seeing the arts and sciences as an essential part of professional practice, hence of preprofessional preparation.

The arts and humanities have gained enrollment from more required work in such fields as history, literature, philosophy, religion, and fine arts. Sometimes these are traditional courses taught in the conventional way by regular faculty members. But some colleges have gone further by mandating the use of original texts (rather than predigested textbooks); written assignments as a means of learning to improve expressive abilities and to foster active involvement (rather than passive learning and memorization); or seminars and discussion sections so that students can express, defend, and modify their own ideas (rather than simply accept the ideas of others). Such guidelines are designed not just to emphasize certain important subject matter but to create the conditions of teaching and learning that make the subject *matter* to students.

Other colleges have been even bolder by requiring interdisciplinary core courses. Roanoke College requires three such courses in different chronological time periods focusing on literature, history, and the fine arts. The University of North Carolina at Asheville offers a sixteen-hour humanities core; the courses are The Ancient World, The Rise of European Civilization, The Modern World, and The Future and the Individual. The University of Nevada at Reno has a three-course Western Tradition sequence for all students; students read seminal writers from the Greeks to the twentieth century, as well as study the American experience. Teams of faculty members and teaching assistants meet regularly to plan and teach these core courses.

Like their humanities counterparts, the natural sciences also have been eroded, as the loose distribution system allowed many students to bypass this entire area or to complete a requirement by taking a "gut" course, a watered-down course such as Physics for Poets (although there are some very good science courses for nonmajors bearing this same name). A report issued by the American Association for the Advancement of Science (AAAS), *The Liberal Art of Science* (1990), calls for half of the curriculum in both four- and two-year colleges to be devoted to the liberal arts, and a quarter of that to be earmarked for natural sciences. Furthermore, it says science education needs "radical reform." Traditional teaching relies on "lectures, textbooks, and perfunctory laboratory activities." The report (p. 29) states that "not only are conventional methods of teaching science ineffective in conveying an understanding of subject matter, but also they create incomplete and inaccurate views of the nature of science and the scientific enterprise, even among high achieving students." Science should be regarded as a liberal art instead of a technical field; be more fully integrated into the general education curriculum; and be broadened to include the aspects of history, philosophy, sociology, politics, and economics of science and technology. Finally, it recommends that science courses should be organized around issues, themes, or problems and taught by professors in small courses rather than in large lectures.

Despite their centrality to modern life and to a solid education, the sciences traditionally have fit uneasily into general education. Their more structured knowledge, reliance on mathematics, and use of the first course as an introduction to advanced work has complicated their role in general education. However, more colleges today are emphasizing science in general education. Some merely raise graduation requirements and demand one to four courses, usually with at least some laboratory component. Others are making some of the changes suggested by the AAAS report. Columbia College developed a two-semester interdisciplinary science course in the spirit of its long-running humanities core, using original science papers to show what scientists actually do. Robert Pollack (1988) describes the first semester as starting with mathematics "taught from the ground up," including number systems, methods of pattern recognition, and the concept of a mathematical model. It then deals with the discovery of nuclear fission; promotes discussion of papers by such luminaries as Faraday, the Curies, Rutherford,

Bohr, and others; and concludes with discussion of two fission papers, accompanied by an on-site demonstration of the fission experiment. The second semester begins with more mathematics, this time emphasizing probability, information processing, and statistics, followed by papers by Mendel, Darwin, and Lederberg leading to Watson, Crick, and the genetic code. Examinations are analyses of other science papers. Pollack reports: "Students are able to summarize and analyze these papers, and they are usually able to propose clever and stimulating next steps in the process. To teach science to a class of scientifically naive students in this way permits us to raise the most serious scientific questions of our day in order to examine the responses of individual scientists. Unanswered questions become the norm, not the exception, since the emphasis is on an open-ended process of model building rather than on the elaboration of a mass of 'known' facts" (1988, p. 14).

A cluster of courses in science, technology, and society is employed at Syracuse University, where students are required to take four science courses. After taking two laboratory courses in biology, chemistry, geology, or physics, students may opt for two more courses: Introduction to Technology and The Social Impact of Technology. In these they learn about technological innovations that follow from basic science and then examine the social and ethical issues that arise in both science and technology. Hunter College operates a science course for nonscientists by focusing on a few key concepts and infusing a strong historical dimension into the first course of a sequence.

*Fundamental Skills.* Skills such as writing, speaking, logical and critical thinking, foreign language, mathematics, and academic computing are increasingly emphasized in curricula today. The experience with recent attempts to improve writing is particularly interesting to examine. Writing is an important skill that is central to all of learning, it is the most widespread aspect of general education programs, and it has received a great deal of emphasis during recent years. So what have we learned? That it is very hard to raise achievement levels, but it can be done with a coordinated effort.

The Consortium for the Advancement of Private Higher Education (CAPHE) awarded grants to several colleges to work on the improvement of writing. Whitworth College required a freshman writing course, but the faculty concluded that was not enough. Whittier extended the requirement to two semesters and concluded that was not enough. William Jewell had students take a proficiency test and assigned them to a freshman writing course according to ability level, they were required to take two additional courses with a significant amount of writing, and a writing center was created to assist them. It still was not enough. As one person put it, they tried simply to "stamp out" bad writing and discovered it was not that easy. With the use of CAPHE funds, each of these colleges subsequently decided on a large and coordinated effort to extend writing across the curriculum and to train faculty with the latest theories and methods of teaching writing. What are those latest methods? Some of the basic tenets of most contemporary approaches are these:

- Writing is like a muscle. It is strengthened with repeated practice and atrophies when not used.
- Writing should be viewed as a process rather than a product; the finished product is a natural consequence of the act of writing.
- Teachers should intervene in the process of student writing by providing useful feedback and expecting corrections to be incorporated in the next draft.
- Coherence, logical development of a line of argument, highlighting main points, and providing supporting evidence are more important than mechanics, grammar, or spelling.
- Writing is an excellent vehicle to teach the skills of critical thinking as well as to promote learning of subject matter in virtually all fields.
- Writing styles vary according to the purpose and audience, and there is no one universal "right way"; students should practice writing for various purposes and audiences.
- Faculty in all departments can learn to give assignments that call for meaningful written responses; to give specific,

useful, and constructive feedback to students; and to design tests that involve effective writing.

At the present time large numbers of faculty members at such diverse institutions as Madonna College, Dillard University, Brown University, and LaGuardia Community College employ variations of this approach. The dean at one institution employing these principles said the writing program was the most notable part of the general education program and exulted, "It works!"

Similar strategies are used to teach other skills. Across the curriculum, efforts are being used to teach speaking at Paine College, mathematics at the Evergreen State College, computing at Washington College, and critical thinking at Jackson State University. The argument made by each of these institutions is that their graduates will be seriously deficient if they lack speaking skills, mathematical proficiency, computer facility, or the ability to think critically. For that reason they made a commitment to train and coordinate large numbers of the faculty to teach and reinforce essential skills throughout the curriculum.

A somewhat different approach has been taken in regard to teaching foreign language. Whether or not to require students to acquire a foreign language is one of the most divisive issues regarding the development of skills, with passionate arguments on each side. Proponents assert that one must know a foreign language to get an inside view of another culture, and opponents counter that much language learning is simply memorization and that most students do not go far enough to understand other ways of thinking. And there is the ever-present question of what requiring a foreign language will do for (or against) admissions. Without resolving this eternal academic debate, we can merely note that many colleges adding or raising academic requirements simply set standards (typically facility at the first, second, or third year of college-level work) and then offer the courses to implement the program. Several institutions, however, have taken other approaches. Some have adopted the oral proficiency approach, in which most instruction is oral, students get a lot of practice speaking, and professors grade spoken discourse. There is evidence that this technique is effective, and often whole departments receive training as oral instructors and examiners. Another approach was developed at Illinois Wesleyan University, where the language faculty are developing expertise with interactive computer and video systems and developing their own instructional programs. This allows students to obtain more practice, the essential element in acquisition of a skill, without increasing inordinately the amount of time the faculty must spend with them.

Flagship or elite institutions may take other steps. The University of Minnesota College of Liberal Arts established a requirement for students to complete two years of college-level foreign language instruction. Ostensibly a graduation requirement, it functions informally as an entrance requirement, because students may complete part or all of the work in high school and take other courses at the university. On the other hand, students may take the first year of language instruction at the university, but they do not get college credit for it. This policy by the flagship institution is one reason why over two hundred more high schools throughout the state added foreign language courses. It illustrates how a curriculum change by a single institution can help raise the level of education across an entire state.

**Higher Standards and More Requirements.** College faculties are rediscovering that all courses are not created equal, that some fields of knowledge are more important than others. Some knowledge or skills are regarded as so important that colleges are making them a requirement for graduation. Subjects such as history, literature, mathematics, and science are specified as large numbers of institutions raise their academic standards. Sometimes higher standards are imposed for admission or for advancement to upper-level study. Of course, there is vigorous debate about what standards are proper and whether they should be applied at entrance (where they might assure minimal preparation for college instruction) or at graduation (where they might raise the level of college instruction). Critics fear that higher standards, especially at entrance, might limit access to higher education. There is also disagreement about whether requirements strengthen education by exposing students to areas they might not otherwise take or weaken quality by forcing students into classes they do not want to take. The campus debates are being won by those who favor higher standards and more specific requirements.

Reflecting students' flight to quality during the 1980s, many leading liberal arts colleges have gradually and consistently raised entrance requirements. Macalester College and DePauw University, for example, have seen their applications increase, and they have become more selective. The same phenomenon can be seen in the public liberal arts colleges, including St. Mary's College in Maryland, Northeast Missouri State University, and Mary Washington College in Virginia. The average SAT or ACT scores of their freshmen students have risen dramatically.

The situation is very different in public institutions that have an open-door policy, but even there standards are on the rise. Florida has mandated a "rising junior" examination that students must pass in order to demonstrate they are qualified to pursue upper-level studies, and students in Texas's public colleges must demonstrate proficiency in basic skills — reading, writing, and mathematics — in order to continue their studies. The assumption is that once students recognize they must pass a test to complete their studies, they will master the necessary skills. There is enormous controversy around these new policies, in large part because they raise questions about two opposing ideals: quality and equality. Opponents argue that the policies deny access to students for whom education should be regarded as a right. They also argue that the need for educated people is so great that it is unwise to bar further study from individuals who are enrolled in college. This policy has the greatest impact on minority students, who are the most educationally disadvantaged. The passing rate on the test for Florida's black and Hispanic students is reported to be significantly lower than for white students ("State Notes," 1990). The policy requires those students who, as a group, enter college with less developed skills not only to make the gains expected of more successful students but also to make up all the deficiencies resulting from their prior education.

Although this policy and its rationale are easy to state, they are very difficult to implement. They place an enormous burden on the technical aspects of testing, and there are controversies over which test to use, how to construct a fair instrument, where to set a cutoff point, how many chances a student may have to pass, and what kinds of assistance are provided to help students succeed. Whatever the eventual fate of rising junior exams, mandated testing, or more curricular requirements as a means to increase quality, many proponents sympathize with the sentiment of Robert McCabe, president of Miami-Dade Community College: Higher standards may be the only way to keep the open door open.

The City University of New York is reportedly taking another approach. ("CUNY Officials Propose New Academic Standards," 1991). It intends to raise the level of quality while maintaining its policy of guaranteeing admission to any graduate of the New York City public schools by requiring that applicants complete a college preparatory program. Those who do not meet the requirements will have to complete comparable courses at one of the system's twenty-one campuses. The specific requirements are being determined by faculty members from CUNY and the public schools and are expected to be approved by the system's trustees so they may be phased in beginning in the fall of 1992. Currently, about half of the students attending four-year campuses have completed a college preparatory program, although a much smaller percentage at the two-year campuses have done so.

*Tighter Curriculum Structure.* The trend is away from loose distribution requirements that students may satisfy with a large number of courses. Increasingly, colleges are deciding on the qualities they think educated students should possess, and they are designing more purposeful curricula to achieve those goals. Three different mechanisms reflect this principle: (1) specific courses in an academic field, such as Western civilization or American history, that all students must take; (2) a limited set of specially designed courses that meet specific purposes; and (3) interdisciplinary core courses that are taken by all students. In practice, most new curricula use some combination of these mechanisms.

In 1978 Harvard University adopted a set of graduation requirements that were expected to foster "the 'knowledge, skills, and habits of thought' that are of general and lasting intellectual significance." Ten semester courses in five substantive areas are required. In literature and the arts, three courses are specified: literature, fine arts or music, and the contexts of culture; in history, two courses: one on some aspect of the modern world and another on the historical process and perspective; in social and philosophical analysis: one course on social analysis and another in moral and political philosophy; in science and mathematics: one course in physical science and mathematics and another in biological and behavioral science; and in foreign cultures: one course on Western Europe or a major non-Western culture. In addition, proficiency is required in writing, mathematics, and a foreign language. Further, specific criteria established by a college-wide committee and subject matter subcommittees allow them to review course proposals and to approve courses that meet the criteria. In this way students are directed to valued goals and guided through a carefully designed set of courses. Approximately 150 specifically targeted courses constitute the general education curriculum, down from the roughly 2,500 courses among which students previously could select. Despite the continued criticism of the Harvard Plan, the core courses continue to be oversubscribed by the students, suggesting that it plays better with the undergraduates than in the media.

A very different approach to a more purposeful curriculum is Brooklyn College's highly touted model of general education. All students must complete a set of ten interdisciplinary core courses that are designed and taught by teams of faculty members: Classical Origins of Western Culture; Introduction to Art and Music; People, Power, and Politics; The Shaping of the Modern World; Mathematical Reasoning and Computer Programming; Landmarks in Literature; Chemistry and Physics;

Biology and Geology; Studies in African, Asian, and Latin American Cultures; and Knowledge, Existence, and Values.

During the past decade many colleges have opted for a tighter curriculum. Barbara Hetrick, vice president at Hood College, reported that as a part of the revised curriculum that was implemented in fall 1990, the faculty "adopted learning objectives for the Core and its various subsections. . . . This is important for three major reasons: we can now explain to students, prospective students, and the general community why students are required to take a Core and why they are required to take these particular requirements; they will help ensure that all courses in a category meet the same objectives (it was chaos before); and we have a sound basis for the assessment of the effectiveness of the Core" (personal correspondence, Feb. 13, 1990).

Students at Maryland's Mount St. Mary's College take six interrelated core courses in Western history, literature, and philosophy and then spend a year studying American culture to examine comparisons and contrasts. Many institutions, including Bemidji State University and Catonsville Community College, have tightened their distribution requirements. Often they also provide a clearer rationale for the requirements, establish criteria for general education courses, and empower a college-wide committee to approve courses that meet the criteria. All of this makes for a tighter and more purposeful curriculum.

*The Freshman Year.* Entering college is an important transition, but until recently colleges have been relatively cavalier about it. They viewed the freshman experience with "a kind of social Darwinism," in the words of John Gardner, the driving force behind this innovation. Today new students are receiving more attention to their intellectual and personal development, stronger advising, and better orientation to college through specially designed freshman seminars and related programs.

There are two basic types of freshman seminars, each of which seems to be effective. The first type follows the tradition of perhaps the best known version, University 101, operated at the University of South Carolina since 1972 and replicated widely.

The goal is to foster the overall development of students and assist them to make a good adjustment to the university. The focus is on three topics: themselves, the campus, and higher education. A teacher is expected, first, to create a sense of community among the class, utilize group building activities that promote social interaction and self-disclosure, and create conditions so that students look forward to the course. There are units on such topics as library research methods, planning for the choice of a major and career, learning about campus resources, study skills, getting along with others, and whatever the instructor and group decide upon. A combination of lecturing, discussion, and group activities is encouraged, and students write frequently. Some variations of this model at other institutions make the seminar available to those who want it, and others require it of all freshmen. The amount of academic credit awarded varies from none to regular course credit.

Southwest Texas State University launched a version of this kind of seminar in 1986 with sixteen sections, expanded it to forty sections the next year, and taught the entire freshman class in 1988. The objective of this one-credit course is "primarily motivational" and designed "to create commitment," according to the instructor's manual. Secondary objectives include:

- To focus attention on the process of growing up, establishing an identity, shaping a career and a life
- To raise the question of what constitutes a good life; to help students think through their values and their goals
- To present a comprehensive view of a university education
- To present the rationale for the required courses; to make the case for broad learning
- To explore with our students the points of connection between a university education and a fulfilling life
- To explore the relation between their university study and their informed, well-thought-out personal goals (Gordon, n.d., p. 4)

Instructors are encouraged to play the role of skilled facilitators rather than the usual subject matter experts.

A second, though related, conception is a freshman seminar with a more academic emphasis. The argument for this form is that freshmen often are overwhelmed by veteran students in many of their courses, and it helps to have a course made up of only new students. Further, the usual introductions to the academic disciplines do not provide a broad enough focus to intellectual life; a topical course drawing on a range of disciplinary perspectives constitutes a better introduction to the life of the mind. By concentrating on the close reading of texts, discussion in small groups, and frequent writing of papers, students can develop valuable skills essential to the rest of their study. These groups, too, seek to foster a sense of community, and the instructor may serve as the academic adviser of students in the seminar.

Marietta College introduced a mandatory freshman seminar with a substantive intellectual focus in 1990, as a part of its new general education program. Similar efforts exist at such diverse places as Broome County (Community) College and Seton Hill College, which requires a year-long course.

Although generalizations are difficult because of the variety of programs, there is strong evidence that they work. Fidler and Hunter (1989) reviewed many research reports and concluded that, in general, freshman year programs seem to improve the academic performance, satisfaction, and retention of students. In addition, they seem to increase the knowledge and use of campus services. And they note some evidence that "faculty-student relationships, communication skills, and study habits may also be positively affected" (p. 224). During a time when traditional-age students are more scarce, freshman year programs are a popular way for colleges to serve students better and to maintain enrollment by enhancing retention. Special first-year programs also work for nontraditional students.

*The Senior Year.* The other major transition for college students is out of college and into the world of work, graduate or professional school, or some other activity. Many institutions expect seniors to take a senior seminar or to complete a significant project that integrates much of their education, demonstrates sophisticated skills, or culminates in a "capstone" experience.

Here, too, there are alternative models. Ohio University adopted a three-tier general education program that deals with skills (tier one), distribution of academic disciplines (tier two), and an interdisciplinary senior synthesis (tier three). Approximately seventy-five senior seminars are offered on a variety of topics. Hope College has a senior seminar that is more personal and seeks to draw out a student's own values as well as to foster intellectual integration. Students are expected to write a "life view" paper that is both disciplined and personal. A Task Force on the Undergraduate Experience at Northwestern University (1988, p. 28) recommended a senior year project or research experience for all students. "Student research and 'senior theses' represent one option for the senior project; other options might include a senior performance or recital, one or more senior seminars, or an extended essay done by the student through independent study of one or more quarters." The report noted that many departments already offer such an opportunity, and it simply recommends broadening it.

A very different approach is utilized at Wheaton College, which established a Center for Work and Learning to assist its liberal arts students to become more familiar with the world of work. According to a grant proposal (1985), the center seeks to "create new links between the liberal arts and the world of work through a program which integrates an explicit learning component into work and internships; develops courses with a required experiential component; creates a program to bring executives, labor leaders, and experts on the world of work to campus; and institutes faculty internships." Although not focused solely on seniors, this is another effective way to assist the transition of students into life after college.

Muhlenburg and Susquehanna Colleges require both freshman and senior seminars. They are regarded as helpful mechanisms to both launch and complete the overall college experience.

*Global Studies.* Because of the growing interdependence of peoples around the globe in regard to economic systems, environmental protection, national security, and a host of other issues, colleges are stressing the study of other cultures. A study by the Educational Testing Service (Barrows, Clark, and Klein, 1980) identified three aspects of global sophistication: knowledge of other countries, positive attitudes toward international affairs, and empathy for other peoples and cultures. These are in varying degrees goals of many new global studies programs.

In the past, the focus of international programs has been on specialties in international relations or the study of some geographical area of the world. Typically they enroll a few students who major in these programs. The emphasis today is to insert global studies into the general education curriculum taken by all students. This is done primarily by means of two different mechanisms: requirement of a course dealing with other cultures or infusion of global perspectives into courses across the curriculum.

Several institutions require students to take a course on other cultures, most of which deal with Western civilization, the tradition out of which our culture developed. Although such courses provide the ideas, history, and culture of the West, however, they are not likely to help students to understand the revolutionary changes taking place in the Soviet Union, the trade barriers between Japan and the United States, the religious fundamentalism in the Middle East, or poverty in Latin America: implicit aspirations of the global studies agenda. More is needed.

Several institutions that have revised their curricula have specified that students study an unfamiliar non-Western culture. Few, however, go as far as Goshen, the Indiana Mennonite college, which requires students to travel to a non-Western country to get a first-hand experience with a radically different way of life. But several, such as Western Maryland College, do require students to take a course on the developing world.

The Consortium for the Advancement of Private Higher Education has provided support to several private colleges for the development of an infusion model. The College of Holy Cross determined the focus of its project would be China. It recruited ten faculty members from as many departments to participate in the program, which included a year-long seminar on the culture and history of China, elementary language learning, a month-long trip to China for sight-seeing and to meet faculty colleagues, in-depth orientation and structured debriefing, and opportunities to integrate knowledge and insights into courses offered the following year. By all accounts, it was a successful effort that strengthened the college's Asian Studies program by infusing it throughout the curriculum.

With minor variations on this theme, St. Joseph's College developed a core course on Mexico, St. Michael's College focused on Japan, and the University of San Diego concentrated on two areas of strategic importance to it, Latin America and the Pacific Rim. The University of the Pacific established a new School of International Studies, drawing largely from faculty members throughout the existing departments. These approaches represent a kind of tightly focused approach to global studies, where a country, region, or particular program is utilized.

More of a shotgun approach was employed by Concordia College (Moorhead, Minnesota). Following a series of lectures and workshops on global studies, faculty members were encouraged to apply for grants to support foreign travel and study leading to the development of new or revised courses reflecting their learning. A total of forty submitted proposals that were subsequently funded. Following their various travels, they taught courses containing the new material. They then participated in a Global Studies Teaching Conference in which each person gave a brief presentation about the changes in their teaching and the apparent effects on the students. According to Peter Hovde, the director, the conference was "a productive opportunity for interdisciplinary communication and cooperation" that brought faculty together in a common endeavor. Because the program involved roughly a quarter of the entire faculty, large numbers of courses, and a sharing of the experiences in a common forum, it had a significant impact on the instructional program.

A recent study by Richard Lambert (1989) indicates that most international studies (apart from foreign language) are not evenly distributed. They tend to consist largely of history and literature courses and to focus on geographical areas, they are heavily Eurocentric, and they are concentrated in four-year colleges and universities. Such courses are more likely to be taken by students majoring in the humanities and spurned by those in the natural sciences and career fields. Requiring specific courses in general education or infusing them throughout the curriculum are useful ways to extend global sophistication among all students. Whatever specific mechanisms are utilized, institutions that are revising their curricula are placing greater emphasis on global studies.

*Cultural Diversity.* Another trend is heightened attention to cultural pluralism in America and the West and the incorporation of new scholarship on these topics into the core curriculum.

As usual, the simplest mechanism is to require a course. For example, the University of California, Berkeley, requires a course on ethnic minorities, not unexpected for a campus in which the majority of students are now non-Caucasian. The University of Tennessee, Knoxville, requires a course selected from an approved list dealing with either gender or racial issues.

Another common approach is to infuse the "new scholarship" in courses across the curriculum, particularly in the core. This stands in opposition to the dominant pattern of the 1960s, when the trend was to create majors in Women's or Ethnic Studies, which functioned like ghettos of the converted. The trend now is to "mainstream" the knowledge and perspectives, so that all students can better understand cultural diversity. For example, San Jose State University adopted a policy that, insofar as possible, all general education courses are expected to address contributions of women and ethnic minority groups, according to Leon Dorosz, associate academic vice president. He notes that evaluation questions given to students in general education courses ask how ethnic/gender issues were addressed. In addition, the university mandates a course on cultural pluralism that deals with comparisons of at least two distinct cultural groups; this requires students to do more sophisticated analysis, comparison, and contrast rather than simply to recognize the issues and contributions of women and cultural groups.

The project on Engaging Cultural Legacies of the Association of American Colleges states in the proposal that colleges should help students "address the complexity that is part of their cultural inheritance; the disparate and often conflicting sources of their traditions; the values, commitments, questions, and tensions that are intrinsic to any rich tradition; the difficulties of framing judgments that draw on inherited values" (Association of American Colleges, 1989, p. 2). The project involves fifty–four diverse institutions working with nine other mentor institutions to create sequences of core courses that deal with the multiplicity of cultural heritages.

***Integration of Knowledge.*** Integration, according to Harlan Cleveland, is what is higher about higher education. Most people agree that students should not simply learn various bits of knowledge but should also make relevant connections between them and with the rest of their lives. Unfortunately, the students are usually left to make such connections on their own. An iron law promulgated by Jonathan Smith of the University of Chicago puts a different light on the matter: "A student shall not be expected to integrate anything that the faculty can't or won't!" What he means is that integration should be a central part of instruction and that professors should both teach and model that kind of thinking. Without explicit training, students are not likely to make relevant connections. Deliberate attempts to integrate knowledge are found in many reformed curricula.

Perhaps the simplest mechanism is a broad-gauge course that includes interdisciplinary perspectives, such as the two-semester sophomore course called Cultures and Traditions used at Wabash College for fifteen years. The first-semester students study the unfamiliar culture of ancient China and then the roots of their own heritage in the ancient Greeks and Hebrews. During the second semester they study Western civilization from the medieval period through the process of "modernization." They end by returning to China and examining its recent attempts to move into the modern world. The course is taught by a cadre of faculty in discussion sections of about fifteen students. Similar approaches have been recently established elsewhere, such as the new humanities course at Utah Valley Community College called Ethics and Ideals.

Some colleges foster integration by linking two or more courses that students take simultaneously. Whittier College offers students the option of satisfying its requirements in World Civilizations and in Contemporary Society and the Individual by either taking pairs of carefully coordinated courses in different disciplines or team-taught courses offered in consecutive semesters. Faculty members must work together to plan and teach jointly these related courses that differ significantly from the usual separate courses. California Lutheran employs a cluster of two regular courses and a third that bridges them— typically an English course that involves students in thinking and writing about the topics of the other two courses. Because the professors plan their work collaboratively, they are able to help students make connections across the courses that would otherwise not be possible.

Another variation on this theme is the use of interdisciplinary core courses or sequences. Hiram College organizes much of its general education "not around traditional departmental questions, but rather, around more universal ideas, problems or issues. . ." Groups of three or four faculty members from two or more disciplines organize a collegium that studies a substantial topic. Each collegium organizes and teaches three courses, all of which the twenty-five to thirty students take during the year. Sample collegia are The Idea of the West, The Origin of Life, The Progress Paradox, and The Environment: Ecology, Economics, and Ethics.

A more intense educational experience is what might be termed a "learning community." Pioneered by Patrick Hill, former provost at the Evergreen State College, it is based on the observations that learning is an individual (but not necessarily solitary) activity and that it can be more effective when done as a part of a community of learners. LaGuardia Community College annually offers about ten different communities, which constitute the primary responsibility for each of the twenty-six to twenty-eight students and three faculty members. Separate topics are designed to appeal to liberal arts and business majors; for liberal arts students The Concept of Freedom clusters introductory courses in philosophy and a social science with an English writing course. For business students, introductory courses in economics and business and an English writing course are joined. The learning community helps overcome the isolation of students and faculty. Roberta Matthews (1986, p. 46) writes: "Because learning communities encourage continuity and integration in the curriculum, students learn more from courses experienced within the community than they would from taking each course as a discrete entity taught with no outside references. . . . [Further, they] offer the closest facsimile of dormitory life to commuter students in nonresidential community colleges."

There is empirical evidence to support her contention. Students taking the composition courses within the cluster have a higher completion rate and half the failure rate, and they receive 10 to 20 percent more "A" and "B" grades. In the business cluster, the completion rate of the economics courses was 5 percent higher and the business course 20 percent higher, and teachers of the two courses assigned 25 percent more "A" and "B" grades than in their discrete courses. Experiences like these are among the reasons the Washington Center at Evergreen State is working with colleges and universities across the state to establish learning communities in all types of institutions. More information about this form of organization may be found in a publication by Gabelnick, MacGregor, Matthews, and Smith (1990).

Several colleges have established whole programs or even subcolleges to create a more integrated education for a small number of students, typically 200 to 500. The Classic Learning Core at the University of North Texas offers, according to Robert Stevens, the director, "a truly integrated and sequenced curriculum of liberal arts requirements for self-selecting students who are willing to agree to a fairly strict succession of courses" (personal communication, Jan. 16, 1990). The curriculum is organized loosely around the three themes of virtue, civility, and reason. The thirty faculty members from nine departments participate in a two-week summer workshop to discuss ideas and plan courses, and they meet every two weeks during the term to construct a common reading list, discuss common texts, and consider means for unifying the learning of their students. Similar efforts are found at George Mason, Miami (Ohio), and California State Polytechnic universities as well as at Gustavus Adolphus and St. Olaf colleges.

Wesley Brown (1989) has assembled a great deal of evidence that demonstrates the effectiveness of the Paracollege, a subcollege at St. Olaf. The students achieved at high levels on standardized achievement tests, demonstrated a great deal of intellectual and personal growth, enhanced their intellectual interests, gained in thinking and communication skills, and were very satisfied with their education. Indeed, Brown (p. 101) concludes that "something associated with their participation in the Paracollege had an effect on their development not shared to the same degree by other students at St. Olaf or, indeed, by most students at other colleges. . . ." This experience is consistent with others who advocate the integration of knowledge, especially if it takes place within a genuine community of learners.

*Moral Reflection.* More than technical expertise is expected of the educated person, and colleges that are revising their educational programs are once again starting to emphasize values. Although implementing any of the programs included in these trends is difficult, the emphasis on values and ethics is particularly tricky. With the exception of a few strict religious institutions, the purpose is not indoctrination nor to get students to adhere to a particular belief system or code of behavior. It is to develop and strengthen the abilities of students to think through value-laden issues, to discuss them intelligently, and to develop the ability to make reasoned judgments about alternatives.

The traditional way of addressing this topic is to require a course in philosophy (or theology in some religious colleges) or, more recently, to offer courses in professional ethics. But a number of new ways are coming into being. A required inter-disciplinary and team-taught core course is a form employed at Louisiana College, designed to teach students about the nature of values, the process by which they are chosen, and their role in the life of an individual. St. Andrews Presbyterian College requires an interdisciplinary course that deals with a global issue and explores controversies and personal values in relation to it. It culminates in a class position paper that reflects common values concerning the issue that emerge from a semester of study and discussion. Los Medanos, a California community college, has a two-semester requirement, Ethical Inquiry into Societal Issues. During the first semester students examine a limited number of topics, such as equality, population, and the environment; during the second they pursue one topic in greater depth.

Freshmen and senior seminars often raise value conflicts and foster greater awareness of the students' own values. These cornerstone and capstone experiences seek to capitalize on the value challenges inherent in the freshman and senior transitions to increase the sophistication of students in thinking through complex issues.

Albion College prefers not to add a course on ethics but to infuse ethics into courses across the curriculum. Frank Frick, director of the Center for Ethics, encourages faculty members to study values related to their disciplines and to incorporate those topics into regular courses. Alverno and Clayton State Colleges have a competency-based curriculum in which valuing is one of the abilities to be developed and assessed. Earlham supports collaborative student-faculty research on themes central to the character of this Friends college, including peace, justice, and race and gender equality. In these ways, several colleges are seeking to develop an educated heart to go along with an educated mind.

*Active Learning.* Students in too many general education courses are treated as passive receptacles; they are lectured to, dutifully take notes, memorize material, regurgitate it on examinations, and soon forget it. Some colleges are trying to change this dynamic by stressing active learning that captures the intellectual excitement of the subject matter.

The courses that emphasize skills development are typically limited in size, often fifteen to twenty students, so that students can practice and teachers can coach them. Writing, speaking, and critical thinking are skills that cannot be developed passively and in large groups. Similarly, freshman and senior seminars are small so that group discussion and social interaction are possible. Interdisciplinary core courses, too, are often limited in size; the University of Arizona has a policy to limit Western Civilization course sections to forty, each of which must be taught by regular faculty members, not teaching assistants. And values courses typically seek to individualize and personalize education by means of case studies, class exercises, personal journals, and other engaging techniques.

Many colleges include active learning as a criterion for approving a course for general education purposes. The burden of proof is placed on faculty members to demonstrate to their colleagues how they will involve students actively in the course. This mechanism allows teachers the freedom to decide what and how to teach while assuring that students are engaged in their studies.

It is more difficult to encourage active learning in subjects that are highly codified, such as the natural sciences, than the less codified humanities, arts, and social sciences, but there are places that are working on that task. Dickinson College (1990, p. 3) submitted a grant proposal for a "discovery approach" that declared that "our faculty proposed an effort to make the science curriculum more personal, interactive, and experiential. Instead of *telling* students about scientific concepts, our goal is to create a learning environment where students can *discover* science just as those involved in science research do; an environment which emphasizes questioning and exploration rather than memorization, conceptualization and comprehension rather than rote learning, and active participation rather than passive observation" (1990 Knight Foundation).

*Extension Through All Four Years.* Typically, general education has consisted of introductory courses and has been relegated to the first two years of college. Students were told they were courses to "get out of the way" so they could get into something more important, their majors. But, increasingly, general education includes advanced courses and extends through all four years. The goals are primarily to build greater depth, to keep the broader purposes in the minds of students throughout their entire college career, to link general education with the major, and to treat certain topics after students have more maturity.

The California State University system has a common requirement among all campuses of forty-eight semester hours in general education, nine of which must be at the upper-division level. One of its special circumstances justifying the upper-level emphasis is that large numbers of graduates (75 percent or more) are transfers from the over 100 community colleges in the state. The forty-eight units are shared with community colleges, with perhaps as many as thirty-five to forty taken at another school. The requirement of nine hours is one means for its several colleges to put their stamp on the general education of the graduates. Southern Illinois University at Edwardsville requires students to take two introductory and two advanced courses from each of three categories: fine arts and humanities, natural sciences and mathematics, and social sciences. The senior capstone experiences discussed earlier are another way this trend is manifested.

*Assessment.* Assessing student learning is increasingly common, both to identify problems that call for change and to determine the extent to which a new curriculum is effective. The basic educational rationale for assessment is stated simply in *Involvement in Learning* (National Institute of Education, 1984, p. 21): "We argue that institutions should be accountable not only for stating their expectations and standards but for assessing the degree to which those ends have been met." Much of the impetus behind assessment is the desire by state leaders to hold colleges and universities accountable for achieving their educational purposes and for expending their funds. Another source of interest is a genuine sense of concern among teachers and administrators that they are achieving the goals they hold dear. Some see a marketing advantage if they can demonstrate that their students are progressing toward valued educational objectives.

Assessment is an endeavor that often leads to discussions of arcane technical topics, such as methodology, tests, sampling, and statistics. But Pat Hutchings and Ted Marchese (1990, p. 14) remind us that "assessment is best understood as *a set of questions* — questions that are not, in fact, entirely new, but that now come at us with greater insistence. At bottom they're questions about student learning. . . ." Faculty members and administrators usually want to satisfy their curiosity about what students learn from their instructional programs and teaching strategies, acquire self-consciousness about their educational assumptions and relationships with students, and maintain integrity by seeing that the consequences of instruction actually match with what they tell students they may expect to gain from an educational experience. In this sense, assessment is a profoundly intellectual — even moral — enterprise that enlightens the very process of education.

Many colleges, whether motivated by their own curiosity and interests or by external forces, are experimenting with various approaches to assessment. Typically, assessment groups discover the need to determine their educational goals, and to do it with enough precision that they are measurable. This is often the most important benefit of the entire process — deciding what students should learn, clarifying the ways individuals think and talk about objectives, exploring what might be acceptable criteria of learning, setting expectations about levels and standards of achievement. All of these issues must be resolved prior to deciding any of the technical matters of instrumentation, sampling, and the like.

Once they reach agreement about educational ends for students, colleges and universities take different approaches to assessing their achievement. King's College embeds assessment in courses, and faculty members seek to measure student progress in regard to each of the college's major learning goals. The University of Connecticut is conducting focus group conversa-

tions with students about their experiences in general education, what they have gained, and their problems. The University
of Tennessee, Knoxville, for over a decade has engaged in a
variety of strategies: departmental studies, administration of
standardized instruments, surveys of student satisfaction, and
senior tests and simulations. Assessment is now a routine part of
the university's planning process. Northeast Missouri State University has conducted a "values added" assessment that measures
student growth in general knowledge during the college years.
Some colleges use an available achievement test, questionnaire,
or personality inventory; others develop a "home grown" instrument, which may lack the professionalism of commercial forms
but is more tailored to the needs of the campus.

Often an institution has a fair amount of existing data in
the admissions office (what is attractive to students, what their
expectations are), registrar's office (what courses students take,
what their grades are, what the graduation rate is), counseling
office (what problems lead students to seek help, what the
important sources of stress are), and alumni office (what walks of
life alumni enter, how well their education has served them, what
they would like to see changed about the college). These materials are often collected and used to gain a fuller understanding
of the student experience.

Assessment can be as confusing as general education
itself. Indeed, the most serious problems of assessing general
education programs typically have more to do with the fragmentation and lack of agreement about basic principles of the
general education program than with assessment itself. Assessment is often a useful strategy for forging closer relationships
between educational goals, general education curricula, and
their consequences.

### Putting It Together: Comprehensive Change

We will conclude this survey of separate trends by noting
that they are just that—separate curriculum components. Many
colleges have taken a piecemeal approach and emphasized one
or more of these elements. Although each trend is individually

important, none of them can create wholeness and coherence. That happy condition comes about when a college develops a comprehensive approach and constructs an overall course of study that is right for its students and true to its history, traditions, and character. Such a comprehensive approach, incorporating several of these trends, can achieve the kind of wholeness that should characterize undergraduate education.

Comprehensive change can be seen at some very different small, private, liberal arts colleges, including Antioch, Eckerd, Hobart and William Smith, Mount St. Mary's, and Seton Hill. Large universities, both public and private, have also made large-scale changes, including American, Memphis State, Ohio, and Syracuse. Some two-year colleges, too, have developed extensive new curricula, including Broome County, Catonsville, Los Medanos, and Miami-Dade.

The University of Minnesota, Morris, is illustrative of a comprehensive curriculum reform that incorporates many of these separate trends. With the assistance of a Title III grant from the U.S. Department of Education, a curriculum planning process was launched in 1986. After extensive study, discussion, and compromise, the faculty adopted new graduation requirements, a different curriculum structure, and learning objectives for general education courses. This marked a turnabout from its previous loose and fragmented curriculum. The new general education curriculum was implemented in fall 1988, and courses were developed or revised as portions of the curriculum were phased in. In addition to a major, students must take ninety quarter units in general education, some prescribed and some elective.

The program is called ProsPer, since its goals are developing both processes of thought and perspectives on the world. The program is guided by explicit learning goals and specific criteria for courses that address each goal. Some of the courses allow students to achieve more than one goal, thereby allowing students to meet part of the general education requirements through electives rather than prescribed courses. The thinking process goals are addressed by the following requirements or their equivalence:

- A freshman seminar focusing on the process of inquiry
- A two-quarter sequence of writing courses
- Two additional writing-intensive courses
- A speech course and one speech-intensive course
- A course on the computer and one with applications
- Foreign language at the level of first-year proficiency

Students are also required to take courses labeled Expanding Perspectives that are grouped in three areas.

1. The Self and Others area includes one course dealing with each of five topics: the self, historical perspectives, different cultures, social institutions, and health and fitness.
2. The Arts area includes a course in analysis and interpretation, one in performance, another in arts and culture.
3. The Physical and Abstract Worlds area includes two courses in the natural world (at least one of which must contain a laboratory) and one in abstract systems.

The Perspectives courses must contain at least one dealing with a non-Western culture, and one must be taken at an advanced level. A college-wide general education committee approves courses that meet the specific criteria established for each of these areas. The Morris campus makes special efforts to explain to students *why* these goals are important and how the course requirements meet the goals.

This general education program, its marketing, and the recognition it is receiving are having a dramatic impact on the institution. It was named as one of the top regional liberal arts colleges and one of the best buys in the Midwest by the *U.S. News and World Report* ("America's Best Colleges," 1989). Its enrollment started to increase before the curriculum revision, but since then applications have skyrocketed, student retention rates have increased, and student test scores have risen dramatically. A cap has been put on enrollment, a luxury that few other colleges can afford. Although the curriculum cannot be given all of the credit for its recent success, it is a central part of the dynamic that has led to both educational excellence and a well-deserved reputation. Morris illustrates what can happen when a college reaches agreement about the vexing issues of content, coherence, commonality, and comprehensiveness — and acts on the agreements to vitalize the heart of college education for all of its students.

## Conclusion

Some critics charge that these changes do not go far enough, are not widespread enough, or are not deeply enough supported. They echo the words variously attributed to Groucho Marx and Talulah Bankhead, "There is less here than meets the eye." I agree that more can and should be done. Many institutions have been untouched by the debate and reform movement, some have only tinkered with the curriculum or made limited or piecemeal changes. Some of the new programs are fragile and not yet fully rooted in the life of the institutions.

Nonetheless, I believe that these several trends, collectively, are transforming the nature of the undergraduate curriculum. Many institutions are deciding on the most important knowledge, skills, and personal qualities their students should acquire, and they are developing curricula to provide instruction to those ends. The development of a more purposeful curriculum designed by colleges to serve valued educational ends is perhaps the most fundamental trend of all.

PART TWO

# Assessing the Impacts
# of the Reforms

# Chapter Three

# Scope and Nature
# of Curricular Changes

The college curriculum has many faces and, like any educational issue, may be analyzed at several levels: its philosophy, policy, or practice (Brubacher, 1977) or in terms of its intent, content, and consequences (Boyer and Algren, 1981). There is the "hidden curriculum," that collection of expectations, norms, and values through which students learn what is *really* important, regardless of the formal curriculum (Snyder, 1971). To put it succinctly: There is a curriculum as offered by the college, as taught by the faculty, and as learned by the student. These conceptual distinctions complicate the task of assessing any given curriculum or its revision.

Studying the results of a curriculum is also fraught with methodological and technical difficulties. The curriculum may look different to an administrator, faculty member, or student. And many methods are available: interviews, questionnaires, standardized tests, learning styles inventories, and institutional data on such factors as retention and grade distributions. Each method has its advantages and limitations.

If assessing a single curriculum is complex, it is even more difficult to assess the instructional programs across many institutions. The task is especially problematic because no two institutions operate identical programs or make exactly the same changes. The real world is a lot messier than our tidy concepts and methodologies presume. Given these tangles, how can we make reasonable judgments about how well new curricula are working?

## Methodology

I cut through this Gordian knot by taking a simple-minded approach. I identified a group of academic leaders at a number of institutions that had been working to improve their general education programs and asked them several questions. The target group included mostly chief academic officers— deans, provosts, academic vice presidents—although occasionally a president or a director of general education was on the list. This group, which I refer to generically here as deans, arguably includes the individuals who are the most knowledgeable about their curricula and the best qualified to report on recent changes and their effects. The major limitations of this approach are that these individuals may lack specific knowledge, and they are far from being objective reporters. Indeed, they may have a personal stake in the success of attempted revisions. Although the evidence from such a survey is "soft," consisting of observations, perceptions, and reports, it does give a useful overview of curriculum changes. Many responses were frank, even critical, and many respondents answered anonymously, although others signed their names.

The information I received was interpreted in light of my own knowledge and experience. My visits to scores of campuses within the last two years and extensive first-hand experience with curriculum change gave me a good perspective from which to view the results. I am the first to argue that we need more data and more objective information to assess the consequences of various forms of general education. My claim is not that this approach yields the last word on the subject but that it is a useful first approximation.

The sample consisted of 305 diverse institutions. It was not a random sample of all colleges and universities but a purposive sample designed not to assess how widely reforms are distributed but to learn what is resulting from curricular changes where they are occurring. It was selected from several sources: recipients of grants for curriculum or faculty development from the Bush Foundation, Lilly Endowment, and Consortium for the Advancement of Private Higher Education; institutions that had attended the Lilly Endowment Workshop on the Liberal Arts to work on general education proposals; colleges with promising programs cited in publications such as the *Chronicle of Higher Education* and reports from the Carnegie Foundation for the Advancement of Teaching and the National Endowment for the Humanities; institutions involved in improvement projects, such as Engaging Cultural Legacies of the Association of American Colleges; and institutions I have known through correspondence or visits. The nature of the changes institutions were making was quite varied: requirements for graduation, structure of the curriculum, revisions in introductory or other courses, and attention to teaching and learning within courses. It turned out that some of the institutions changed only one or two of these components, and others made a comprehensive revision. Although most had implemented changes, some as much as a decade ago, a few were preparing to implement changes or still conducting reviews. The sample, therefore, consisted of a large number of colleges and universities actively involved in a wide range of efforts to improve their general education programs.

The sample was selected to approximate the distribution of colleges and universities, as indicated by the Carnegie Foundation for the Advancement of Teaching (1987). The major exceptions are that specialized institutions (for example, business, engineering, or fine arts institutes) were omitted because general education operates differently in those settings; also community colleges are underrepresented because I wanted to focus on the whole of a baccalaureate education. The sample actually contained slightly larger proportions of research, doctoral granting, and comprehensive institutions than their numbers in the population and slightly fewer liberal arts colleges. The resulting sample represents approximately 10 percent of all colleges and universities in the United States — 20 percent of the four-year institutions. All states of the union were included.

The response to the survey was exceptional. As shown in

Table 3.1. Sample and Response Rate by Type of Institution.

|  | Number Sent | Number Returned | Response Rate |
|---|---|---|---|
| Comprehensive Colleges and Universities I | 75 | 58 | 77% |
| Comprehensive Colleges and Universities II | 33 | 27 | 82 |
| Liberal Arts Colleges I | 49 | 37 | 76 |
| Liberal Arts Colleges II | 61 | 44 | 72 |
| Doctorate-Granting Universities I | 13 | 10 | 77 |
| Doctorate-Granting Universities II | 10 | 6 | 60 |
| Research Universities I | 24 | 13 | 54 |
| Research Universities II | 8 | 7 | 88 |
| Two-Year Colleges | 32 | 24 | 75 |
| Totals | 305 | 226 | 74 |

Table 3.1, a total of 226 returned completed questionnaires, for a response rate of 74 percent. Over half of each type of institution returned the form.

Respondents were asked to complete a ten-page questionnaire concerning their instructional programs, a copy of which is located in the appendix. The questionnaire consisted of structured items in which respondents were asked to check an alternative, as well as open-ended items for individuals to answer in their own words. Topics included descriptions of their programs, the relation of general education to academic majors and student affairs activities, perceived consequences of the revisions, barriers encountered and strategies employed to overcome them, the greatest concern or disappointment, and advice they would give to others. Deans were also asked to send printed materials, not just catalogues and brochures but also unpublished studies, proposals, assessment reports, and similar "fugitive literature." A great deal of this material was received, and it offered valuable insights and interesting "war stories."

## A Typical General Education Curriculum

The proportion of the curriculum allocated to general education appears to be on the increase. In the average four-year college with a semester calendar, the number of credit hours required for graduation was approximately 124. The average number of these hours allotted to general education was reported to be 49.2 credit hours, or 39.5 percent of the total. Among the two-year colleges, the average amount of general education required was 35.8 semester hours out of an average of 62 hours required for an associate degree. Among the deans responding to the survey, 59 percent said that the number of credit hours in the new general education program were more than in the previous one; 39 percent reported that they were the same; and only 3 percent noted that the number of hours were fewer.

Other evidence that general education is playing a larger role in the undergraduate curriculum comes from a series of comparable studies in a few benchmark years. Each relied on a random nationwide sample of four-year colleges and universities. General education constituted an average of 43.1 percent of the total curriculum in 1967 (Dressel and De Lisle, 1969). Just before the student protests erupted, the curriculum was criticized as irrelevant, and many colleges relaxed requirements. In 1974 (Blackburn and others, 1976) the proportion of general education had dropped to 33.5 percent. William Toombs and his colleagues (Toombs, Fairweather, Chen, and Amey, 1989) reported that in 1988 it was 37.9 percent of the total. Although these studies examined different institutions, they were designed to be comparable. On the basis of all of these data, it appears that general education is occupying a somewhat larger proportion of the baccalaureate program, especially among institutions, as those in my study, that are revising their curricula.

Probably more important than the total amount of time, whether on an absolute or proportional basis, is the character of the program. What are the "reformed" programs like? A profile of a "typical general education curriculum" at a four-year college with a semester calendar was developed by averaging credit hour requirements for all such colleges and rounding them off into conventional three-credit courses. The resulting typical curriculum has the following requirements:

- Two courses in writing
- One course in mathematics
- Four courses in the humanities
- One course in fine arts
- Two courses in natural science (four-credit courses with a laboratory)
- Three courses in social science

In addition are several components that are less commonly found. About half the colleges require foreign language averaging three courses (most require either one or two years); somewhat less than half require a speech course; and about 30 percent require a course on computer literacy. In terms of content, this typical program seems fairly comprehensive and broad. In its outlines it approximates the proposal by Cheney (1989) for a fifty-hour curriculum spread over a variety of subjects.

But there is more to most general education programs than this broad-brush outline. They often include special features that attempt to capture the distinctive qualities of the particular college, its heritage, or its students. Another set of questions solicited information about several specific features that are employed. Again in the interest of focusing on the entirety of a baccalaureate degree program, the emphasis was on the four-year colleges. A total of 73 percent have advanced or upper-division courses, 67 percent utilize interdisciplinary core courses, and 56 percent offer courses using original sources. In most cases these features are required, but often they are options available to students who want them. For example, a little over half of the colleges operate freshman seminars, and a little under half have senior seminars or projects; they are required in 61 percent and 55 percent of the cases, respectively.

Most colleges today have a diverse student body, and the general education programs often address this circumstance. Two-thirds of the colleges have honors programs for accelerated students, and slightly more than half offer courses for underprepared students. Some of the honors programs include special sections of courses that feature more reading of classic texts, more discussion, and more written papers. Some of the courses for underprepared students are special sections of mathematics or English, and some are noncredit courses designed to remedy deficiencies from earlier schooling.

Finally, a relatively new phenomenon has arisen in this wave of reform. Rather than require a course on some specific topic, colleges often teach the topic in several courses across the curriculum. These are common parts of new general education curricula, but they do not often show up in surveys or curriculum transcript studies because the content is infused into existing courses. Certain skills, for example, are often taught in this manner. Ninety-three percent of the campus leaders reported some kind of writing across the curriculum, 71 percent cited critical thinking, and 50 percent noted computer literacy. The idea of teaching writing in courses beyond the English department is an old one, but it has enjoyed attention because many people are recognizing that only a concerted college-wide effort will correct the serious deficiencies students have with written expression. Teaching critical thinking abilities is often linked with writing, since thought and expression are so closely intertwined, and the computer is becoming so pervasive that it is increasingly used as a tool for learning subjects of all types.

In addition to skills, several key topics are handled across the curriculum. The majority of institutions in this sample used this approach to teach global studies (63 percent), cultural pluralism (58 percent), ethics and values (57 percent), and gender issues (53 percent); smaller percentages required students to take courses dealing with such topics. The purposes of such courses are for students to acquire knowledge and also to become more sensitive to other peoples and to learn new perspectives that pervade all of their studies. Sometimes students are simply exposed to these perspectives, but often they are required to take a specified number of such courses.

The major advantages of teaching something across the curriculum are that responsibility for teaching important subjects is spread widely among the faculty and that students get reinforcement when certain skills or topics are encountered time and again throughout their education. The main danger of this approach is that the guidelines for teaching these special emphasis courses may be carried out unevenly by the faculty. One dean confessed, "Across the curriculum components are only gradually receiving more than lip service from some of the faculty, partly because of scholarly narrowness, partly because of no budget support for better faculty workshops and better administrative evaluation."

The questionnaire asked about the mechanisms used to implement the across-the-curriculum emphases so that they would become more than lip service. Several are widely employed, including

- Assisting faculty to develop new knowledge or skills, largely through workshops and seminars (75 percent)
- Supporting faculty to develop new or revised courses (65 percent)
- Establishing a writing, speaking, or other resource center to support student learning (60 percent)
- Charging a committee to approve such special courses (48 percent)
- Making the particular emphasis a criterion for general education courses (46 percent)
- Identifying courses with the special emphasis that students can take if they choose (42 percent)
- Requiring students to take a certain number of special emphasis courses (41 percent)
- Appointing an administrator, usually a faculty member, assigned to provide leadership for the program (41 percent)

In combination, these quality control mechanisms help this kind of program to work. Although none of these devices are foolproof, without them, across-the-curriculum strategies are not likely to get much beyond lip service.

In some fundamental sense, each curriculum must be judged in its own particular context, and these aggregate numbers tell little about the operation of any single program. But this "typical curriculum" does give an overall view of the kinds of changes that have been taking place on many college campuses. Collectively, the changes appear to be bringing more rigor,

structure, and quality into the course of study of all undergraduates at these colleges. By and large, this curriculum appears to
be responsive to the charges against the freewheeling curriculum where students are given little guidance about which subjects are most valuable. It requires students to study broadly
across the liberal arts and sciences; it includes an emphasis on
fundamental skills; it teaches some knowledge and skills across
the curriculum; and it includes many special features such as
advanced or interdisciplinary courses, courses requiring original sources, and special seminars for freshmen and seniors. This
happy condition currently is not recognized or accepted by the
American public, even by many academic leaders. Cheney
(1990, p. 34), for instance, states, "Education reform in colleges
and universities has not yet attained the momentum of education reform in the schools." Among this group of institutions,
education reform has indeed attained momentum, as important
changes have been made in the general education curriculum
for all students.

## Consequences of the Changes

"The most sweeping changes ever undertaken in the academic plan and curriculum at California State University, San
Bernardino, will be implemented in the fall of 1989," proudly
proclaimed a brochure (Steinman, 1988, p. 1). At the other
extreme, a respondent to my survey bluntly said the college had
created a "bland cafeteria" program; even that dubious achievement happened only when, after ten years of discussion, the
dean "took the committee off campus, locked them in a room,
and kept them there until a compromise was reached." These
two extremes illustrate the range of degrees of improvement
actually taking place in colleges in this sample, but neither
characterizes the majority of recent reforms. To get a better view
of this matter, the survey asked campus leaders to report on the
consequences of their curriculum changes.

One way of answering the question of consequences is to
see how large the amount of change was. On the one hand, if
only a small change was made, the amount of improvement is

unlikely to have been very great. On the other hand, a large change does not guarantee that it was for the better, although it does make for the possibility of a large improvement. Further, the amount of change does not tell anything about the absolute level of quality; it might be either high or low. (I once belonged to a college fraternity that won a huge trophy for improving our grades more than any other living unit—and we were still dead last! We displayed it prominently, and few knew our true ranking.)

According to these respondents, a substantial amount of change was made in the curricula of their colleges and universities. Fifteen percent of the deans reported that they had made a small change, 42 percent a moderate change, and 42 percent a large change in their general education program. With four out of five deans reporting at least a moderate change, there seems to be a good deal of movement taking place in general education. We must remember that the number of colleges reporting a small change includes several places that are in the midst of reviewing their offerings, and their work has not yet come to fruition.

The amount of change achieved is better understood if viewed in relation to the amount of change planned. As might be expected, aspirations were somewhat higher than achievements; more planned a large change than accomplished it. Eight percent of the deans reported that they planned to achieve a small, 37 percent a moderate, and 54 percent a large change. Although there may be some slippage, the evidence indicates that most commonly an institution gets the amount of change it plans for. That is, among those planning a small change, 81 percent achieved it; among those aspiring to a moderate change, 66 percent realized it; and among those aiming for a large change, 70 percent got what they desired.

The practical lesson for curriculum planners is this: The level of aspiration at the outset tends to determine the magnitude of the change that results. When I visit a college to help kick off a curriculum revision process, I am often asked by a faculty member, "How serious are we about this? Are we just going to tinker with the curriculum, or are we going to rethink the whole

Table 3.2. Impact of General Education on the Institution.

|  | Negative Impact | No Impact | Positive Impact |
|---|---|---|---|
| Institutional identity | 2% | 26% | 72% |
| Faculty renewal | 2 | 27 | 71 |
| Sense of community | 2 | 33 | 65 |
| Public relations, visibility | 1 | 38 | 61 |
| Efficient utilization of faculty | 13 | 37 | 48 |
| Student retention | 6 | 47 | 47 |
| General education budget | 11 | 42 | 46 |
| Student admissions | 2 | 59 | 40 |
| Institutional fund raising | 1 | 62 | 36 |
| Faculty reward structure | 4 | 72 | 24 |

thing?" It is a fundamental question. (My personal experience is that when an administration goes to the expense of bringing in a consultant from out of state and assembles an entire faculty to discuss the issue, something more than tinkering is likely to be involved.)

Few colleges accomplished a larger change than they intended at the outset, whatever the level of aspiration, because the political pressures in the academy conspire to whittle down good ideas that call for significant change from the status quo. This is particularly the case in regard to general education, which touches the interests of so many departments and faculty members. As reformers have learned, it takes an enormous amount of time, energy, wits, and wise strategies to succeed with even a modest curriculum revision. The evidence here is that large and moderate change may be at the end of the rainbow for those who plan substantial change and persevere to achieve it.

The perceived impact of the new program is another way to assess the consequences. Deans were asked to indicate whether it had a "negative impact," "no impact," or a "positive impact" on several other parts of the institution. The percentages of persons selecting each alternative is shown in Table 3.2.

This is a remarkable set of results. First of all, changes in the general education program appear to have produced negative results at very few colleges. For the vast majority they either produced positive impact on the institution or had no impact. Curriculum reformers face a daunting task and many dangers when they embark on the task of designing and implementing a new curriculum. The process, especially at an early stage, often generates fierce turf-protective battles and rancor among individuals before compromises can be effected. But in terms of institutional *results*, curriculum change seems to have produced few negative consequences. There may be other negatives than those included in this list, but these reports indicated that it is a prized "win-no lose" kind of game—precisely the game any educational leader should be eager to play. (It should be kept in mind that a curriculum reform may prove to be very successful, but faculty who are wounded in the process may bear grudges against the faculty and administrative colleagues perceived to be responsible. Reformers may succeed institutionally and lose personally.)

Further, the kinds of positive impacts are noteworthy. More than seven out of ten deans said the new program sharpened the colleges' identity, and nearly two-thirds noted that it developed a greater sense of community. Shaping an identity and developing community around it are activities at the very heart of a college and are essential determinants of its vitality, perhaps even survival. Successful institutions of higher learning today are working on defining their identity, developing a strategic plan, positioning themselves in relation to their competitors, and aggressively marketing their special qualities. The data suggest that these general education reforms involved far more than jiggling graduation requirements or tinkering with courses. In calling everyone's attention to the core of the curriculum, the process of curriculum review seems to have re-called attention to the core values of the entire institution.

How does this happen? For one thing, a revision in the curriculum brings people together from all parts of the institution, they get acquainted with each other, and they work on an important common endeavor—designing the best general education program possible. The task elevates individuals from their particular circumstances and lifts their sights from the narrow confines of their own department to the college or university as a whole. Because general education is the one program that touches all parts of the instructional program, restructuring it (if successful) is a community-building exercise. Further, many task forces conduct their reviews by examining the mission, distinctive features, heritage and traditions, and special qualities of the students and faculty of their own institutions; usually they consciously try to develop a program that is tailored to their particular needs and builds on their identified strengths. The discussions within the committee and with the broader constituencies — faculty, students, administration, alumni, and board — often recall basic values and commitments.

Further, once a curriculum change is adopted, a college usually goes to great lengths to promote it, with articles in the alumni magazine and student newspaper, eye-catching brochures, special mailings to high school guidance counselors and to prospective students, and speeches by campus leaders. The files from my survey are salted by articles from the print media about the new programs of colleges, since they respond to concerns of the reading public. It is not accidental that institutional identity, community, and visibility are common consequences.

The impact of new programs on faculty renewal deserves special comment. Faculty dissatisfaction with low standards, frustration with students' skills, and inability to assume a certain level of what Hirsch calls "cultural literacy" helped to fuel many of the changes. Most faculty suffer their frustrations in isolation, grumble to their colleagues, or struggle with their individual efforts, resulting in an inevitable alienation, often unspoken, from their colleagues and institution, who are not seen as supportive. A curriculum reform process often validates the educational concerns of faculty and supports their impulse toward high-quality education. If the reform is successful, faculty morale increases.

A second reason for faculty renewal is that they have worked together on a valued corporate enterprise. Curriculum change is an inherently social activity, which, at its best, stimulates and vitalizes individuals. Often faculty do not know — or do not know well — their colleagues in other departments or units

of the institution, and this kind of activity gives them an opportunity to discover how much they share.

Third, most institutions conducted faculty development
programs as a part of their curricular changes. Much of the
usual activity for the professional development of faculty is
individual, in such forms as research projects, travel to professional meetings, sabbatical leaves, individual grants, or course
revisions. But here they frequently worked in groups to discuss
proposals, participate in seminars, attend retreats, and develop
new kinds of courses with their colleagues. Gerald Gibson, dean
at Roanoke College (personal communication, 1990), expressed
well the consequences of this activity for faculty:

> Although strategy for getting a new curriculum
> designed and implemented was my most passion-
> ate concern during those first few years at Roanoke,
> I don't think that even I guessed what a tremendous
> impact work on the curriculum would have on our
> faculty. Reading and debating curricular issues,
> then writing grants and planning for implementa-
> tion, placed general studies center stage for our
> faculty, and has provided relief from the academic
> narcissism that majors tend to represent. More and
> more the Roanoke faculty are seeing "education" to
> mean a much broader and richer consequence of
> four years of college and a much sharper Roanoke
> imprimatur than they had thought of its being,
> perhaps ever, but certainly in decades.

Another set of institutional impacts that deserves comment has to do with enrollment and fund raising, areas that have
direct impact on the budget. It is significant that nearly half of
the deans reported that retention increased and over 40 percent
that admissions were favorably affected. This is not what one
would expect from common conceptions of students. Higher
education has adopted a view of student as consumer, and
sophisticated marketing strategies are used to identify the interests of students and prospective students and to satisfy them. In

their zeal to attract students, some colleges appear willing to offer any course on any topic at any place that might conceivably be a market. But the colleges in this survey have stressed educational purposes and *raised* standards, *increased* rigor, *limited* choice. These actions have not turned students away in the vast number of institutions, and in a large minority of cases have actually attracted and retained them. This is important evidence that our traditional conception of students as consumers needs to be revised, that many students are actually attracted to higher-quality education. Students seem to be becoming more sophisticated consumers of education; college officials may have been selling students short. When general education is conceived and presented properly, students seem willing to reach higher and to work harder than many have assumed.

A related area is fund raising, which was reported to have increased in over a third of the cases. It is not hard to see why. A college that has a clear sense of its identity and purposes, cultivates a sense of community around those purposes, makes a commitment to a strong core curriculum that responds to many of today's criticisms, receives favorable publicity for its efforts, has a revitalized faculty, and is attractive to students can make an excellent case for support. This is true whether the institution is private and must rely heavily on support from alumni and individual donors or whether it is public and must rely primarily on state appropriations. Indeed, a member of a newly assembled curriculum review committee at a Big Ten university confided her belief that the only way it can get major new funds from the state is by making a significant improvement in its undergraduate general education program.

A final observation has to do with the 13 and 11 percent who cite a negative impact on the efficient utilization of faculty and the general education budget, respectively. A president at one college lamented that small class sizes required in their first-year symposium, senior seminar, and skill-intensive courses would create a need for more faculty and increase the cost of the program. This may well be the case in those aspects of the program; small classes are necessary to achieve the purposes. Quality *is* more expensive than mediocrity. On the other hand, a

Table 3.3. Changes in Attitudes Toward General Education.

| Changes in Attitudes | Less Favorable | Not Much Change | More Favorable |
|---|---|---|---|
| Faculty | 5% | 33% | 62% |
| Students | 7 | 53 | 40 |
| Administrators | 5 | 25 | 70 |

general education curriculum with less choice allows for more efficient utilization of faculty, because enrollment in required courses is more stable and easier to predict than in a curriculum that permits student choice. This may be why over three times as many deans said the new program had positive rather than negative impact on both the efficient utilization of faculty and the budget. Of course, a transition may take some years to complete before the staffing patterns fall into a new state of equilibrium with enrollment in newly required courses.

We must keep in mind that this sample includes colleges with many different types of curricula and with many different kinds of changes. I suspect that the specific content of curricula is less important than the *process* of conducting a review, agreeing on a program of study and its rationale, and endowing it with the authority of the faculty and administration. Declaring what an institution stands for in terms of general education and placing it in the center of the students' academic program is more important, for example, than whether some particular course is required or not required. The process of renewing and strengthening the heart of the academic enterprise, whatever its particular configuration, is probably most responsible for these consequences.

One other set of consequences has to do with how members of the college community respond to changes in the general education program. The deans were asked to assess the changes in attitudes of faculty members, students, and administrators. As may be seen in Table 3.3, strong majorities of faculty members and administrators became more favorable, as did a large minority of students.

Unlike during the 1960s when radical students agitated for relaxed requirements, more relevant courses, and individualized instruction, change in general education today typically is brought about by an alliance between the leaders in the academic administration and faculty. Not only the impetus but also the planning and operation of new programs are in the hands of these groups, so it is understandable that they might be favorably disposed to what they have wrought.

Students tended to show less change, but most of what did occur was in a positive direction. The fact that student attitudes were less likely to change for the better may be because students played a less prominent role in changing the programs. It may also be that the rationale for the changes and the benefits are sometimes not well explained to students. In addition, it may be simply a matter of timing. Faculty and administrators who have spent years discussing and planning the change may see the benefit of a new program before students even experience it.

The conclusion that must be drawn is that many positive results and few negative ones result from the process of revising the general education curriculum. The very process of revising general education, however formidable and difficult, is a major vehicle for institutional renewal.

## Significance of the Changes

Beyond descriptions of the new general education programs and perceptions of their consequences, I was curious about their educational significance. Of course, educational significance is difficult to assess, but some approximation may be made by asking deans to make judgments about the consequences of the efforts they reported. Obviously, there is nothing infallible about these judgments, but like the respondents' perceptions, they provide useful information for assessing the changes.

This issue was probed by asking respondents for their overall judgments about the extent to which the new general education programs resulted in various outcomes. The results

Table 3.4. Various Outcomes of New Programs.

|  | Not Very Much | Somewhat | Quite a Lot | Very Much |
|---|---|---|---|---|
| Higher-quality education | 5% | 35% | 41% | 20% |
| Greater curricular coherence | 13 | 28 | 34 | 25 |
| Faculty renewal | 16 | 32 | 32 | 20 |
| More active learning | 20 | 35 | 26 | 19 |
| Revitalized institution | 16 | 40 | 27 | 18 |
| Greater appreciation for racial and cultural diversity | 21 | 35 | 26 | 17 |

shown in Table 3.4 indicate that the vast majority of colleges report improvement on a range of educational outcomes.

Higher-quality education for students, greater coherence for the curriculum, and renewal for the faculty were judged the most frequent results; the majority of respondents checked the top two categories for each of these. Since greater quality and coherence are central goals of the reform movement, in one sense it is no surprise that they resulted in most of these colleges. But it is one thing to talk about those goals, and it is quite another to hear from our informants that they actually resulted from the various changes that were made. Even though these judgments must be characterized as informed opinion rather than the results of actual tests, they do suggest that the kinds of changes in college curricula that were described above appear to be having generally positive effects.

The dominant impression from these data is one of moderate improvement. The middle categories—"somewhat" and "quite a lot"—were chosen by over six out of ten of the deans in regard to each item. While the vast majority noted at least some improvement in each of the categories, the amount of improvement was not dramatic. This is reasonable, since the curriculum is just one part of a college, and although it is central, improvement in the quality of the education is dependent on many other factors. These data may also reflect the fact that many of the revised curricula stopped short of having maximal impact by avoiding the use of requirements. That is, although writing and critical thinking across the curriculum were widespread, some colleges did not make them curricular requirements, allowing many students to avoid such courses. Similarly, many colleges offering interdisciplinary core courses or courses using original sources did not require them. By providing options, they made it possible for students to avoid taking courses that were designed to have significant educational impact.

Active learning and greater appreciation for racial and cultural diversity were the two categories with the least reported improvement. Even so, about four out of five deans reported at least some improvement. More active learning may have resulted from colleges making that a specific goal for general education courses, sometimes a criterion for approving them. Further, the emphasis on skills such as writing and critical thinking that require students to assume responsibility for actually doing things, and the small classes found in freshman and senior seminars as well as skill courses, make it more difficult for students to be passive spectators. And as we have seen, many of the revised curricula include a greater emphasis on cultural diversity and the study of other peoples. At the same time, it must be noted that higher education has been white-dominated and lecture-dominated, with a few important exceptions, for its entire history. Nobody should underestimate the difficulty of altering the course of this history.

Another area of concern is the relationship between the general education program and academic majors. The departments have the power to advance their own interests at the expense of general education, and part of the reform agenda is to strengthen the core and to make it coherent in the face of centrifugal forces of the departments. As many have learned, the protection of departmental turf and of the academic majors are important barriers to reforming general education. When asked to judge the relation between general education and the majors, only 3 percent of deans said they thought general education weakens the majors on their campuses. This is an important finding. Despite all of the calls for improvements in the general education curriculum and the actions to strengthen it, deans believe that they have not eroded the majors. This should be a reassuring finding for faculty who fear that strengthening general education might weaken the majors by drawing resources away from instruction in the academic specialties.

Indeed, most respondents, 65 percent, profess that there is a "healthy balance" between general education and the majors. Many had worked to create a better balance precisely by strengthening general education. The dominant kind of change was to assure that students are knowledgeable about a wide range of subjects, aware of cultural diversity, skilled in writing and critical thinking, and able to relate ideas with other fields of study. Would not students with such qualities be welcomed by teachers in any field? Would they not make teaching more stimulating and exciting? Would not that kind of education be a wonderful complement to mastery of any specialty? That seems to be what the deans report to be happening on nearly two out of three campuses in this survey.

In fact, the majors may be strengthened by general education changes. How can this happen? Some departments, especially in the humanities, proliferated courses during the 1980s in search of enrollment. At one institution a new freshman seminar gave faculty members the opportunity to drop courses that were uncertain to attract sufficient enrollment in favor of a secure seminar on a topic of their interest. These courses became vehicles to recruit majors to their department. The humanities division at another college conducted a seminar on recent feminist scholarship, and several faculty incorporated this cutting-edge scholarship into their specialty courses. The increased enrollment associated with the new curriculum at another college gave each department a larger number of students majoring in their fields. These are examples of ways the ferment surrounding general education has had beneficial results for some major programs, results that perhaps contribute to the deans' sense that the reform did not weaken the majors.

A third of the respondents reported, however, that the majors weaken general education. Some deans noted that departmental interests tend to subvert general education in the assignments of faculty, the press to conduct research, and the reward structure that slights teaching and advising of nonmajors. One person said that each of the alternatives would be accurate on his campus, depending on the particular department. Two said neither characterization was accurate, one observing, "There is precious little interaction at all, certainly not a 'healthy balance.'"

For years I have argued that a strong general education program is compatible with strong academic majors. In the words of Ernest Boyer (1987, p. 290), "Rather than divide the undergraduate experience into separate camps — general versus specialized education — the curriculum at a college of quality will bring the two together." Here is some evidence that improvements in general education need not be made at the expense of the majors, although the task of obtaining a healthy balance is complex.

One other way to examine the significance of the changes was to ask the deans, "How close is your general education program to *your own ideal* one for your students, faculty, and institution?" Thirty-nine percent said quite or very close, 42 percent said somewhat, and 20 percent said not very close. Further analysis revealed that a number of the group most unhappy with their program were in the process of revising it; their unhappiness was part of the impetus to launch a review, not a conclusion after a reform. Some also were new to their positions and saw further improvements they would like to make in the curriculum they had inherited.

The rest of the respondents were fairly evenly divided between seeing the program as only somewhat close to their ideal on the one hand and quite or very close on the other. Since deans are often initiators of curriculum reviews and are responsible for managing the process of change, it is not surprising that a good number reported that the result turned out to be close to their ideal. By the same token, the fact that so many reported the program to be only somewhat close to their ideal is due to the fact that they do not have their way. Deans cannot bring a curriculum into being by fiat; they, like other participants in a curriculum review process, must make compromises. Their original expectations were fairly high (at least to judge from the amount of change originally planned), and often a new compromise curriculum falls short of everyone's personal ideal.

What are the major reasons for the deans' assessments of the closeness to their ideals? Those reporting the program is *not* close to their ideal give the usual litany of criticisms expressed in Chapter One. Hear the views of deans from different types of institutions.

- Community college: "It represents the simplest political solution without taking on the issues of structure, coherence, and commonality." "Too many bricks (individual courses) and not enough house (cohesive, integrated, core program)."
- Comprehensive college: "[It is] too much of a smorgasbord; [it] omits cultural diversity, global perspectives, interdisciplinarity, skills across the curriculum." "It is a 'lowest common denominator' approach."
- Research university: "A big state university will never have the kind of intensive general education experience that a smaller teaching college offers. But even in comparison with other big universities, we have a long way to go."
- Liberal arts college: "[Disappointment] that more new courses were not created, that too many old ones were modified or not changed at all, and that we are regressing back toward the starting point." "The actual changes in pedagogy in the classroom have been small."

These are important cautionary tales that should be taken to heart by curriculum review task forces that want to learn from the mistakes of others.

What about those deans who *are* in basic agreement with their college's general education? In general, these individuals report much improvement, especially when seen in the context not of a platonic ideal but of the practical constraints of politics, resources, and type of institution.

- Community college: "It reflects my sense of what a community college can and ought to do to prepare its graduates for the contemporary world: to understand it, criticize its deficiencies, and resolve to ameliorate them."

- Comprehensive college: "As chair of the revision committee and now dean of the program, I have a sense that we progressed as far as we could have." "We are making the most efficient use of time and resources with a clear focus on what is good for students."

- Research university: "[We have] the best possible approach for the entire university at this time. Ideally I prefer a core curriculum of the required kind, but this is not a possibility in [our] near future, and we have a very good program that is possible to achieve and will make a difference here."

- Liberal arts college: "It raises important questions of personal identity and values within a context which emphasizes community and community standards. It stresses skill development and gives students much greater interaction with faculty than before."

Chester Case, president and previous dean at Los Medanos College, reflected over a longer time frame than many, as that community college introduced its distinctive three-tier curriculum over a decade ago. He observed that there is a "reversion over time to the conventional and a drift from the spirit of the original program." He also noted, "There is a gap between what we do and my ideal of an explicit, relentless emphasis in the content and pedagogy of each course on the rationale for general education... and an exploration of its relevance for the student—a 'meta-message' about the program." He reminds us that any change is in danger of eroding unless its purposes are kept in mind and faculty and students are true to them in their daily work. Unless the spirit can be kept alive, even the best curriculum may lose its vitality and, thereby, sow the seeds for others, concerned with quality and coherence in the future, to overthrow it.

### Comprehensive Versus Piecemeal Change

Some colleagues who have had an opportunity to examine the above reports wondered if the deans might have portrayed events too positively. They suggested that administrators might give more positive views than, say, faculty members. If so, that would not surprise survey researchers who have long known about social desirability and other technical factors that affect the results. Despite the existence of what is called "response bias," survey research has proven to be a useful tool in studying a wide variety of people and settings. There is no reason to assume that academic administrators are a special breed for which it is inappropriate. One of the ways to handle response bias is to do analyses among subgroups, since there is little reason to assume that it operates differentially among groups of respondents. Indeed, the most striking findings from this survey are derived from analyses between groups in this and the next two chapters.

*Curriculum Components and Supports.* I was interested in whether different kinds of curriculum change might be differentially associated with various educational practices or consequences. Might institutions making large-scale change engage in different practices or derive greater benefits than those that had adopted a more modest change? In order to answer this question, we looked at the size of the change that was reportedly made in the general education program. Eighty deans reported making a large change, seventy-seven a moderate change, and thirty-two a small change. Although the definition of these terms was left to the respondents, those reporting a small change focused on one (or a limited number) of the components, such as a writing program. Those indicating a large change altered many components and adopted a more comprehensive reform. Then we analyzed these groups in relation to other items in the questionnaire. The size of program change was positively related to a revealing configuration of factors. This kind of analysis has the advantages that it is less subject to response bias and it offers insights into the factors responsible for effective change.

A large change was more likely than a small one to include certain curriculum components, especially those that affect the pedagogy of individual courses. Further, it more frequently emphasized a coordinated approach to the teaching of

**Table 3.5. Curriculum Components and Supports Associated with Size of Change in General Education.**

|  | Small Change | Large Change |
|---|---|---|
| Curriculum components offered: |  |  |
| Interdisciplinary core courses | 47 | 72 |
| Courses using original sources | 31 | 58 |
| Freshman seminar | 38 | 48 |
| Senior seminar, project | 28 | 38 |
| Across-the-curriculum themes offered: |  |  |
| Writing | 62 | 91 |
| Gender issues | 25 | 61 |
| Cultural pluralism | 28 | 61 |
| Ethics or values | 28 | 61 |
| Global studies | 34 | 60 |
| Computer literacy | 34 | 49 |
| Curriculum supports provided: |  |  |
| Faculty committee for general education | 25 | 74 |
| Administrator responsible for general education | 12 | 55 |
| Major systematic faculty development program | 9 | 50 |
| Policy of active learning in courses | 25 | 50 |
| Student services furthering purposes of general education "quite a lot" or "very much": |  |  |
| Academic advising | 48 | 87 |
| Orientation | 19 | 63 |
| Admissions | 16 | 35 |

certain subjects across the curriculum. A large change also more often employed stronger curriculum supports — such as policies, governance, and faculty development — than a small one.

As shown in Table 3.5, large curriculum changes more commonly offered interdisciplinary core courses, courses that employed original sources rather than textbooks, freshman seminars, and senior seminars or projects. The majority of them also utilized a variety of across-the-curriculum emphases, including writing, gender issues, cultural pluralism, ethics or values, and global studies; nearly half taught computer literacy in this fashion. All of these program components involve not simply changes in the content but also in the pedagogy of general education. That is, interdisciplinary core courses typically involve reading, discussion, and the making of connections among different subjects. Courses that stress original sources, too, typically include a good deal of give and take and exploration of alternative interpretations of the texts. The seminars presume small classes with an abundance of classroom dialogue and interaction. In each type of course, students usually are expected to develop their own views and to defend them in discussions with the teacher and classmates. These kinds of changes, especially if they are coordinated throughout the curriculum, involve more careful attention to what goes on in the classroom—and often meaningful changes on the part of individual faculty—than simply altering graduation requirements.

Most general education programs, even revisions, include a distribution of study across the various academic disciplines as well as the development of such generic abilities as writing and mathematics (Toombs, Fairweather, Chen, and Amey, 1989). But this does not tell the whole story. Many of them also have additional special features, such as freshman and senior seminars and study across the curriculum, that are often difficult to detect in catalogue studies. Apparently it is these additional matters, especially when they require serious attention to classroom pedagogy, that characterize comprehensive changes.

Another related point: Not only did institutions with large-scale change offer these options but they more often *required* each of them of students. For example, cultural pluralism was required in 6 percent of the institutions making a small change and in 46 percent of those making a large change. Requiring such study, especially in an across-the-curriculum format, necessitates a much more complex implementation process—guidelines to assure that they are serving similar ends, assistance to faculty members, monitoring many disparate courses—than simply providing them as options. It is understandable that the respondents would regard such efforts as a large change.

A large change also was more likely to provide strong supports for the general education curriculum. Half of the campuses reported having a systematic faculty development program of major proportions targeted specifically for general education. This is about five times as many as colleges making a small change. One of the reasons for this association is that comprehensive change of many curriculum components is likely to require developing new types of courses, such as freshman or senior seminars, or courses that incorporate perspectives across the curriculum. Another reason is that a large change is riskier than a small one, and faculty development may reduce the risk by assisting faculty to learn new material, develop courses, and assist each other in implementing the curriculum. Or perhaps it is simply that deans regard a major program of faculty development that complements a curriculum change as a more significant change than the same curriculum change without the faculty development effort.

Governance supports, too, tend to be stronger for more comprehensive revisions. About three-fourths of them organized an institution-wide faculty committee to oversee the general education program. Most such campuses assigned an administrator responsibility primarily for general education, so that she or he would have a clear focus of authority and not be distracted by a host of competing claims on his or her time and attention. These arrangements provide for greater central authority over the program and allow for the possibility of more coherence than in the small-change group.

Deans from colleges making comprehensive changes in general education also were more likely to report that a series of student services were coordinated with the curriculum and furthered its purposes: academic advising of students, orientation, and admissions, in particular. These are all services that present students with information about the academic program and, equally important, about its rationale; a major change in the curriculum requires staff working in these areas to adapt their presentations to the new realities. Each of these offices is involved in setting expectations of students about the curriculum, and each can play a major role in helping students to approach a new curriculum in a positive, even enthusiastic, way. Also, it is easier to market a more purposeful and structured curriculum than a purposeless and shapeless one. Indeed, a structured one needs explanation in order to convey the purposes to prospective students and for a student to plan a sensible course of study.

*Curriculum Outcomes.* A number of reported conse-quences also were related to the size of curriculum change, as shown in Table 3.6. Attitudes of administrators, faculty mem-bers, and students were more favorable toward general educa-tion where there were large changes. Reports of greater educa-tional outcomes came from places that made large changes: higher-quality education, greater curricular coherence, more faculty renewal, greater appreciation for diversity, more active learning, and a revitalized institution. Like the changes in at-titudes, these differences are dramatic; over three times as many respondents in large-change institutions reported substantial improvement in each of the outcomes as in small-change institu-tions.

Comprehensive curriculum change was more likely than small change to have a positive impact on various aspects of the institution. Faculty renewal, institutional identity, public rela-tions, and a sense of community were cited by 74 percent to 85 percent of the deans, much more often than their counterparts at small-change institutions. Even on items where less than half of the respondents at large-change institutions reported a positive impact—for example, admissions, fund raising, and the faculty reward structure—such impacts were more common than at small-change colleges. Finally, the programs that had been changed a lot were closer to the dean's ideal, probably because a larger change gave him or her a better opportunity to influence the curriculum.

It is noteworthy that the size of the curriculum change was *not* related to certain variables that some might expect. For example, the size of the change was not correlated with whether the new program had increased or decreased the total number of semester credit hours of general education required for grad-uation. Nor was the size of change related to the balance be-tween general education and the academic majors.

The lesson to be drawn from this analysis is this: If a little bit of reform is good, more is better. Those institutions that

Table 3.6. Outcomes Associated with Small and Large Changes in
General Education.

| | Small Change | Large Change |
|---|---|---|
| Attitudes toward general education more favorable: | | |
| Administration | 42% | 89% |
| Faculty | 29 | 85 |
| Students | 26 | 49 |
| "Quite a lot" or "very much" change in: | | |
| Higher-quality education | 19 | 82 |
| Greater curricular coherence | 22 | 80 |
| Faculty renewal | 19 | 72 |
| Greater appreciation for diversity | 19 | 63 |
| More active learning | 16 | 61 |
| Revitalized institution | 9 | 64 |
| Positive impacts on: | | |
| Faculty renewal | 44 | 85 |
| Institutional identity | 41 | 85 |
| Public relations, visibility | 19 | 82 |
| Sense of community | 36 | 74 |
| General education budget | 23 | 64 |
| Retention of students | 16 | 58 |
| Admissions | 16 | 47 |
| Fund raising | 25 | 45 |
| Faculty reward structure | 3 | 36 |
| General education "quite" or "very" close to dean's ideal | 9 | 60 |

made the largest, most comprehensive changes—presumably doing the most serious and boldest thinking about the nature of instruction at the heart of undergraduate education—derived the greatest benefits for their students, their faculty, and their own functioning. The process of strengthening general education curricula is like a pebble dropped in a pond. Ripples radiate out from it and impact all other parts of the educational enterprise. A comprehensive revision tends to make a larger splash than a smaller one.

## Institutional Differences

How did these various factors differ among institutions? One might expect different kinds of institutions to operate different kinds of curricula and to experience different consequences. Liberal arts colleges, for example, are often regarded as more favorable to general education and more fertile grounds for curriculum reform than research universities. For this analysis, the Carnegie classification was compressed, and comparisons were made among four groups: all liberal arts colleges, all comprehensive institutions, all combined research and doctorate-granting universities, and the community colleges.

Institutional differences, in fact, were found, but with a surprising twist. That is, large change was reported in 79 percent of the community colleges, 52 percent of the combined research and doctorate-granting universities, and 36 percent of both comprehensive and liberal arts colleges. The higher proportion of comprehensive change in community colleges may reflect a sampling artifact. Few two-year colleges were included in proportion to the entire population, and the ones selected may have included a disproportionate number of those making large revisions. Similarly, a number of liberal arts and comprehensive institutions were included because they had received grants to work on specific general education projects; a number of those may have had little intention of making a major overhaul. An alternate explanation is that curriculum change that features the liberal arts and fundamental thinking skills may appear to be a larger and more impressive change in community colleges, which have been vocational in orientation, and in research universities, with their graduate and professional priorities.

In terms of components of general education curricula, community colleges were much less likely to offer a freshman seminar and somewhat less likely to offer interdisciplinary core courses or those using original sources. However, if any of these components were offered, both community colleges and research–doctorate-granting universities were more likely to make them optional than to require them. That may be because these institutions tend to have greater diversity of academic programs and types of students; requirements for all students in all programs tend to be anathema in these contexts. A letter from a senior academic administrator in one major university expresses this view well. "We have seven undergraduate colleges, each of which deals with the issue (general education) in its own way. And, in addition, the variety of options available to students is such that virtually none of them pursue the same path through their undergraduate years" (anonymous, 1990).

In terms of the several outcomes discussed above, there was only one statistically significant difference between institutions: in the amount of positive change in the attitudes of administrators toward general education. Ninety-four percent of the community colleges reported more positive attitudes, as compared with 84 percent of the research and doctorate-granting universities, 70 percent of the comprehensive institutions, and 58 percent of the liberal arts colleges. That order may reflect a kind of continuum of commitment to the liberal arts and general education. That is, the community colleges are the most vocational in orientation, and the liberal arts colleges are the most "purist." These results may reflect the growing appreciation of the liberal arts—and the general education programs where they are featured—among administrators who have been more strongly oriented to career preparation. Whatever the reasons, more positive attitudes toward general education among administrative leaders, especially in settings that have been less than hospitable to liberal learning, may be one of the most important long-term consequences of the reform movement. Such individuals may provide additional leadership for strengthening general education programs in coming years.

No other differences, statistically speaking, were found among the major types of institutions on any of the outcome variables. That is, there were no differences in the reported changes in attitudes of faculty and students toward general education, in educational benefits, in institutional impacts, or in the closeness to the dean's ideal.

In summary, while there are a few differences in the character of curricula at different kinds of institutions, they appear to be few and not terribly significant. And in terms of reported consequences of the changes, there are virtually no institutional variations. It appears that the benefits of general education reform are more related to the size and character of the changes than the kind of institution. Comprehensive change is possible in all kinds of institutions, although more common in these community colleges, and it seems to be powerfully related to a number of valued educational and institutional outcomes.

## Conclusion

Some observers think that little is coming out of the general education movement, even on campuses that have been working on improvements. The reports we have directly from the campuses indicate, however, that colleges and universities that have changed their general education curricula—as a group—have derived important benefits. They tended to improve the quality and coherence of education for students, renew faculty members, and strengthen aspects of their institutions. A more purposeful and tighter general education curriculum with a grounding in the liberal arts and sciences produced valuable benefits in most cases. In many cases the benefits were slight, but in the majority of cases they were reported to be rather substantial. Although one must issue a disclaimer that past results do not guarantee future performance, it seems that the quality of higher education may be improved if additional colleges review and improve their curricula.

To be sure, some colleges that talk a good game of reform are in fact only tinkering with distribution requirements or taking a few cautious steps away from the status quo. Those making small changes are few in number in this sample, and they report minimal improvement in their programs and relatively few benefits.

Lest we be too quick to judge them, we should acknowledge the value of small efforts. Some curricula are in good shape and, frankly, do not need much change. Further, campuses where common experiences, coherent curricula, or cross-disciplinary dialogue among the faculty are rare may find it useful to cultivate small improvements. A group of faculty members may be working, for instance, on a freshman year program, perhaps reading the literature, studying what other institutions are doing, and offering a few courses on an experimental basis to students interested in them. Another group may be developing a writing program and another one discussing the "canon" and its critique. Such small-scale efforts can build knowledge, experience, trust, and enthusiasm; the faculty involved in them may become leaders for expanding the program. Spawning small-scale efforts is thus a valuable strategy toward more comprehensive change.

Yet those colleges that adopted comprehensive change reaped the greatest benefits—for their students, their faculty, and themselves. They were more likely to adopt policies and programs that called for changes in the conditions of teaching and learning within individual courses, not just in curriculum requirements and structures. And they strengthened the curriculum with a variety of structural supports. My conclusion is that since achievements generally are consistent with their plans, colleges should be encouraged to think in a comprehensive way about their general education programs and to consider devising bold plans. Indeed, to judge from those that have taken this route, it seems to be very much in their self-interest to do so.

*Chapter Four*

# Faculty Development Programs and Strategies

Faculty development is the other side of the coin from curriculum reform, an essential ingredient in any serious attempt to improve general education. The faculty are responsible for the curriculum, and they are the only ones who can implement a change in it. Conscious efforts to foster their professional development promote improvements in general education in four separate ways.

First, these efforts assist the review and redesign of the curriculum. Curriculum review task forces and their faculty colleagues learn about the widespread dissatisfaction with the current state of affairs, consider issues in the debate about the quality of undergraduate education, learn what other colleges are doing to foster improvement, explore alternative curriculum models, and make informed choices among proposals to improve conditions. Some reviews of general education are initiated by a faculty development committee, discussed at specially designated professional development days, and supported by professional development funds.

Second, once a new curriculum is approved, faculty development is once again called upon as individuals prepare for new teaching responsibilities—for example, to teach writing in various subject matters or to design courses that incorporate more international or multicultural content. Faculty members are often willing to participate in these important initiatives, but they look for assistance in doing so.

Third, after a curriculum is implemented and operating more or less well, it needs to retain its vitality. Faculty members may find it useful to recall the original purposes and rationale of the curriculum, review their courses individually or collectively, assess the progress of students, consider refinements in the program, and otherwise nurture the program. Especially if it has a distinctive quality, the distinctiveness needs constant care and feeding, because the pressures in the academy are to return to more standard forms. As one reformer declared, "This college was most distinctive the day that it opened; all the changes have tended to return it to the status quo."

Finally, sometimes a college decides not to alter its graduation requirements or curriculum structure but to concentrate instead on improving the quality of teaching and learning that takes place within the existing structure. A series of seminars, workshops, and small grants assist faculty to acquire new ideas and to express them in engaging ways in their courses.

In all of these ways, faculty and curricular development are closely intertwined. Indeed, it makes little sense to alter curricular structures or requirements unless faculty members rethink at least some of their courses in light of the purposes of the new framework. Simply reshuffling the same old courses does not constitute a genuine reform. By the same token, it also makes little sense to support the development of faculty if their gains are not reflected in some way in the curriculum. Their own growth and learning should be reflected in what they do with students. Genuine reform in a curriculum requires that faculty members be given time, resources, and support to learn new material, revise their courses or design new ones, and develop new approaches to their teaching.

## A Brief History

The concept and practice of faculty development have evolved in three different phases. Historically, faculty development has meant mechanisms to help faculty master their subject matter specialties and keep up to date in their fields; sabbatical leaves, travel to professional meetings, research grants, and assistance in completing advanced degrees are typical practices.

A second phase emerged during the 1970s that emphasized the improvement of teaching and learning (Group for Human Development in Higher Education, 1974; Gaff, 1975; Nelsen and Siegel, 1980). Retreats and workshops introduced newly developed exercises and activities to faculty members so that they might become more conscious of the attitudes and values affecting their instruction, consider alternative teaching strategies, systematically analyze and design their courses, and practice honing their instructional skills.

We are now into a third phase in which the goals and methods of both subject matter knowledge and pedagogical improvement are brought to bear in furthering institutional priorities, such as implementing a new curriculum, serving a new student clientele, or conducting an assessment of student outcomes. Various approaches and strategies previously used to advance teaching and learning in general are used for particular purposes, such as implementing a new curriculum.

Unlike earlier efforts to promote the development of faculty with programs that support individuals regardless of their teaching assignments, programs to achieve institutional purposes require a large amount of collaboration, coordination, and commonality of effort. That is especially true when it comes to designing and implementing a new general education program. Actually, some of these new programs regarding faculty development and curriculum revision are simply recent attempts to restore the wholeness that united them at an earlier time. Lionel Trilling illustrates this by recalling his experience as a college teacher at Columbia University through the 1930s, 1940s, and 1950s: "I inhabited an academic community which was informed by a sense not merely of scholarly, but of educational purpose, and which was devoted to making ever more cogent its conception of what a liberal and humane education consists in. It has been possible for there to be. . . a concern with questions of what is best for young minds to be engaged by, with how they may best be shaped through what they read—or look at or listen to—and think about" (1980, pp. 45–46).

Over the decades Trilling was a leading professor in Columbia's core Western history and literature course, Contemporary Civilization. That holistic experience merged his intellectual interests with his interests in teaching and learning, the development of his teaching with the development of the curriculum, his own development with the development of the community. It would have been impossible to conceive of any of these as antithetical. But in recent decades these several aspects of the faculty role have become severed, and it takes a conscious effort to put them back together. Hence, faculty development today is often a means of restoring wholeness in faculty life as well as in undergraduate general education.

## Types of Programs

Even though faculty development *can* facilitate improvements in general education, it is important to learn the roles it actually played in revisions of the curriculum. The survey asked whether the institution had a "*systematic program* to develop faculty knowledge or skills to strengthen general education." Although the phrase "systematic program" was highlighted, the definition was left to each respondent. What I had in mind was some form of organization, an assigned leader, adequate budgetary and other resources, and a program of activities with both variety and continuity. Seventy-one respondents, or 32 percent, said yes, they had a major program, and 78 respondents, or 35 percent, reported having a modest one. Seventy-five, or 34 percent, said they had no systematic program, although several did offer a few activities. This represents almost as much variation as the questionnaire format allowed in terms of the use of faculty development for improving general education.

I was interested in how many faculty members teaching general education courses had been involved in faculty development. The deans reported these estimates: 13 percent indicated fewer than 10 percent of the faculty, 29 percent said 10 to 29 percent of the faculty, 26 percent checked 30 to 49 percent of the faculty, and 32 percent reported 50 percent or more of the faculty had been involved. This is a great deal of variation: Nearly a third of the institutions involved the majority of their general education faculty, and most managed to engage a sizable minority.

Faculty development programs served two different ends. (1) The improvement of subject matter knowledge — for example, to help faculty teams to design and teach interdisciplinary core courses — was the focus in 56 percent of the colleges. Most of these colleges offered seminars, retreats, and workshops on intellectual issues, common themes, or particular texts as well as traditional activities, including providing leaves, research support, and travel for individual faculty members to update or extend their knowledge. (2) The focus on developing a new or strengthened pedagogy and enhancing student learning was found in even more colleges, 74 percent. These colleges drew upon the techniques developed during the 1970s (Bergquist, Phillips, and Quehl, 1975, 1977) to assist faculty members in improving teaching and learning, typically adapting the seminars, workshops, retreats, and their exercises to their own particular general education programs. Obviously, these are not mutually exclusive purposes, and many colleges had both emphases.

Given the wide variety of instructional programs offered at the colleges in this sample, it should be no surprise to learn that they employed a wide variety of faculty development activities. Here is a sampling of the most notable features of the programs:

- Summer seminars on various subjects
- Workshops on great teaching, learning styles, and applying student development models to instruction
- Faculty conferences, retreats, and work days to plan and develop curricular materials
- Small grants, release time for course development to incorporate writing, computers, and multicultural and other topics

- Travel to attend professional meetings on curriculum and instruction and to visit programs at other institutions
- Visits by consultants, speakers, and experts
- Mentoring and peer coaching
- Team teaching, with experienced faculty members paired with less experienced ones in a core course
- Development of interdisciplinary teams dealing with such topics as multicultural perspectives, gender issues, critical thinking, and writing across the disciplines
- Significant training prior to teaching first-year symposiums and senior seminars
- Use of a teaching and learning center to stimulate discussions, provide information, and consult with individuals
- Weekly staff meetings of those teaching in the freshman Western Heritage and senior Judeo-Christian Perspective sequences
- Training in textual analysis, group critique, and discussion skills
- Conversations among individuals in the professional departments and those in the humanities and sciences

A close reading of the comments on the questionnaires reveals several additional points of interest about faculty development activities. First, these activities were often supported by grants from private foundations and public funding agencies. Fortunately, a number of organizations provide funds to support faculty as they implement new instructional programs. Private sources mentioned include the Bush Foundation, Lilly Endowment, and Mellon Foundation as well as the Consortium for the Advancement of Private Higher Education. Public agencies include the National Endowment for the Humanities, Fund for the Improvement of Postsecondary Education, Title III for developing institutions, and Title VI for international education. Considering that some institutions were included because they received such grants or their grant-funded work was noted in publications, this result is hardly surprising.

Second, several deans indicated that, whatever they already were doing in regard to faculty development, a special extra effort was needed to bring about significant change in general education. Several said they were planning a more extensive faculty development program, as their curriculum proposals and revisions advanced. A few, however, conditioned their commitment to the receipt of outside grants. It is apparent that most deans with faculty development plans thought that additional programs and funds to support individual faculty members were needed to effect change in the general education curriculum.

It is noteworthy that some colleges had adopted a policy that requires faculty teaching certain components of the curriculum (for example, freshman seminars, skills courses across the curriculum, interdisciplinary core courses, and senior seminars) to participate in specified development activities. The rationale is that these special types of courses call for knowledge and teaching strategies that are different from usual courses, and faculty members need special assistance to teach them effectively. Further, different courses that satisfy the same curriculum requirement should address similar educational goals. Groups of faculty members must meet and develop guidelines that provide both commonality among a group of courses, such as freshman seminars, and flexibility for individual instructors to adapt them to their own strengths and interests.

Recruiting enough individuals from the faculty to offer enough courses or sections to meet the needs of the student body can be a serious problem, especially at a large university. For example, in order to require a freshman seminar limited to twenty students, one large university would have to offer 185 sections. Apart from questions of educational value, this would be an enormous personnel and logistical matter. Usually such considerations are handled by the curriculum review committee before a proposal is approved. Nobody wants a faculty member to teach a freshman seminar, for example, who does not want to—not the faculty member, not the department chair, and most of all, not the students. Although there are cases of a curriculum being approved without the faculty to staff it, typically, by the time a requirement is adopted, the faculty and administration have a pretty good idea that enough individuals are available to staff the necessary courses.

One of the maxims of faculty development is that the activities should be designed and executed so as to involve participants, to make the activities so interesting and useful that everyone wants to participate. Building on the intrinsic motivation of faculty and offering activities that have practical applications as well as theoretical underpinnings are ways some programs used to engage faculty. However it is accomplished, the faculty development program must be an example of excellence if faculty are to come forward and teach excellent general education courses.

Finally, several colleges reported a fair amount of faculty development programming that was not directed specifically to the needs of general education. This makes sense, because faculty members have a number of professional needs that deserve support, of which general education is only one. However, some colleges have not conducted an extensive faculty development program directed specifically at strengthening general education simply because they have been unwilling to reconsider the use of existing funds. One college that I visited had had an endowed fund that generated income used to give small grants to individual faculty. Although this doubtless produced useful benefits to individuals, it was redirected to support group as well as individual efforts and to specify that individual grants be awarded for the design or revision of courses to implement the new curriculum. Faculty leaders of curriculum change sometimes have been pleasantly surprised to learn that they actually have more resources available than they expect simply because they can redeploy existing sums.

Several individuals mentioned aspects of their faculty development that are now standard principles of good practice at many institutions (Gaff, 1975; Eble and McKeachie, 1985; Schuster, Wheeler, and Associates, 1990). These include faculty commitment and ownership, good leadership, a standing faculty committee to design and oversee the program, a full- or part-time faculty director with time to plan and organize activities, an organizational "home," institutional commitment, assessment of activities, and provision of adequate resources. Like any effective program, these faculty development efforts built on faculty interest, encouraged self-reflection, made room for individual interests and styles, and relied on carrots rather than sticks for incentives.

How effective were these various programs? The deans were asked that question; 34 percent said they were very effective, 61 percent judged them as moderately effective, and 5 percent regarded them as not very effective. How did respondents know whether their programs were effective or not? Several of the most positive respondents cited evidence of success, such as

- Faculty satisfaction: "Faculty love the program and rank it among our highest priorities." "Faculty rave about [it]." "Numerous faculty have commented on the importance of the workshops and financial support to create freshman seminar courses and transform courses to meet cultural diversity and writing intensity requirements."
- New priorities: "People are thinking and talking about these issues who had not been before." "The most significant outcome is widespread cross-departmental discussions."
- New courses: "Eighty-five faculty completely revised their general education offerings. . . ." "Faculty [made positive] self-reports and evaluations as to their impact on their teaching in interdisciplinary, honors, and general education courses. . . ."

Programs are often differentially effective. A dean from a comprehensive institution rated her college's program as very effective but provided a more detailed breakdown. "Significant success in raising the level of commitment to and enthusiasm for teaching challenging core courses within integrated program; varied success in transforming teachers' pedagogical effectiveness; moderate success in expanding and deepening teachers' knowledge; significant success in building collaborative and cooperative ethic within and across disciplines; significant success in upgrading quality of instruction in core program."

Jan Bowman, the faculty chair of a committee responsible for bringing forth a new general education curriculum at California Lutheran University, cited several kinds of evidence about the effectiveness of its decade-old cluster program that joins writing courses in the English department with courses in other disciplines: "(1) Positive assessments by four NEH consultants and evaluators, (2) positive evaluations submitted to the program coordinator after each faculty workshop, (3) changes in teaching styles and practices as evidenced by course outlines and materials, faculty-led workshop presentations, and classroom observation, and (4) student satisfaction with their learning experience in Cluster courses."

A time dimension is involved in these responses. Some faculty development programs were just beginning, and their effectiveness could not yet be assessed, while others were well established. One person whose college has long operated a program expressed what was implied in other responses by saying that professional development had become "an institutionalized expectation." Chester Case of Los Medanos College took a longer view. After about a decade of his college's operating a distinctive general education program, he observes that "things wind down, new faculty rotate in, administrators move to other assignments. There is a very short half-life to hot curricular ideas—they need to be refired very often. . . ." Several "old-timers" observed that faculty development is needed not just to implement a more coherent curriculum but to keep it vital throughout its life.

## Types of Curricula

The evidence from the survey indicates that faculty development is associated with the nature of the general education program adopted. This conclusion is reached by comparing the answers of respondents at the seventy-five institutions operating no systematic faculty development program with the seventy-one where major programs were in effect. In virtually all cases, the answers from the group with a minor program fell between those of the more extreme categories.

Table 4.1. Curricular Changes Associated with Faculty Development.

| | No Systematic Program | Major Program |
|---|---|---|
| Large change in general education: | | |
| Planned | 42% | 68% |
| Achieved | 28 | 65 |
| Faculty development: | | |
| Half or more of the faculty involved | 3 | 48 |
| Program regarded as very effective | 3 | 67 |
| Required special types of courses: | | |
| Interdisciplinary core courses | 25 | 55 |
| Courses using original sources | 11 | 46 |
| Freshman seminar | 15 | 42 |
| Senior seminar, project | 12 | 32 |
| Required across-the-curriculum themes: | | |
| Writing | 36 | 75 |
| Ethics or values | 17 | 55 |
| Global studies | 20 | 38 |
| Cultural pluralism | 16 | 35 |
| Computer literacy | 13 | 28 |
| Gender issues | 9 | 25 |
| Had policy of active learning in courses | 23 | 55 |

As shown in Table 4.1, a major program of faculty development was related to the scale of programmatic change in general education both planned and actually achieved. Among those with a major faculty development program, 68 percent of the deans reported planning a large change in general education, and 65 percent said they actually made a large change. In contrast, among those with no systematic faculty development effort, 42 percent said they planned a large change, and 28 percent said they made a large change. Not only is a major effort of faculty development related to the size of reform both attempted and achieved, but also there seems to be less slippage from original plans than at the colleges with no systematic faculty development.

Whether a college operated a major or modest faculty development program was related to the number of faculty members involved, which was probably also related to the scale of the curriculum revision. In colleges with a major program, 48 percent reported that half of the faculty members teaching general education were involved; in the colleges without a systematic program 3 percent said that many of the general education faculty were involved. A dean at a research university noted that "whenever there is a 'program,' the atmosphere changes, people become more readily involved, expectations change." This is one of the reasons why a systematic program is valuable and why it is related to the scale of change in the curriculum.

Similarly, respondents associated with major faculty development programs judged them as more effective; 67 percent said their programs were very effective and 33 percent moderately effective. Among those without systematic programs, 3 percent said they were very and 9 percent moderately effective. Some of the deans said their programs were differentially effective. One from a comprehensive college noted that the program was only moderately effective for the faculty less actively involved and very effective for those more actively involved. Another from a research university lamented, "Those who need it most have not taken advantage of the program." At a community college the writing-intensive effort was reported to have continuity featuring regular workshops, good publicity, effective follow-up, coordination with a nearby university, and a formal approval process for courses. In contrast, "other general education faculty development (activities) have been one-shot efforts and therefore less effective."

Certain components of revised curricula were also related to the existence of a major faculty development program. Specifically, interdisciplinary core courses, courses dealing with original sources, freshman seminars, and senior seminars were all more likely to be required if there was a major emphasis on faculty development. These are distinctive courses that few faculty members have designed or taught previously. If they are to be implemented as intended, many faculty need assistance and support in preparing them.

Similarly, curricula featured more across-the-curriculum themes at institutions with a major faculty development program. Further, more of them with a bigger stake in faculty development involved required courses, rather than options for students. Writing, ethics or values, global studies, cultural pluralism, computer literacy, and gender issues — all taught across the curriculum — were strongly associated with faculty development. These are especially difficult, even controversial, topics that require great sensitivity and skill to bring off well. When faculties approve such curricula, it is usually with the explicit understanding that they will be supported in developing the capabilities to implement them. Indeed, more than one faculty has approved a faculty development component at the time they approved a new curriculum requiring them to recast their courses to incorporate these themes.

One particularly intriguing aspect of some general education programs is a policy that courses should employ active learning, with less lecturing, memorization, and passivity on the part of students. A total of 41 percent of the respondents in the survey said that their general education program included such a policy for at least some components. It is noteworthy that those with a systematic faculty development effort were much more likely to have such a policy than those without. This may be because such a policy implies providing assistance for faculty to develop alternatives to the lecture. Lecturing is so pervasive in collegiate instruction that a major effort is needed for most faculty to put students and their initiatives at the center of instruction. Or the policy might have been enacted because the faculty, as a result of involvement in discussions and workshops on teaching and learning approaches, determined that a curriculum needs both substance and an engaging pedagogy.

It is apparent that faculty development is associated with the nature of the general education curriculum. It is a major strategy for change, and its absence acts as a major constraint on what is possible. This is why most deans were so eager to support the development of the faculty in regard to general education.

## Outcomes

It is time to ask about the consequences of formal programs of faculty development. Although not focusing on general education programs, other scholars have discovered that faculty development tends to have important influence on the professional lives and teaching behavior of faculty members. Michael Siegel (1980, p. 135) concluded from interviews he and William Nelsen conducted with over 500 individuals, mostly faculty members, at twenty liberal arts colleges that "the impact of the faculty development projects has been quite positive and substantial." Barry Morstain and I (Gaff and Morstain, 1978) found that the overwhelming majority of faculty members who participated in a variety of teaching improvement activities at quite varied institutions said they received the following benefits: increased motivation for teaching excellence, support for their own ideas or practices, greater awareness of their teaching assumptions, information about additional resources for use in their teaching, a broader understanding of faculty development, and new perspectives on teaching and learning. Eble and McKeachie (1985, p. 223), after studying the impact of faculty development grants from the Bush Foundation at thirty diverse institutions, concluded from their questionnaires, interviews, and campus visits, "We believe that faculty development programs not only enhance student learning but also can maintain and increase the satisfactions of teaching and of belonging to a community of learners."

These studies have looked at development of all faculty, not just those working in general education programs, but our concern here focuses on the impact of faculty development on faculty members, curricula, and students in general education. In keeping with the more generic assessments, we found that a systematic program of faculty development is associated not with just the characteristics of general education curricula but with their outcomes as well. The differences in general education outcomes between colleges with no systematic faculty development program and a major one are summarized in Table 4.2.

This is a fairly dramatic set of results, which indicates that a number of the benefits for students, faculty, and the institution are associated with faculty development. In general, this suggests the practical wisdom of operating a systematic program for the professional development of the faculty in implementing

Table 4.2. Outcomes Associated with Faculty Development.

| | No Systematic Program | Major Program |
|---|---|---|
| Attitudes toward general education more favorable: | | |
| Administrators | 52 | 84 |
| Faculty | 49 | 83 |
| Students | 21 | 51 |
| Quite a lot or very much change in: | | |
| Faculty renewal | 23 | 89 |
| Higher-quality education | 40 | 82 |
| Greater curricular coherence | 38 | 77 |
| More active learning | 24 | 68 |
| Revitalized institution | 27 | 68 |
| Greater appreciation for diversity | 35 | 55 |
| Positive impact on: | | |
| Faculty renewal | 48 | 88 |
| Institutional identity | 58 | 87 |
| Sense of community | 51 | 79 |
| Public relations | 48 | 75 |
| Efficient utilization of faculty | 36 | 65 |
| Admissions | 21 | 65 |
| General education budget | 32 | 62 |
| Retention | 24 | 58 |
| Fund raising | 20 | 57 |
| Faculty reward structure | 12 | 42 |
| General education quite or very close to dean's ideal | 20 | 57 |

a curricular revision. Indeed, it suggests that it would be foolhardy for a college to attempt a significant reform of general education — especially if it involves many new kinds of courses — *unless* it is committed to substantial faculty development.

In colleges with a major faculty development program, the attitudes toward general education became more favorable for larger proportions of administrators, faculty members, and students. This may be because individuals involved in workshops, seminars, or retreats, for example, may strengthen their own attitudes toward general education. Among like-minded colleagues sympathetic to the ideal of a broad general education, they may see its role in the full education of students and its centrality in the life of the college. This is certainly one of the primary goals of many faculty development programs.

Another possibility may be that participation in faculty development activities, particularly the communal type frequently found in general education revisions, exposes individuals to the positive attitudes of others, which ordinarily are not expressed. Ordinarily there are few forums for discussion of general education on college campuses, and therefore it is natural to perceive little faculty or administrative interest. When forums are created, individuals can see that there is a greater reservoir of good will than is generally known.

Another set of outcomes has to do with more fully realizing the large purposes driving general education reform. Having a major faculty development effort was positively related to campus leaders saying that the following results were achieved quite a lot or very much: faculty renewal, higher-quality education, greater coherence, more active learning, a revitalized institution, and greater appreciation for diversity. The straightforward interpretation of this set of variables may be most accurate; the faculty actually learned how to implement a general education curriculum that made a difference with students. For example, faculty members at the University of Nevada, Reno, attend a month-long seminar on issues related to their new Western Tradition sequence that focuses on a series of classic texts from the Greeks to the present. The faculty discuss various interpretations of the books and learn about the history of the periods in which they were written. They decide on common features (for example, texts, grading, and pedagogy) of these interdisciplinary core courses, develop syllabi, and devise their own individual variations on the common themes. The several courses feature two hours of lectures and an hour of discussion per week, and the different groups of lecturers and discussion leaders meet regularly to discuss substantive issues and practical matters in the courses. Without assistance, it is unlikely that faculty would have been able to coordinate their separate courses, learn content from one another, or generate the enthusiasm for this centerpiece of the new core curriculum. Faculty development may improve the conditions of teaching and learning and thereby produce more benefits from a curriculum change.

A major faculty development effort also was related to a number of institutional impacts: faculty renewal, institutional identity, sense of community, public relations, efficient utilization of faculty, admissions, general education budget, retention, fund raising, and faculty reward structure. Here, too, the obvious interpretation is that faculty development aided many institutions to implement the kind of programs that produced this range of benefits. And lacking the faculty development part of the reform puzzle, colleges were much less likely to put together a coherent general education that produced important educational and institutional benefits. This suggests that a systematic faculty development program produced larger ripples in the general education pond than a smaller effort. As was true of large comprehensive curriculum change, a major program of faculty development can make a large splash that impacts on other aspects of institutional functioning.

One impact, which was discussed in Chapter Three, deserves special comment: faculty renewal. The renewal of faculty was reported as a positive impact at 88 percent of the colleges with a major faculty development program contrasted with 48 percent of those with no systematic one. The amount of impact can be seen in another item. Eighty-nine percent of the institutions with a large faculty development program said faculty renewal occurred quite a lot or very much, contrasted with 23 percent of those lacking a systematic program. This is a very sizable difference, which underscores the conclusion of William Nelsen (1981, p. 46), "Changing curriculum is, of course, primarily for the benefit of the students, but the *process* of change and preparation may have greater meaning for the faculty." Professional growth and development is a major result of the changes in general education among these colleges and universities, especially those that offered the most opportunities for faculty.

Finally, the deans were more likely to report that the general education program resulting from the reform effort was closer to their own ideal if it was accompanied by a major faculty development effort. As we have seen, faculty development is a major vehicle for achieving a large-scale change in the curriculum and is associated with many important general education components. If a dean has the program and resources to support the faculty, he or she can more closely approximate his or her own ideal. Without that element, there is less likelihood that the faculty will pull together in the general education curriculum. They may mean well and work hard, but they will simply go their own individual ways, which does not necessarily add up to a coherent curriculum that has maximum impact on students or the institution.

The existence of a major faculty development program is one thing, and its effectiveness is something else. But we found that these two were, in fact, positively correlated. That is, respondents at colleges with a major faculty development program reported that it involved a larger proportion of the faculty, and they were more likely to regard it as effective than those at colleges with modest or no systematic programs. Thus, the judgments of effectiveness of faculty development—not just its existence—were positively related to all of the above outcome variables.

Institutional type was *not* related to the existence of a major program of faculty development; major programs were reported just as frequently among community colleges, liberal arts colleges, comprehensive institutions, and the combined research and doctorate-granting universities. The type of institution was related to the proportion of faculty who were involved and to the perceived effectiveness of the effort. Half or more of the faculty teaching general education courses participated in 49 percent of the liberal arts colleges, 38 percent of the community colleges, 23 percent of the comprehensive institutions, and 5 percent of the research and doctorate-granting universities. This result appears to be largely a function of size; a larger proportion of faculty in a small liberal arts college can be involved than is the case at a large research university. In terms of effectiveness, 69 percent of the community colleges reported their program was very effective compared with 34 percent of the liberal arts colleges, 27 percent of the comprehensive institutions, and 24 percent of the universities. It seems that major faculty development efforts can be operated in all kinds of institutions, but the proportion of individuals they reach and the perceived effectiveness of the program may be moderated by institutional conditions.

At this point I would like to offer another interpretation about faculty development, one that may tie all of these findings together. It is that colleges that operate a major program for the development of their faculty exhibit greater sensitivity to the needs of individuals — faculty members, students, and administrators — than those who lack such a program. This sensitivity and care for the development of individuals may underlie interest in both the general education of students and the development of the faculty and may also include the "people skills" to orchestrate a large and successful change in the core of the curriculum.

What evidence is there for this hypothesis? Some of it comes from an inspection of other items in the questionnaire. The two groups of respondents were compared in terms of their answers about what factors should be addressed in an evaluation of a general education program. There was no difference between the groups regarding the importance of student mastery of content, of their acquisition of skills, or of faculty effectiveness. The deans from colleges with major faculty development programs, however, more frequently favored addressing student satisfaction, changes in students (value added), faculty satisfaction, and institutional vitality. They seemed to believe that the feelings of students and faculty, growth of students as individuals, and a vital institution to support individuals were more important considerations than their counterparts without systematic support for the faculty.

Similarly, as we have seen, the colleges with strong faculty development programs disproportionately offered freshman and senior seminars, and they more frequently required them rather than offering them as options. It is as though more of them consciously rejected the "sink or swim" approach to students going through these two key transitions and opted for a mandated program to assist them. They seemed to exhibit greater sensitivity to the needs, dangers, and opportunities facing students in these critical transition points. Similarly, they more frequently offered across-the-curriculum instruction in writing, cultural pluralism, and ethics or values, and these, too, were more likely to be required than optional. These colleges seem to acknowledge that communication is essential for all students; that sensitivity to people is important, regardless of their race or gender; and that consciousness about ethics and values is central to the educated person. In all of these ways, such institutions expressed concern for their people.

Finally, those colleges with a major faculty development effort are more likely to have an administrator with primary responsibility for general education (51 percent versus 31 percent) as well as an institution-wide committee to oversee it (65 percent versus 41 percent) than those without one. They seem to appreciate the magnitude of the task of coordinating many individuals and molding them into a communal enterprise. And they tend to provide the authority to see that general education is implemented as intended. This new central authority—both administrative and faculty—may be necessary for individuals to reap the fruits of a sound general education program.

Perhaps what faculty development does best of all, then, is to put a human face on curriculum reform. Students are people who must be challenged, yes, but they must also be supported to reach higher achievements; they need rigor but also personal engagement. Faculty must assume their responsibility for general education, to be sure, but they, too, must be aided in developing knowledge, skills, and confidence—confidence in their own selves and in their colleagues. The fundamental importance of people may be the most important connection between faculty development and general education.

### Conclusion

Larry Goodwin, dean at St. Scholastica College, launched a curriculum review with a strong personal statement, declaring: "The key to curriculum revision is faculty development. We do not really revise—or better, *reform*—a curriculum just by adding or subtracting courses. What is required for a reformation is the energy that is born of a common commitment to a common goal. What is required is thinking about how we teach, as well as what we teach, about how students learn, and about how we evaluate their learning; what is required is a willingness to be self-critical and to learn from one another; in short, what is required is new wine as well as a new wineskin. The bulk of our work over the next several years should be with ourselves as teachers." (Sept. 1989)

We can now agree with Goodwin. Faculty development is not simply something "nice" to do. The evidence indicates that it is a very important strategy for strengthening general education by changing a curriculum, by improving the nature of teaching and learning within courses, and by keeping the focus on the people at the heart of the enterprise—students and faculty members. Simultaneously, it helps to increase the quality of education for students, to vitalize the institution, and to renew the faculty. As such, it is in everyone's self-interest to operate a substantial program that supports the professional growth of the faculty as teachers of general education.

# Chapter Five

# Educational Benefits for Students

The purpose of the curriculum and of the faculty and their development—indeed, the raison d'être of the college itself—is to promote the intellectual and personal development of students. We have seen that changes in general education programs have provided important benefits to institutions and to faculty members. Now it is time to explore their value to students, the ultimate beneficiaries.

Students have been conspicuous by their absence in this wave of reform. During the 1960s and early 1970s, students were a visible and driving force for curriculum change. Their protests against irrelevant courses, mediocre teaching, and unjustified requirements contributed to the widespread relaxation of requirements and to the adoption of educational alternatives such as experimental colleges, individualized learning contracts, and calendars permitting travel and other experiential learning. This time the reform movement is being led on campuses by faculty members and academic administrators; students are seldom included as full partners in the process of reviewing and revising the curriculum. Students sometimes are included on task forces working on curriculum change, but often student members are few and they are not central to the work. A change should be made: They should be full partners and given important assignments, their contributions should be heard, and they should be key liaisons to the student body. Such task forces could survey students about their experiences with general education and ideas about improvements, invite graduates to talk about how their education related to their lives after college and to offer suggestions for changes, consult with the student government and with other student leaders, and publish occasional articles in the student newspaper about important issues and progress of the task force. Students, no less than faculty, should know which problems are being discussed, which changes are proposed and why, and what is expected of them. Ideally, they should understand the changes, have a positive view of them, and have a sense of ownership of the new program. While some institutions do employ students in these ways and get a good payoff, others do not.

In a sense, the concern for students, specifically for the quality of their education, is sparking the public debate and driving the reform movement, so it may seem odd to say that they do not have much of a presence in campus changes. However, students as the presumed beneficiaries of something to be *done for or to them* are often treated as an abstraction and not as real live individuals. A curriculum review task force seeking to improve the education of students without including them in the process is reminiscent of the mythical individual who loves humanity but not necessarily people. Further, many curriculum task forces do not bother to gather data from their own students. If they would pay attention to students and their experiences, such groups could discover their educational goals and values, positive and negative experiences with general education, and valuable suggestions for improvement. Not only can students provide useful experience, ideas, and suggestions, but the very act of soliciting their views lays the basis for student support for the changes that are made. Some colleges that have taken students seriously and involved them in meaningful ways from the beginning of the process right through to full-scale implementation have reaped valuable benefits. Student understanding, acceptance, and commitment to the new program can go a long way in assuring its successful implementation.

Students often play a formal governance role in approving—or rejecting—proposed curriculum changes. For example, one task force spent a long time developing a proposal for a comprehensive change and submitted it to the Academic Policies Committee. Student membership was equal to faculty, and after the faculty members discussed the issues, the chair asked for students to comment on the proposal. Several task force members held their breath for fear that students might speak against it and doom their work. But one by one they spoke from their own personal experiences about the value of a proposed freshman seminar, the importance of having more writing and speaking, the benefit of a planned computer requirement. Later the task force learned that the student government had discussed the proposal with student members of the task force and unanimously instructed its members to support the plan. Having had a voice in the process of developing the proposal, the students were in a position to lend their very substantial support in a crucial vote. The strong support of the students was not lost on the faculty when they subsequently debated the proposal and approved it overwhelmingly.

There is abundant evidence, although it is not widely appreciated, that students want their colleges to provide more than preparation for a career; they also want a broad general education. Joseph Johnston, Jr., and his colleagues (forthcoming) reviewed several studies and concluded: "In study after study the collective level of support for general education is only moderately below that for goals relating to career preparation, and high enough to indicate that many, probably most, students are acknowledging major goals in both categories." The authors state that many students themselves are not clear about what they mean by general education: They report ambivalence and confusion, which, as we saw in Chapter One, is very common among academics at large. Whatever conceptions they have, their preferences may or may not be what their professors expect or what their colleges offer. But the authors point out that students clearly want more than preparation for a career. They suggest that general education seems to mean for students a configuration of four qualities: a broader intellectual horizon, stronger cognitive skills, getting along with other people, and personal growth.

Michael Davis and I discovered (Gaff and Davis, 1981) that although most students in diverse institutions wanted to achieve a broad general education, they regarded their colleges' general education programs (which were primarily in the form of loose distribution requirements) to be ineffective. Only 20 percent said they were very satisfied with their general education curricula, compared with 40 percent who were very satisfied with their electives and 52 percent with their majors. Further, they reported that the majority of their general education courses, which were largely a miscellany of introductions to the academic disciplines, failed to achieve any of the most common purposes ascribed to them: providing a broad intellectual foundation; challenging their own ideas, assumptions, or attitudes; stimulating their curiosity to learn more about those fields; or mastering new methods of intellectual inquiry. Although the study is dated, the results echo among today's students in colleges that have not revised their distributive studies. In such places, student dissatisfaction can be a useful force for improvement.

This chapter examines aspects of students' experience with the new approaches to general education, with particular attention to the benefits they derive from them. It concentrates first on the educational outcomes that students are reported to gain from the revised curricula. Second, it looks at where students gain the most and the least. That is, I relate the magnitude of reported student gains to various aspects of the curricula, to a variety of factors that support the curriculum, and to other outcome measures.

### Estimated Educational Value

Perhaps the most important question, the "bottom line" on their education, as it were, is what students learn. Ideally, one would have direct measures from students about the achievement — knowledge, skills, and personal qualities — resulting from their education. Unfortunately, that information is not available across the sample of institutions used in this book. And even if it were, it would be methodologically difficult, if not impossible, to attribute any gains to students' experiences in general education and not to any of their other experiences. For this book, then, I used a proxy for direct measures by asking deans to estimate the extent to which the current general education program resulted in greater educational value. Three areas in particular were used to infer educational value: higher-quality education, greater curricular coherence, and more active learning.

The choice of the three items used as global measures of educational value deserves comment. Higher-quality education and greater curricular coherence are more or less self-evident indicators of educational excellence. More active learning is a bit different. Astin (1985b, p. 133) has called involvement "the key to effective education," and he cites considerable empirical evidence that student learning and individual development tend to be related to the amount and quality of involvement. This item about active learning is an indicator of academic involvement.

Estimates about these matters are difficult to make, especially since the key terms were defined by each respondent, and their answers may vary among different types of students, different types of learning, and different components of the programs. But deans may reasonably report higher quality if students are required to pass courses dealing with history and culture, to learn mathematics and science, to write in several courses, and to learn about other peoples, especially where such requirements did not exist previously. They might perceive greater coherence if the curriculum has a clearer and more widely understood rationale, individual courses meet specified educational criteria, and students are expected to draw relationships between content in various courses. And more active learning may be inferred if that is a criterion used to approve general education courses; if students must utilize skills such as writing, speaking, and computing; or if courses involve reading and discussing original texts. The rather broad categories provided on the questionnaire allowed respondents to give rough estimates, which, as we shall see, were useful at least for comparative purposes.

Evidence directly from students surely informed some responses to these questions, because 61 percent of the respondents indicated that their general education programs either had been evaluated or were in the process of being evaluated. Information from students typically is included in such assessments. Other evidence underlying their judgments probably includes the usual range of reports, informal conversations, anecdotes, and other information available to academic administrators, such as course enrollments, student evaluations of courses, and retention data. In any event, the value of a measure such as this, in the final analysis, is determined by its utility, so let us look at the results.

Deans were asked, "To what extent would you say the change in your current general education program resulted in the following *consequences*?" In regard to higher-quality education:

- 20 percent checked "very much"
- 41 percent said "quite a lot"
- 35 percent indicated "somewhat"
- 5 percent said "not very much"

In terms of greater curricular coherence:

- 25 percent said "very much"
- 34 percent noted "quite a lot"
- 28 percent said "somewhat"
- 13 percent said "not very much"

Concerning more active learning:

- 19 percent said "very much"
- 26 percent replied "quite a lot"
- 35 percent said "somewhat"
- 20 percent reported "not very much"

The good news from this analysis is that the vast majority of deans reported at least some progress in each of these areas that figure prominently in the national debate.

The bad news is that the magnitude of the improvement is, on average, not large. About two of five colleges reported no more than somewhat of an increase in the quality of education and curricular coherence; the gain in active learning was even less. This is not too surprising, since many institutions made small or moderate changes in their curriculum and operate no faculty development program or a modest one. The major reason for weak results from any educational intervention is simply that the intervention did not really take place; modest changes may not have the power to alter the educational value of a curriculum very much. Further, significant improvement cannot be produced by the snap of one's fingers, and some of these programs are not very old. It may be well to keep in mind the dieter's dictum: It takes a long time to put on weight, and it takes a long time to remove it.

Furthermore, the natural flow of a curriculum change starts with the faculty and administration fashioning a change, the faculty acquiring new learning and developing new or revised courses, and often the college offering courses on a pilot basis before beginning implementation of the program. Then it takes four years for a student generation to pass completely through the entire curriculum. The students are the last to feel the impact. Also, there is slippage translating purposes into curriculum structures and then into individual courses—especially, as we have seen, at campuses with modest or no faculty development programs; the impact on students may be less than desired.

Nonetheless, these findings are consistent with the changes in attitudes toward general education that we discussed in Chapter Four. Recall that more positive attitudes were reported more often among administrators and faculty members than among students. A picture of large and significant benefits for faculty members and institutions is beginning to take shape, a picture that also shows more modest benefits for students, from the perceptions of deans.

One of the reasons for the more modest impact of general education on students may be that general education values and goals are not carried beyond the classroom. Academic life is often separated from the rest of student life, and researchers (Feldman and Newcomb, 1969; Chickering, 1969, 1981; Wilson and others, 1975; Astin, 1977) have shown that curriculum and courses have the greatest impact on the lives of students when classroom learning is consciously supported and reinforced throughout the rest of student life.

That is why the survey asked the respondents to estimate "the extent to which the purposes and values of general educa-tion are furthered" by a selection of activities in the general domain of student services. Although academic deans may an-swer differently from student affairs deans, the perceptions summarized in Table 5.1 are revealing.

The most striking thing about these data is how little most of these student services were reported to serve general educa-tion ends. Only in regard to academic advising and study skills did as many as half of the deans check either "quite a lot" or "very much" to describe their contributions. The reasons for their answers are informative. Several individuals observed that gen-eral education is "not viewed as a primary objective by the student affairs staff" or that "student affairs does not enjoy a high level of trust on the part of the faculty here." One dean noted that "academic advising, the most effective of these activities, is a *faculty* function and not a support activity." Another bluntly stated, "When [our school] controls the activity, such as Orienta-tion to College courses, academic development, and various learning laboratories, the purposes of general education are reached," implying that they are not reached otherwise. One noted that the student affairs staff "tend to support student choice rather than the principle of requirements."

Table 5.1. Student Services Furthering General Education.

|  | Not Very Much | Somewhat | Quite a Lot | Very Much |
|---|---|---|---|---|
| Academic advising | 4% | 24% | 43% | 29% |
| Study skills, tutoring | 12 | 35 | 37 | 16 |
| Library | 12 | 41 | 30 | 18 |
| Orientation of students | 12 | 42 | 32 | 15 |
| Campus convocations | 44 | 30 | 18 | 8 |
| Admissions | 39 | 35 | 17 | 8 |
| Residence halls | 50 | 37 | 11 | 2 |

The above comments reflect a tendency to partition the campus into an in-group and an out-group. "We" academic staff are good, responsible, and effective; "they" in student affairs are not. Some comments on the questionnaire reflect stereotypes indicative of the invisible wall that separates academic life from the nonacademic side of college life, a division reinforced on many campuses by separate administrative organizations that seldom intersect. As we will see, this arrangement has negative consequences for general education.

Advising is perhaps most logically and closely related to the curriculum, as its purpose is to help students plan their course of study. At its best, faculty members or professional advisers work with students to clarify their goals, explain requirements and their rationale, explore alternative courses of study, and plan their programs. But advising, unfortunately, is often not at its best. Some faculty members are assigned so many advisees that they cannot know the student and his or her goals; others do not take advising responsibilities seriously; a few may be uninformed about requirements or their rationale. More commonly, individuals have a narrow view of the role of an adviser and regard the signing of a registration card as the most significant activity. Good advising is hard work and time-consuming; it often involves "trench warfare" over general education, with students wanting to satisfy a requirement as easily and conveniently as possible and the adviser trying to explain the educational significance of various aspects of the curriculum.

Special assistance with study skills is also closely related to the content of general education. Study resource centers can offer assistance with writing, mathematics, reading, study habits, test-taking strategies, and personal counseling; tutoring is typically provided as needed. These are not simply remedial services found at open-admissions colleges, but they are common at all types of colleges. In many places, these services are underutilized by students, especially by those who need them the most. Further, the staffs of offices providing them often struggle with limited resources, lack recognition or respect, and labor with a sense of holding second-class citizenship.

The library and student orientation, like most of the services, were perceived with wide degrees of variation, but overall their patterns were similar. One might expect that the library would be particularly responsive to the curricular needs of general education, building useful collections in global studies or cultural diversity, for example. Although some appear to have done so, many seem not to have made much of a special effort. My impression is that library collections are about as fragmented and incoherent as the laissez faire general education curriculum. After all, book orders are requested by dozens of separate departments and scores or hundreds of individual faculty members, many of whom have been notorious for valuing their specializations over general education. Therefore, although general education may be strengthened in the curriculum, it may take a second order of effort to change traditional values and practices of the library, and this may be true of other support services as well.

Orientation typically focuses on assisting students to make a successful transition to college rather than on academic or curricular matters. If academic issues are included, they usually center around requirements for particular majors or preprofessional programs, rather than general education. Further, orientation is often planned and coordinated by student rather than academic affairs staff who may have less knowledge or interest in general education. The lack of effective orientation or advising leaves students wondering why they must take any particular course. Randy Bass (1981, p. 127), a student who served on a curriculum reform task force during his entire four years at the University of the Pacific, put it this way: "It is rare for a student to be educated in the process and meaning of education itself. Students are told to take three 'humanities' courses, but may never know what the meaning of 'humanities' is. A student may acknowledge that to know a foreign language or laboratory technique is important but may never comprehend why."

Admissions, convocations, and the residence halls were regarded by the academic deans as particularly non-contributory to general education. It is conventional wisdom among admissions officers that apart from certain majors, students seldom choose college because of the curriculum. This is especially true in the case of general education, which, with loose distribution systems, tends to be quite similar in most colleges. As a result admissions officers and their promotional materials seldom feature the general education goals or curriculum. This reality demeans general education even before a student sets foot on the campus and contributes to the mindset that it is not as important as the major. On the other hand, some colleges, especially those with comprehensive and distinctive programs, have featured general education in their admissions presentations and publications and helped to create positive expectations among new students. When I was at Hamline University, the admissions staff featured the Hamline Plan — a comprehensive and coherent general education curriculum — in publications and presentations. Students were attracted by the general educational goals and by the freshman seminars, the advising system, the writing and speaking programs, and the cultural breadth courses. This shift in admissions strategy paid off, because in two years freshman enrollment increased by a third, and the class increased in measures of quality and diversity. This success with admissions, combined with improved retention, produced a record enrollment, which in turn meant larger budgets and higher morale (see Carter, 1989).

Convocations, theoretically, can similarly serve to reinforce and extend certain values of the curriculum, but apparently they have little impact in most places. One respondent commented that "it is difficult to get students to seek out. . . cultural events." Among the colleges with residence halls, they, too, are said to make little contribution to general education. Indeed, from the point of view of these respondents, residence halls seem to be a virtual disaster area, as 50 percent of the respondents reported their contribution was "not very much."

What are the reasons for this unspectacular set of results? The reason most often mentioned by the academic deans is that these student support services were not coordinated with the curriculum. Problems exist on both sides of the aisle. One respondent said, "The faculty has not really looked at general education seriously in this way," and another on the other side observed, "We don't have a tradition of student affairs people thinking in terms of academic programs." One person spoke for many when she noted, "We haven't involved these other campus programs as much as we would like—but we're working on it."

It is important to point out that this is not so much a criticism of individuals as a reflection of the way the academy works. One respondent wrote, "[Our] co-curricular programs are among the strongest in the nation for an institution of this kind—comprehensive residential university with an active graduate school (M.A. and Ph.D.). However, they have not been particularly oriented to the liberal education program. . . . [Our] intention is to change that situation." Leadership to provide more effective coordination can be provided by either the academic or student affairs side of the equation—preferably by both.

Different offices provide most of these student services and as in any bureaucracy, there may be little awareness of how changes in one area, such as the curriculum, call for changes in another. The problem is compounded in colleges because academic and student affairs usually are administratively separate. This managerial division is particularly deep, with faculty members and student affairs staff creating negative views of each other, as we have seen, that are reinforced by little understanding or interaction. It takes special efforts to bridge the world of the faculty and the academic administration with that of the student affairs administration. If such efforts are not made, more than one college has found that their rigorous general education program is undercut by the admissions and orientation staffs, who give a higher priority to promoting "warm fuzzies"—a warm place, friendly and caring people, a safe environment—than to the intellectual goals that the college values and the curriculum that serves those ends.

Several respondents, on the other hand, rated student services as effective in furthering the goals of general education and cited reasons for this state of affairs, most frequently that student affairs and academic affairs were administratively joined and worked together toward common goals. Others cited specific collaborative efforts of faculty as well as academic and student affairs administrators, including the following.

- "The Vice President for Student Affairs served on our General Education Task Group. . . and the statement of general education goals expresses the University's commitment to integrating the efforts of academic affairs, student affairs, and campus programs in educating our students."
- "Personal development activities are part of graduation requirements, and student life area reports to academic vice president who coordinates general education."
- "The Coordinator of General Education is given a major role in the New Student Orientation Program."
- "Advisement. . . has worked well. Also, the College's learning center has actively provided tutorial and other services to support the core curriculum."
- "At [this] College student affairs and academic personnel share academic advising responsibilities. Both teach in the freshman core course."

These efforts create, in the words of one person, "a kind of institutional envelope for general education." Chapter Seven discusses more examples of ways institutions are addressing the goals of general education beyond the curriculum.

### Correlates of Gains in Educational Value

Apart from examining the overall increase in educational value, we need to analyze the correlates of the reported gains. The results will give us a better understanding of factors in general education that are associated with different educational outcomes (as perceived by campus leaders) and suggest actions that might enhance the benefits for students. For the purpose of this analysis, I created an educational improvement scale by combining the answers to the three questions about quality, coherence, and active learning. Each question was answered on a four-point scale, meaning that the educational improvement scale ranged from 3, if all questions were answered by "not very much," to 12, if all were answered by "very much." The entire sample was divided into two groups, reporting high and low increase in educational value. The high improvement group consisted of 85 colleges scoring a total of 9 to 12, and the low improvement group contained 111 colleges scoring 3 to 8. These two groups were then compared on the other items of the questionnaire. Three distinct sets of factors are associated with reported gains in educational value: aspects of general education and its revision, mechanisms that support the curriculum, and other outcomes related to student gains.

*Aspects of General Education.* Several aspects of the general education curricula that are related to the improvement of education for students are summarized in Table 5.2.

Students were reported to have gained the most educational benefit from curricula that were planned and changed most comprehensively. Typically, such comprehensive changes come about from a serious long-term analysis of the deficiencies

Table 5.2. Aspects of General Education Associated with Reported Educational Improvement.

|  | Amount of Improvement | |
|---|---|---|
|  | Low | High |
| Large change in general education: | | |
| Planned | 33% | 78% |
| Achieved | 22 | 65 |
| Required special types of courses: | | |
| Interdisciplinary core courses | 32 | 56 |
| Advanced courses | 35 | 55 |
| Courses using original sources | 15 | 41 |
| Freshman seminar | 25 | 38 |
| Senior seminar, project | 14 | 35 |
| Required across-the-curriculum themes: | | |
| Writing | 50 | 75 |
| Critical thinking | 30 | 64 |
| Ethics or values | 20 | 50 |
| Cultural pluralism | 21 | 41 |
| Global studies | 23 | 35 |
| Gender issues | 9 | 24 |

in the current program and wide-ranging explorations of the possibilities for improvement. One standard step involves creating a fairly clear vision about what constitutes an educated person and then securing widespread agreement about the importance of working together to cultivate those qualities among students. The curriculum is usually designed to nurture the knowledge, skills, and attitudes that the institution most highly prizes. It should not be surprising that such revisions are associated with more educational benefit for students than those programs undertaking less visionary and more modest improvements.

Certain specific aspects of the changed general education programs were also related to the amount of reported educational gains. Most of the high improvement group required interdisciplinary core and advanced courses significantly more than the low improvement group. These are typically more demanding than introductory disciplinary courses, either by the level of work or by the expectation that students will not only learn material from disparate fields but integrate it, too. A minority of the programs that were reported to yield high improvements (but significantly more than the rest of the colleges) required courses using original texts rather than textbooks, as well as freshman and senior seminars. These special types of courses are all staples of the current debate and reform movement; it now seems that they are associated with educational gains, at least as seen by these reporters.

The high improvement group also adopted across-the-curriculum requirements more than the group reporting less improvement. Specifically, the majority of them require writing and critical thinking; a minority require courses dealing with values, cultural pluralism, global studies, and gender issues. These kinds of courses stress skills, habits of the mind, and such personal qualities as empathy and sensitivity to others that are central to most concepts of an educated person. These courses obviously have subject matter, because one thinks critically about *something* rather than in a vacuum, but they emphasize more than content, as they seek to help students to acquire the thinking, expressive, personal, and interpersonal abilities to function on their own. In other words, the student treated as a receptacle to be filled with facts seems less characteristic of those institutions reporting the greatest gains among students.

One other thing stands out. Requirements are more favored at the high improvement institutions, both as special feature courses and as across-the-curriculum courses. Imposing a curriculum requirement on students is a very serious matter, but it appears, from what the deans say, that these requirements produce beneficial results. For example, students who are weak in writing might wish to avoid taking courses with written assignments, but a writing requirement makes them confront their difficulties and work on strengthening this essential ability. It should be noted that the low improvement colleges often offered these same types of courses as options, but they were less likely to require them. For example, approximately half of each group offered freshman seminars; among the low improvement group half of these courses were optional, but among the high group three-quarters were required. Similarly, 55 percent of the low and 58 percent of the high improvement groups offered cultural pluralism courses, but more of the high improvement group mandated them.

Requirements are not greater only for students; they apply to the faculty, too. That is, when students are free to decide which courses they want to study, faculty members are relatively free to offer what they want to teach. But if students are required to take certain kinds of courses to meet certain specified educational goals, then the faculty must see that their courses teach to those goals. The faculty at high improvement colleges seem to have imposed greater discipline on themselves—as well as on their students—than their counterparts in the low group.

Securing the cooperation of faculty members to incorporate across-the-curriculum themes into their courses is a major complication of this approach. As we saw in Chapter Three, several mechanisms have been introduced to facilitate faculty compliance with the intention of these programs. Both groups of colleges supported the faculty in acquiring new knowledge or skills and in developing appropriate courses, but the high improvement group more frequently required students to take a certain number of special emphasis courses and to make writing, critical thinking, or similar emphasis a criterion for general education courses. These practices made certain that *all* students would have to grapple with the issues or sharpen their skills. Also, high improvement institutions more frequently appointed an administrator to lead the program, a director of writing or women's studies, for example. In short, the high improvement colleges took stronger steps to see that the benefits reached beyond faculty members and their individual courses into the common learning experiences of students.

It is instructive that the degree of perceived educational improvement was not related to the *amount* of general education required for graduation. The amount of time devoted to general education is a major issue in campus curricular discussions, and in fact, the number of semester credit hours required among colleges in this sample varies greatly.

*Support Mechanisms.* A range of activities and programs on a college campus can either support or weaken a revised curriculum. A number that we have already discussed differentiated the high and low improvement colleges; they are summarized in Table 5.3.

Faculty development, as we saw in Chapter Four, is powerfully related to the nature of general education and its successful revision. These findings suggest that it also increases the educational value of a curriculum. High improvement colleges were more likely to have a major program, to involve larger proportions of the faculty, and to operate a program regarded as very effective by the deans. More extensive efforts by the faculty — and by more of them — to understand their students, develop sensitivity to their learning styles and stages of development, explore ways to motivate and involve students, hone their instructional skills, keep up to date with scholarship, and revise their courses seem to have paid off in improved education available to students.

This finding is consistent with the results of Eble and McKeachie's (1985, p. 205) study: "Even though grants for individual scholarly activities are valued, curricular change, work-

Table 5.3. Support Mechanisms Associated with Educational Improvement.

| | Amount of Improvement | |
|---|---|---|
| | Low | High |
| Systematic faculty development: | | |
| Had major program | 17 | 48 |
| Over half general education faculty participated | 21 | 45 |
| Regarded program as very effective | 17 | 49 |
| Had policy of active learning in courses | 26 | 59 |
| Support services furthered general education quite a lot or very much: | | |
| Advising | 68 | 82 |
| Study skills | 47 | 63 |
| Library | 34 | 63 |
| Orientation | 34 | 69 |
| Convocations | 16 | 40 |
| Admissions | 20 | 35 |
| Residence halls | 6 | 18 |

shops, and other programs involving faculty members working together to achieve common objectives may be more cost-effective for the institution in terms of their impact on student learning."

At some colleges the faculty adopted a policy that general education courses must involve active learning or other pedagogical practices that actively engage students. Such a formal policy was reported in about four out of ten institutions in the entire sample, often implemented by means of a general education committee that uses active learning as one criterion for approval of courses. Some colleges have a sunset provision, under which courses are approved for a certain number of years and then must be reviewed to assure their conformity with the policy. Committees typically review such evidence as syllabi, reading lists, assignments, and examinations in making their judgments. The policy of active learning is also supported by various faculty development activities, such as workshops, seminars, and collaborative planning and teaching of courses. Some colleges have been successful in enlisting faculty to the program who are particularly skilled in engaging students actively in their courses, and some use special student evaluations of general education courses to assess compliance with the policy.

When asked how this policy was implemented, one candid dean spoke for the majority by answering, "with difficulty." Even though it is extremely difficult to monitor, however, the policy may be useful in taking an institutional stance about the kind of teaching and learning that is valued. It establishes a normative expectation for the faculty that may function like a conscience. A conscience does not guarantee that one will always act honorably, but it makes one feel guilty when its dictates are ignored and thereby secures greater compliance than would occur without this beneficent spur. Over the long term, students, too, may come to count on being more responsible for their own learning.

Those colleges in the high improvement group were over twice as likely to have such a policy for active learning than those with lower results. Despite the obvious difficulties of implementing and monitoring such a policy, it does seem to offer a significant benefit in terms of this measure of educational value.

Another support mechanism is the coordination of student services with general education. Although student services were generally not closely coordinated with the general education curriculum, those colleges which had the greatest coordination and support for it reported greater benefits for students. This suggests that if colleges can find ways to hitch the various student services — orientation, advising, admissions, convocations, and the like — to the curriculum, they might further the education of students.

*Other Outcomes.* The educational improvement scale was related to other reported outcomes of general education, which are shown in Table 5.4.

More favorable student attitudes toward general education were positively associated with educational improvement. Attitudes and learning interact with each other: If students approach a task with positive attitudes, learning is facilitated; if they view the learning experience as positive, favorable attitudes develop.

Table 5.4. Other Reported Outcomes Associated with
Educational Improvement.

|  | Amount of Improvement | |
|---|---|---|
|  | Low | High |
| Attitudes toward general education more favorable: | | |
| Students | 26 | 58 |
| Faculty | 45 | 80 |
| Administrators | 56 | 86 |
| Positive impact on: | | |
| Faculty renewal | 57 | 90 |
| Institutional identity | 61 | 88 |
| Sense of community | 51 | 84 |
| Public relations, visibilty | 44 | 82 |
| Student retention | 34 | 65 |
| Efficient utilization of faculty | 42 | 60 |
| Admissions | 41 | 59 |
| General education budget | 37 | 58 |
| Institutional fund raising | 28 | 53 |
| Faculty reward structure | 13 | 40 |

Also, in the high improvement group the attitudes of faculty members and administrators toward general education more often became favorable. Positive views of teachers and administrators can exert strong and favorable influence on students, especially if, as we have seen, they are associated with large changes in the student's general education programs.

Educational improvement was also associated with all of the institutional impacts connected with curricular change discussed in Chapter Three. One is tempted to interpret these findings as indicating that each of these factors contributes, directly or indirectly, to improved education for students. That is, a vital faculty is more effective than a tired one; a sharp institutional identity conveys clearer expectations, values, and priorities to students than a fuzzy one; education is enhanced with a sense of community. And so on through the list. But we should also allow for the reverse: Students who are more actively engaged and learning at a high level contribute to the renewal of their professors and to the communal well-being. Indeed, in the

best of all possible educational worlds, there is a synergy between these institutional features and the effective performance
of the students.

One variable that was *not* related to the educational improvement scale, however, is institutional type. Significant differences did not emerge among responses from academic leaders
across the community colleges, liberal arts colleges, comprehensive institutions, and combined research and doctoral granting
universities. This does not mean that the student experience or
the quality of learning may not vary by type of institution, but it
does indicate that all types of institutions reported about the
same degree of educational improvement with their new general
education programs. All kinds of institutions can become better, and all have sources of resistance that work against meaningful improvement.

## Conclusion

The true benefits of a college education to students and to
society become apparent only with the passing of years—even
decades. Unfortunately, if we wait that long to assess them, the
results are not available to use for shaping courses of study for
the other generations in college or about to enter. A short-term
estimate, although far from the final word, is helpful in getting a
quick reading on the consequences of new, more highly structured curricula. According to the reports of these deans, their
students derived greater educational value from revised general
education curricula, including higher-quality education, more
coherence, and more active learning. The absolute amount of
gain, however, was not great, but neither was it objectively measured; gains in actual student outcomes might have been
greater—or less—than deans thought.

Perhaps more important than the amount of reported
increase is the configuration of factors that indicate where
students were able to derive the greatest and least benefits.
Greater improvement in education was related to several aspects
of the curriculum change, including a large-scale revision, required special courses, and required themes across the curricu-

lum. Improvements were also related to support mechanisms, including a policy of active learning, a systematic faculty development program and close coordination of student services with the general education curriculum. Finally, reported improvements were correlated with positive attitude change among students, faculty, and administrators, as well as a number of specific institutional impacts.

This familiar pattern of relationships has been discussed in the last three chapters from different vantage points. Academic leaders from colleges that are making large-scale curriculum changes and establishing systematic faculty development programs to vitalize general education curricula seem to be more convinced that they are raising the quality of education among students than are their counterparts at institutions making more modest adjustments in their programs.

One of the major limitations of this study is that the information was provided by academic leaders, whose eyes filtered what we could learn. One reviewer of this manuscript went so far as to suggest that the results are "more compelling in describing the attitudes, values, and operating styles of college and university administrators" than in accurately assessing curriculum changes, faculty development, or enhancement of educational value for students. This serious concern has lurked in the background throughout the last three chapters, and it needs to be addressed directly.

Of course administrators want to believe that their labors are effective and producing valuable educational and institutional benefits. Although respondents may have shaded some of their responses that called for personal opinion or perceptions, a number of items called for simple factual information describing the curriculum and its changes. There is little reason to expect biased reporting about whether the curriculum includes freshman seminars, interdisciplinary core courses, or writing-across-the-curriculum requirements, for example. Also, when they gave more subjective perceptions and opinions, they often were asked to explain the reasons for their answers, and their responses were informative and quite reasonable.

Further, there is some evidence that the respondents did

not systematically present a rosy picture. Several items were not answered by individuals, suggesting that many respondents showed restraint when they lacked information or the item did not pertain to them. This fact gives more confidence in the answers that were provided. In addition, when answering questions about the problems they encountered and advice they would give to others, the respondents gave frank comments. They did not pull their punches when talking about protection of turf, arguments over which departments might win or lose, stubbornness of individuals, the long time required to reach agreement, and some of their own disappointments with the final results.

More important, whatever the absolute level of the responses, the comparisons among the high and low responses produced a consistent pattern of results. The patterns make sense and are consistent with at least my own experience. For example, I have been on campuses that have made quite modest curriculum changes, and it is difficult to see much impact. But where large-scale changes have been introduced, I have seen the kinds of benefits—for students, faculty members, and the institution—claimed by these campus leaders. Even though individuals may tend to see their campuses positively, the most compelling evidence in this survey comes from the comparisons between groups of respondents—for example, those with large and small curriculum change, those with no faculty development program and a major one, those where students reportedly benefit the most and the least. In fact, it would not be credible if a slight change was found to have a large payoff. Although the responses to the questionnaire may be shaded positively, I believe that we can have a reasonable amount of confidence about the kinds of programs that are producing the most results and the kinds that are producing the least.

Certainly it would be more reassuring if these results were related to independent information, to actual achievement measures of students. However, that information is not available in this study, nor in any that have been completed. Although views of campus leaders about gains in educational value are only estimates that cannot substitute fully for more direct information, and although the measure used in this chapter is a holistic one, these are useful early findings. Overall, they lend support to the dominant trends reshaping the undergraduate curriculum these days. They also suggest that further research on the links between student gains and general education curricula might be fruitful, more fruitful than indicated by previous research on student development during the college years, which has tended to neglect the curriculum. More refined questions may be pursued whereby particular kinds of outcomes—writing and critical thinking skills, understanding history or science, or having a global perspective, for instance—are related to particular types of curricula.

Even though we are far from having the last word on the matter, the conclusion I am drawn to is this: Comprehensive curriculum rethinking and change—especially if the new curriculum is well supported by such means as systematic faculty development efforts, an active learning policy, and a closely coordinated set of student services—are responsible for the greatest improvements in the general education of students. Serious efforts to strengthen general education apparently are as much in the students' best interests as they are in the best interests of faculty members and institutions.

Let me close with a few more words about self-interest, a concept I have used to close the last three chapters. Long-term institutional change seldom occurs for altruistic reasons; self-interest is the greatest motivator known to bring about significant change. If changing general education can be shown to be in the interests of students, faculty members, and institutions, that fact should be more important in stimulating meaningful reform than all of the dispassionate analyses or passionate calls in the world. That is why I have been interested in working toward those conclusions.

But let me be clear that I am not talking about willful, self-centered, hedonistic self-interest nor immediate gratifications. What I have in mind may be called "enlightened self-interest." For students this may mean studying something important that they might find unfamiliar, difficult, and even unpleasant. It may mean developing skills that do not come easily, such as critical thinking, analyzing value-laden issues, solving mathematical problems, or writing. But seen in the context of preparing for a full, productive, and satisfying life, such study may pay off in an expanded knowledge of the world, greater self-consciousness, and a bigger "tool kit" of skills to cope with unknown challenges they will surely face in the future.

Similarly, many faculty members identify their own interests with their departments, their courses, and their specialties. They naturally seek to advance the interests of their department at the expense of others within the institution, but no department, or faculty member, can be strong and secure in an institution that is weak or unstable. Further, most faculty chose their careers because of their interest in ideas, learning more, and teaching others about them; they have interests in ideas that transcend their own specializations and that are connected with ideas in other disciplines. General education, as we have seen, gives them an opportunity to learn, get fresh ideas from other fields, be stimulated by their colleagues—in short, experience and enjoy ongoing growth and renewal. In the end, they, like their students, may be better specialists because of the enrichment that comes from seeing the larger picture and connecting their knowledge with that of other fields.

Institutions, too, sometimes operate as though something other than undergraduate general education is a priority—majors, graduate education, research, service. Policies, budgets, governance, and day-to-day activities often reveal a tilt away from general education. But those that have revised their curricula, particularly in comprehensive ways, have reaped many important benefits, tending to strengthen the institution in specific ways, thereby making it more advantageous to all. Whether one thinks in terms of a sense of identity or community, of student enrollment or faculty renewal, of stature or finances, a strong general education program benefits all individuals.

But enlightened self-interest is always a matter of interpretation, and since it differs from what many of each group immediately think of as their interests, it involves a constant dialogue with students, faculty members, and institutional leaders. Nonetheless, I believe that these findings should be very helpful as educators try to think their way through the current debate and consider how they can both improve the quality of undergraduate general education *and* achieve other objectives they value—in specialties and majors, graduate education, or research.

# PART THREE

# Sustaining Improvements in General Education

# Supporting Quality
# General Education Programs

As an ideal for undergraduate education, a broad general education along with either an academic specialization or career preparation is captivating. But the ideal has always fit uneasily in the modern university, because general education typically receives short shrift—not because individuals openly attack the ideal but because it is squeezed out by the press of more highly prized activities. Historically, the university has prospered by emphasizing research over teaching, professional preparation over liberal learning, graduate training over undergraduate education, specialized knowledge over holistic understanding, and departmental interests over institutional interests. The university model today has spread to infuse other kinds of collegiate institutions, including liberal arts colleges and comprehensive institutions.

But what has worked in the past may not in the future. A better balance may be necessary if the university expects to continue receiving support from the taxpayer, the donor, the legislator, the corporate leader, or, most especially, the undergraduate student and his or her family. The very success of the university may make it necessary to accommodate the public's demand for a more rigorous education for all undergraduates.

## A Historical Note

This century has witnessed periodic attempts to breathe new life into the ideal of general education by buttressing its practice. Three different approaches have been used historically to create a more favorable environment for the practice of general education: reconceptualizing and restructuring of existing programs, creating different types of institutions, and establishing subcolleges within existing institutions. The first can be illustrated by Columbia University, which, during the general education revival after World War I, established an interdisciplinary core course focusing on the study of culture and history from the ancients to the present. Drawing on senior faculty members from various social science departments, Contemporary Civilization, as the course came to be known, stressed the study of classic books in small discussion sections. Its success led to the introduction of similar year-long core courses in the humanities and natural sciences. But the introduction of majors at Columbia in the 1950s and the growth of research saw the science and humanities cores reduced to one semester each; senior faculty concentrated on their departmental programs, and teaching assistants took their place in the undergraduate classroom. Interest in the core has recently resurfaced and led to a stronger commitment to Contemporary Civilization and to the reintroduction of a year-long science core.

Reforming existing curricula is the most common approach in the contemporary period of reform. As we have seen throughout this volume, colleges today are strengthening their own general education offerings in a variety of ways. Academic leaders are finding it necessary to design a series of institutional policies, structures, and procedures to provide stronger support for general education. Below are a number of such supports that have been mentioned throughout this book:

- Faculty development programs that promote dialogue across departments and divisions, promote the acquisition of new knowledge, foster the development of new or revised courses, and coordinate across-the-curriculum approaches
- Appointment of an administrator with primary responsibility for the coordination of the entire general education curriculum and/or administrators of key parts of it

- Organization of an institution-wide faculty committee to provide oversight for the curriculum as a whole, approve courses, assess the program, and act as a watchdog for its interests
- Establishment of criteria for courses within curricular components, such as freshman seminars, interdisciplinary core courses, disciplinary introductions, and across-the-curriculum emphases
- Assessment of the consequences of curricula to determine how well the program is working, make mid-course refinements, and keep original purposes in front of the community

These are very important steps, but it is doubtful that they are strong enough, or enduring enough, to assure the long-term survival of current reforms, given the prevalence of competing academic priorities. For example, a dean from a leading liberal arts college stated bluntly, "No college-wide faculty committee can offset the power of the departments." And the rewards for research and writing—grants, speaking invitations, consulting opportunities, job offers—outstrip the rewards for excellence in teaching.

A second approach is the establishment of new colleges championing alternative curricula. Although the number of students directly affected is small, the reforms developed in experimental colleges have often found their way into more traditional institutions. For example, Antioch College was moribund when it was radically reorganized into a very different college in the early 1920s. The new curriculum featured cooperative education in which students alternated between periods of off-campus work and periods of traditional study in a range of liberal arts subjects within a highly intellectual community. This distinctive program attracted an exceptional student body and excellent professors, and the college became a leading liberal arts college. Nevertheless, despite the work program's success with students, who derived enormous intellectual and personal benefits, it created tension between academic life and practical experience for the faculty, many of whom thought students needed more academic study. After a period of exporting its unique brand of experiential education through off-campus centers and graduate and professional programs during the 1960s and 1970s—and in the process nearly going bankrupt again—Antioch is currently enjoying another rebirth. It closed all but three of the off-campus centers to concentrate on the Yellow Springs campus, strengthened finances, raised funds, and built new structures. The college adopted a comprehensive new general education curriculum that recaptures its traditional values, including an international experience that will go into effect fall 1991. The new curriculum is part of a dynamic that includes expanded enrollment, several new faculty members, and an endowed chair for the work program. Antioch is busy reestablishing its distinctive educational program.

Other experimental colleges with distinctive curricula were established during the 1920s and 1930s. Swarthmore developed an honors program; Bennington relied heavily on individualized education and advising; St. John's adopted a great books curriculum; Sarah Lawrence stressed student-centered education. The progressive theories of education of John Dewey and others guided many of these experimental efforts. During the 1960s, alternative institutions were created at such places as the University of California, Santa Cruz, with its several cluster colleges, each emphasizing different areas of knowledge; Empire State College with its individual learning contracts for nontraditional students; New College in Florida with its accelerated and highly demanding curriculum; and Evergreen State with its reliance on learning communities and student initiative in designing and carrying out curricular contracts. Community colleges sprang up all over the United States in the postwar era as different kinds of institutions that stressed vocational instruction, general education for transfer purposes, and a range of community services. For a time, community colleges were created at the rate of over one per week.

During this revival of general education, however, the creation of new institutions with alternative approaches to the curriculum is not a common strategy. Two facts militate against this approach: The limitation of resources precludes establishing more institutions, and access to higher education, though never perfect, is largely achieved by means of the large number of institutions that already exist. The conviction today is that existing colleges and universities should offer the best quality education they can, not that more institutions are necessary.

A third tack is to establish subcolleges within existing units, rather than creating entirely new institutions. This strategy was adopted by the University of Wisconsin when Alexander Meiklejohn established the Experimental College in 1927, a two-year lower-division program focusing on key eras in Western civilization. Meiklejohn believed that the proper unit of analysis is a civilization, and students studied a number of problems and themes in ancient Greece, Europe, and contemporary America. It was housed in a dormitory to create a living-learning environment extending beyond the classroom. The program ended in 1932 with the departure of Meiklejohn.

Robert Maynard Hutchins at the University of Chicago argued, similarly, that the university was not a hospitable setting, because it stressed scholarship, graduate training, and professional preparation to the detriment of undergraduate general education. A separate college with its own faculty, integrated curriculum, team-planned courses, original texts, and interdisciplinary study was created during the 1930s. A faculty and administration committed to this vision of education was assembled, and they taught a talented group of students. Despite the demonstrated success of both of these "colleges within a college," both Wisconsin and Chicago found them to be costly, divisive, and lacking strong defenders among faculty and administrative leaders beyond the small group of participants. When their leaders departed, despite the demonstrated success with students, the Experimental College was closed (it has since been revived as an integrated studies program), and the college at Chicago was more fully integrated into the rest of the university (it retains much of its earlier flavor with interdisciplinary core courses).

During the 1960s and 1970s, many institutions created "cluster," "residential," "experimental," or "alternative" colleges, including the University of Michigan and Western Washington

State, Sonoma State, and Hofstra Universities. Some of these alternative colleges have survived, more or less as intended, often by making accommodations with their larger and more powerful "hosts." Some have been recast to serve new populations, such as older adults; some have failed due to shifts in student interests away from the liberal arts in the 1970s, the departures of original administrative and faculty proponents, scarce resources, and conflict about their educational philosophies. Although subcolleges may well be suitable vehicles to introduce comprehensive change for small groups of students and faculty, and although some of them have survived, it is apparent that separate small units are not organizationally strong enough to assure permanence. Their survival depends on the willing support of the larger institution, and when conditions change for the institution, it can easily reorganize the small unit out of existence.

The creation of small-scale alternative instructional programs remains an alluring approach for general education leaders today. Several institutions have established alternative structures to provide more holistic, integrated general education, including Gustavus Adolphus College, the University of North Texas, and George Mason University. Nonetheless, the focus of concern during this wave of reform has not been the creation of alternative units on the periphery of the institution for a small number of students. Today's efforts to reform general education, for the most part, have remade the mainstream curriculum for the benefit of all students.

The pattern emerging from this brief foray into the history of general education reform is one of a visionary educator calling for a better way to provide a broad general education for students, the establishment of new curricula and pedagogy supported by new structures, only to be assaulted by continuous attacks on behalf of traditional academic values and ways of operating. In some cases, the reforms were abandoned; in some cases they were modified to fit more comfortably within traditional frameworks; and in some cases the new approaches persevered in more or less recognizable forms.

The historical lesson is clear: New general education curricula need to have strong academic supports if they are going to continue for the long haul. We need to find ways to give a solid foundation for the new curricula so they can avoid being undermined by the competing priorities, other values, bureaucratic structures, and political underpinnings of the American university. Frederick Rudolph (1977, p. 253) described the problem this way: "Concentration was the bread and butter of the vast majority of the professors, the style they knew and approved, the measure of departmental strength and popularity. Breadth, distribution, and general education were the hobby horses of new presidents, ambitious deans, and well-meaning humanists of the sort who were elected to curriculum committees by colleagues as token support for the idea of liberal learning."

Will colleges and universities make the changes in academic structures necessary to be truly supportive of current reforms in general education curricula? Or will they give only token support, which will ultimately undermine the revised curricula, however effective they may be, and thereby sow the seeds of discontent that will blossom into another general education revival a decade or two in the future? The answer to that question is not yet known. On the one hand, reformers should not underestimate the magnitude of the task and the weight of historical evidence against reversing the course of the modern university. On the other hand, Rudolph, who chronicled the evolution of the modern university and its curriculum that prizes specialization and vocationalism, concluded his analysis on a hopeful note: "The time may be at hand when a reevaluation of academic purpose and philosophy will encourage the curricular developments that will focus on the lives we lead, their quality, the enjoyment they give us, and the wisdom with which we lead them. If such a development does take place,... perhaps, once more, the idea of an educated person will have become a usable ideal." (1977, p. 289)

To achieve this end, conventional academic values and practices of colleges must be reconsidered and modified. Without changing the larger context within which a curriculum is embedded, curriculum change on most campuses will produce no lasting effect. The history of general education—with its episodic cycles of reform followed by erosion of the changes—teaches us that the gains that have been made by literally hundreds of colleges and universities in the last decade are in danger of being washed away. Today's reforms are threatened by the very same campus conditions that had to be purposefully overcome in order to establish changes: dissolution of agreements about the qualities of mind and habits of thought desired for students, fragmentation of academic community, centrifugal forces of departmentalism, and the allure of research or other priorities.

## Creating a Deeper Structure of Academic Supports

Although many people seem to have discovered that general education is the core of a college education for all students, it often does not function as the core of the institution itself. On the contrary, general education often has a low priority, even on campuses that boast of recent "curriculum reforms." A number of additional structural changes are necessary to sustain and maintain the reforms that have painstakingly been made. If the ideal of general education is to become a central feature of the actual operations of the colleges, more is needed than simply changing the curriculum, however comprehensively. I fear that probably the few academic supports mentioned above will not be enough; what is needed for lasting improvement is a more pervasive, deeper, and supportive structure.

Such a structure would entail, above all, five key elements: (1) shaping of a new generation of faculty to hold liberal and general education values, (2) developing a faculty culture that takes undergraduate teaching and pedagogy seriously, (3) creating a community of learners among faculty and students, (4) devising ways to make shared authority work in the instructional program, and (5) infusing general education purposes throughout the academic departments. Changes in these areas, collectively, would create an academic organization that consistently and persistently supports the educational purposes and values embodied in new formal general education curricula.

*Creating a New Professoriate Committed to General Education.* The United States has a rare opportunity to recast the professoriate and its role in colleges and universities. This is because large numbers of retirements are anticipated in the near future, and the largest infusion of new professors in three decades will have to be trained, recruited, and nurtured. It is possible to prepare college professors interested in broad intellectual currents, capable of offering courses that are inclusive of diverse ideas and people, and committed to the general education of students. The attention of most scholars in this area, however, focuses largely on what might be labeled "pipeline issues": the number of expected retirements, the training and recruitment of large numbers of replacements, and ways to encourage enough individuals, and particular kinds of individuals (for example, ethnic minorities), to enroll in graduate schools (Bowen and Schuster, 1986; Bowen and Sosa, 1989). These are very serious concerns and must be addressed, but they beg the even more serious question of what the next generation of faculty will be like—their minds, teaching capabilities, and personal qualities. Answers to this question will determine the kind of education the faculty will be able to provide for future generations of college students. We need to seize this first opportunity in three decades to recast the professoriate—truly a historic moment that far transcends simply the filling of slots.

Unfortunately, the graduate schools of major universities, which are the training ground for future faculty, typically do not embody and inculcate general education values. Quite the opposite: They embrace their antithesis. An evaluation of Columbia's renowned general education program states it well. Although finding the students, faculty, and alumni "strongly supportive of the core curriculum," the chair of the Commission on the Core Curriculum, Theodore deBary, wrote in his transmittal letter, "general education faces unparalleled challenges today, and its value needs to be vigorously reaffirmed against the erosive effects of several powerful trends in academic life today—the ever more intense specialization and fragmentation of learning; the entrenchment of departmental structures in university administration; the stress on research and publication at the expense of teaching. . .; and the widespread assumption that 'selective excellence' is to be found in individual displays of highly visible scholarship rather than in shared programs of collegial instruction based on a coherent educational philosophy." (Commission on the Core Curriculum, 1988) These "powerful trends" are strongest in graduate programs at the major universities. In the best of all possible worlds, graduate schools—more accurately, graduate departments—would place more emphasis on general education values: holism, connected learning, wide-ranging intellectual analysis, a focus on teaching and learning. But, alas, they are unlikely places to foster such values. Even departments in the liberal arts pay homage to narrowly specialized learning, departmental prerogatives, the priority of research, and individual achievement.

The task of nurturing liberal and general education, therefore, falls upon employing colleges and universities with undergraduate programs that are more hospitable to these values. These values include an emphasis on breadth, the connectedness of knowledge, and holistic learning, as well as on specialization; the coordination of departmental and individual interests with the larger needs of the institution; prizing teaching and work with students as well as research; and honoring shared programs of collegial instruction as well as individual achievements, such as journal articles, books, and artistic productions. It is not necessary to reject traditional academic values, but it is necessary to keep them in check so that they do not crowd out general education.

Faculty members are the bearers of academic values, and to the extent that academic values work against general education, the faculty is part of the problem. But they are part of the solution, too. On every campus are faculty members sympathetic to general education who can "adopt" what is too often an orphan program and nurture it to health and success. They may provide such leadership through formal programs of faculty orientation, curriculum reviews, instruction in general education programs, or faculty development activities. Or they may do it informally and individually through lunch-time conversations, discussions of scholarly work, team teaching experiences, mentoring younger colleagues, committee discussions, and the hundreds of other ways of being one of those most valuable of commodities, a good colleague.

It is noteworthy that often the faculty most imbued with general education values are the older ones. Many colleges have hired large numbers of faculty in the last decade or two in professional areas as they established market-responsive career-oriented programs. Even in the liberal arts fields, many young faculty members are trying to establish a scholarly reputation in their specialties, and many institutions have raised standards for tenure to include higher publication expectations. And because for many years general education has tended to rely on loose distribution requirements, new faculty members are less often themselves products of coherent and rigorous general education programs than their older colleagues. The older generation is in a unique position to pass on their wisdom as a gift to their colleagues before they retire. Of course, younger faculty may not be receptive to the wisdom of their elders if it is offered in a high-handed manner, but such communication can be done with sensitivity and mutual respect and in ways that foster growth.

In the last analysis, though, received knowledge is not as educationally effective as personal experience. The fact of the matter is that many faculty members have never participated in "shared programs of collegial instruction based on a coherent educational philosophy." There is simply no substitute for becoming a part of such an enterprise and experiencing what it is like. That is why Catonsville Community College provides release time and mentoring for faculty preparing to teach interdisciplinary core courses; the College of St. Benedict offers training to faculty members prior to their teaching a first-year symposium and senior seminar; and Eckerd College holds weekly staff meetings for those teaching in the freshman Western Heritage and senior Judeo-Christian Perspective sequences. Teaching such integrative courses is so different from the usual practice of teaching isolated courses that faculty members experiencing it for the first time often report that it transforms their professional lives. Some have told me that they literally are unable to derive the same kind of satisfaction they once did from the solitary approach. It is from such experiences that faculty members see the value of general education to themselves and to their students, that they are able to truly understand and support general education. Only when general education is seen to be in the long-term best interests of the faculty members will its long-term success be secured.

Special policies, structures, and practices are necessary to keep the attention of faculty members and administrators focused on the heart of the enterprise. Such mechanisms as cross-disciplinary seminars, assignment of administrative responsibility, ongoing faculty development, creation of new forums for faculty to discuss the substance and process of general education, developing mentor relationships between junior and senior faculty teaching general education courses, discussions of the results of assessments — these and similar mechanisms are elements of good practice in general education. Moreover, they are essential foundations for lasting reform.

*Taking Teaching and Pedagogy Seriously.* General education programs, however well designed they may be, are not likely to thrive, or even survive, without the active involvement of interesting and effective teachers. The effectiveness of teaching in general education is to a large degree the reflection of the value an institution places on teaching in general. Although the vast majority of individual faculty members and many colleges and universities do take teaching seriously, the academic profession does not.

College faculty members typically prepare for their careers by obtaining a doctor of philosophy, a research degree, in some subject at a major university. Anna Wasescha, my research assistant for this project, asked provocatively, "What happened to the 'philosophy' part? It is more accurate to say that they receive a specialized degree in a discipline than something more broad, thoughtful, comprehensive." During their training, graduate students often learn from the faculty that teaching is a lower priority than research and that research — not teaching — is the route to career success; few students do practice teaching, and even fewer receive supervised assistance in learning to teach well; seldom do they encounter the extensive professional literature on teaching, learning, student development, and similar topics; and they have little practical knowledge about how to plan a course, prepare a syllabus, or evaluate students. They do not even learn about the history of higher education or the corporate realities of colleges and universities, topics central to their chosen vocation. In extreme instances, thinking about such issues is regarded as unworthy of a serious scholar, and discussion of pedagogy is disdained. Efforts to create alternative degrees oriented more to preparing college teachers have not been successful, and although *some* departments in *some* universities do offer training for *some* teaching assistants, the nation is left with Ph.D. training programs that ignore teaching at best and discourage analysis and discussion of pedagogy at worst.

Teaching-oriented colleges traditionally have tried to provide a corrective to this research model through campus-based faculty development programs that emphasize teaching and learning issues. But many of these colleges are adopting the research model, too, as they pursue visions of a grander reputation, greater stature, and more visibility. Faculty at predominantly undergraduate colleges are increasingly expected to conduct research at the leading edge of their disciplines and to publish in refereed journals; standards for tenure, promotions, and salary increases are being altered to include published research. The dean of one of the most respected liberal arts colleges in the country (who shall remain anonymous) confessed, "I am very concerned that in the past ten years or so, the amount of budget support for developing faculty as teachers has fallen dramatically, while the support available for scholarly activity has increased dramatically." She was requesting funds from a foundation to establish a new center for learning and teaching that would provide a range of activities designed to redress the balance.

Paul Lacey (1990, p. B1), professor of English at Earlham College, has reflected on this state of affairs: "As I compare what is being said and done to recruit and prepare the next generation of teachers with my own experience as a graduate student and beginning teacher 30 years ago, I am impressed by a sense of what Yogi Berra called 'deja vu all over again.'" He urges us not "to repeat past mistakes," but rather to establish a "professional culture that takes teaching seriously" and to put into practice what we have learned about teaching and learning during recent decades.

What does this mean exactly? Three things. First, it means resurrecting the venerable ideal of the teacher-scholar (Nelsen, 1981). Nelsen illustrates the concept of a teacher-scholar by quoting from the Davidson College faculty handbook (p. 7). "Ideally the college professor would be a widely respected scholar excited about learning and capable of communicating this excitement to others, a teacher deeply concerned with the welfare of students and eager to have them learn and grow, one who teaches imaginatively both by books and by personal example, a demanding yet compassionate person who respects the moral worth of students and their potential for growth. While no one teacher is likely to realize all these attributes, the College must continually seek to recruit men and women who strive to do so to the greatest possible extent."

Such an ideal may seem more appropriate to teaching-oriented institutions, such as liberal arts colleges, than to universities with a research mission. But that is not so. At Stanford University, outgoing president Donald Kennedy (1990, p. 1) noted that although teaching and research are both important, "The relative weight has shifted over time, as the relatively new term 'research university' suggests." He continued: "I believe we can have superb research and superb teaching, too. We need to talk about teaching more, respect and reward those who do it well, and make it first among our labors. It should be our labor of love, and the responsibility of each one of us."

Seeking to position the university for the next two decades, he declared, "It is time for us to reaffirm that education — that is, teaching in all its forms — is the primary task, and that our society will judge us in the long run on how well we do it." Kennedy is reported (Mooney, 1991) to have announced $7 million in new programs to reward and improve undergraduate teaching. The funds are to be used to give raises and bonuses to excellent teachers, give graduate students course preparation stipends and awards for teaching, support young faculty members in carrying out innovative teaching, and improve interdisciplinary courses.

Other research universities are taking steps to elevate the status of undergraduate teaching. Syracuse (Diamond, Gray, and Roberts, 1991) launched a multiyear campaign to elevate the importance of teaching through a survey of faculty members and administrators, a conference for deans and department chairs (the first since the 1940s), and a number of follow-up conversations within colleges and departments. Action plans have been prepared, and implementation has begun to improve the evaluation of teaching, give it more weight in personnel decisions, and enhance its effectiveness. Other universities have joined this endeavor, including Berkeley, Carnegie Mellon, Massachusetts, Northwestern, Ohio State, and Michigan. Thirty-five others are participating in the survey, which elicits views about the relationships between teaching and research, perhaps a first step toward elevating the importance of teaching. Teacher-scholars are needed in all kinds of institutions, especially those that aspire to strong general education programs.

Second, taking teaching seriously means recognizing that teaching and learning are complex activities that are worthy intellectual challenges. In the words of Parker Palmer (1990, p. 11), "Good teaching is . . . a maddening mystery." Every teacher should know the gist of the professional literature dealing with principles of learning, student development, learning styles, test construction, and the like. But more, she or he should become what Patricia Cross (1986) calls a "classroom researcher" by trying different approaches to introducing concepts or theories, engaging students in analyzing issues and imagining alternatives, and helping students to develop their own ideas and express their views. By setting goals, carefully selecting strategies, assessing the results, and reflecting critically on the whole process, teachers can hone their pedagogical skills. They can learn their strengths and weaknesses and develop into the most effective teachers possible.

Third, taking teaching seriously requires that the institution support faculty members in their quest for perfecting the craft of teaching, designing improvements in their courses, and fostering the development of students. In part, this involves a faculty culture that values discussions among faculty members about students and their learning, forums to consider new pedagogical ideas, classroom visitations by colleagues, and provision for assistance with teaching and learning with no stigma attached to it. It also involves formal faculty development programs that, as we saw in Chapters Four and Five, seem to foster the renewal of faculty members as well as learning among students. Such benefits alone should assure that all colleges take conscious steps to foster the continual development of faculty members as teachers as well as scholars.

Unfortunately, some institutions do not provide such assistance, and others have hit-or-miss programs, often because of a lack of funds. Although understandable, this reasoning is regrettable; such support should be seen as a necessary and routine cost of doing business. The importance of providing such assistance to support the continual renewal of faculty can be likened to an insurance policy on a building. No board of trustees would think of building a structure and then failing to carry insurance to guard against risk of damage to it, yet a long-term faculty member represents a substantial investment, too, that needs to be protected. For instance, assume that a new assistant professor is hired at age thirty for the salary of $25,000, plus a fringe benefit package amounting to 25 percent of the salary. Further assume that the individual receives salary increments of 5 percent per year for thirty-five years until reaching age sixty-five. The total amount of investment in that one faculty member totals $2,822,510. The investment in an entire faculty runs to hundreds of millions of dollars at even a small college. Formal and informal programs that promote the development of faculty are a kind of insurance policy to keep this hypothetical individual — and others like him or her — alive and vital throughout his or her career. What is more, by acquiring more experience and wisdom, human beings become more valuable as they grow older.

In short, adopting the model of the teacher-scholar, inquiring into the teaching-learning process, and providing positive assistance to faculty members to enhance their pedagogy are all ways of taking teaching seriously—and securing stronger support for effective instruction in general education.

*Developing a Community of Learners.* Learning is an individual activity but not necessarily a solitary one. Indeed, one usually learns best when part of a supportive environment of fellow learners. A community of learners is one way of characterizing a college or university at its best.

Unfortunately, community is in short supply on college campuses. Maintenance of a community is virtually impossible at institutions with tens of thousands of students, but there are forces that fragment even small ones that enroll a few hundred. Indeed, the phrase "organized anarchy" was coined by educational researchers (Cohen and March, 1974) to characterize the way the modern university operates, and that phrase is accepted as a useful characterization by scholars. The divisions between the liberal arts and professional programs on many campuses; the multiple departments (and sometimes schools) as the loci of academic authority; the diversity of students in terms of age, race, gender, and ethnicity—these and other centrifugal forces operate against the development of true academic community and give the appearance of anarchy.

In the academic arena, departments often provide a sense of community, where faculty members and their major students are most involved, share similar values, and establish common bonds. Many colleges have discovered that a coherent general education program can constitute another basis for community for both faculty and students. A curricular philosophy and learning goals—if clearly stated, forcefully articulated, and reflected in the courses taught by professors—can create the basis of community. Also, subcommunities often flourish (for example, in freshman seminars, across-the-curriculum programs in writing or global studies, interdisciplinary core courses, and other components of general education). Similarly, subcolleges, integrated studies programs, and honors colleges often constitute powerful learning communities that magnify the effects

of individual professors and students. Academic support programs such as writing centers with peer tutors to work on
expression or computer centers where numbers of students
congregate to work on assignments also constitute communities
with clear educational foci.

Ernest Boyer, having argued for a core curriculum that
focuses on concerns of all people and that strengthens common
bonds, took the logical next step when the foundation he heads
(Carnegie Foundation for the Advancement of Teaching, 1990,
p. 7) sketched the outline of an academic community in which
such a curriculum might best function. "The goal as we see it is
to clarify both academic and civic standards, and above all, to
define with some precision the enduring values that undergird a
community of learning." He proposed six principles that collectively provide the basis of community. A college or university
should be:

> First, an educationally *purposeful* community, a
> place where faculty and students share academic
> goals and work together to strengthen teaching and
> learning on the campus.
> Second, an *open* community, a place where freedom
> of expression is uncompromisingly protected and
> where civility is powerfully affirmed.
> Third, a *just* community, a place where the sacred-
> ness of the person is honored and where diversity is
> aggressively pursued.
> Fourth, a *disciplined* community, a place where indi-
> viduals accept their obligations to the group and
> where well-defined governance procedures guide
> behavior for the common good.
> Fifth, a *caring* community, a place where the well-
> being of each member is sensitively supported and
> where service to others is encouraged.
> Sixth, a *celebrative* community, one in which the
> heritage of the institution is remembered and
> where rituals affirming both tradition and change

are widely shared [Carnegie Foundation for the Advancement of Teaching, 1990, pp. 7–8].

This ideal of community attempts to balance the common good with the needs of each individual. Since the prevailing academic assumptions and arrangements today tilt so much toward the individual, the thrust of Boyer's work is to stress greater community, especially in the strengthening of general education curricula. The relationship between general education and community cuts both ways: Establishing a coherent general education program fosters a sense of community and, by the same token, general education benefits from operating within a genuine academic community. The enemy of general education is fragmentation and those advocates for special interests that are unable to subordinate their particularistic views to the common good. If coherent general education programs are to survive, the academic culture must become more supportive of such central concerns as community, pedagogy, and liberal education to balance the more common manifestations of individualism, scholarship, and specialization. General education both sustains these qualities and draws sustenance from them.

*Making Shared Authority Work.* One of the basic principles in the governance of colleges and universities is that of shared authority. As articulated and approved jointly by the American Association of University Professors and organizations of colleges and universities, the principle holds that professors should be consulted in regard to a number of important institutional decisions made by the president or board of trustees. Also, it calls for essential academic decisions — for example, graduation requirements, curriculum, faculty personnel decisions, academic standards of students — to be vested with the authority of the faculty, subject to review by the administration and, if appropriate, by the trustees. This principle (like general education values, the importance of teaching, and community) has retained its rhetorical value even as it has tended to break down in practice.

Nowhere is shared authority more important than in the general education program, since it touches virtually all depart- ments. Authority is so widely dispersed that it is extremely difficult to fashion a coherent course of study. (France's Charles deGaulle, faced with diffusion of authority after World War II, lamented the difficulty of governing "a country that makes 265 kinds of cheese.")

Academic authority is typically delegated to separate col- leges, and, within colleges, to departments. The result is that no individual department, by itself, has the power to create a high- quality and coherent general education curriculum. However, a department does have power to veto or undermine a construc- tive initiative if it does not suit its purposes; lacking positive power, departments are quick to use their negative power. It is a curious and perverse twist of fate that shared authority, origi- nally designed to empower the faculty and give them a legiti- mate role in the most important decisions affecting the institu- tion, operates in practice to cause gridlock and to prevent the exercise of their collective responsibility.

This is why William Schaefer simply throws his hands in the air. The former executive vice chancellor at UCLA and executive director of the Modern Language Association, the nation's largest professional organization of humanities faculty members, put it this way:

> Within most colleges and universities the concept of shared governance tends to break down when the issues are monumental. The faculty, which lacks the time and support staff to undertake careful analyses and to propose constructive change, looks to the administration for action whenever the issue is larger than a loaf of bread. But recognizing that the chief administrator who proposes significant curricular change is inevitably attacked as med- dling with the faculty's prerogatives, few presidents or chancellors are brave enough (or foolish

> enough) to undertake such action on their own. . . .
> Thus most institutions simply back off from initiat-
> ing changes of the size and complexity proposed
> here [1990, p. 130].

Although the faculty has authority and responsibility, it often fails to exercise either for the good of general education.

There is an administrative failing on the other side of this coin. As academic organizations have grown larger and more complicated, boards of trustees have tended to appoint presidents who are good managers. Recently they have also stressed the importance of fund raising, as institutions have grown enormously costly to operate. Educational leadership has thus declined in importance as managing and fund raising have increased. It is no accident that colleges are underachieving their educational potential; the absence of strong educational leadership from the top administrators combines with the diffusion of authority among the faculty. Together they hasten the fragmentation of the curriculum and, ultimately, the educational experience of students.

What is to be done? If general education is to be strong, institutional leaders need to assume responsibility for it. As we have seen, several colleges with new programs of general education have created central administrative offices, such as dean, director, or coordinator of general education, to provide administrative leadership. About three out of five of the institutions in my survey reported having such a position. Also, administrators of curriculum components — often faculty members released from some teaching responsibilities — have been appointed to positions such as dean of first-year students at Reed College, director of writing at hundreds of institutions, coordinator of interdisciplinary studies at Defiance College, and director of Leadership, Ethics, and Values Program at North Central College. Many institutions have established college-wide committees of faculty to provide oversight of general education, rather than leaving decisions to dozens of more or less autonomous departments. These committees can be found at such institutions as San Jose State University, Metropolitan State University

(Denver), Morraine Valley Community College, and Texas Lutheran College. Such committees typically establish guidelines for courses and review proposals from departments to assure that they are consistent with college-wide policies and intentions; they represent important structures to give greater authority and responsibility for general education.

These are important steps, but one must candidly ask if these new structures are enough. I doubt that they are sufficient to build a solid and durable basis of support for general education. Let me suggest a three-prong strategy to provide a stronger power base for general education.

First, administrators need to exercise educational — not simply managerial — leadership, articulate the importance of a high-quality and coherent general education program, and take steps "to revive the responsibility of the faculty *as a whole* for the curriculum *as a whole*" (Association of American Colleges, 1985, p. 9). Several examples come to mind. General education was made a priority by several academic deans, even when there was not much grass-roots demand from the faculty or the students. Lloyd Chapin at Eckerd College in Florida and Jose Gonzalez at Inter American University in Puerto Rico organized the review, spoke strongly for improvements, recruited key faculty members to participate, and kept the process on track. Ann Ferren at American University chaired the ad hoc review committee and, as assistant provost for academic development, encouraged faculty involvement and assisted in the implementation of the new curriculum. Robert Hess, president of Brooklyn College, decided that a faculty-approved curriculum change simply forged an expedient political solution, and he told the faculty that they could do better. With his encouragement, the faculty subsequently fashioned and adopted a truly significant core curriculum that has served as a national model. (When is the last time you remember a president telling a faculty that their decision about a curriculum was not adequate?) Peter Seldin and his associates (1990) have assembled many splendid suggestions for how administrators can contribute to the improvement of undergraduate teaching.

Second, faculty leadership is equally crucial. Many individuals have come forward to chair or serve on curriculum review committees that fashion new college-wide programs. Although rooted in their own departments, they tend to have, or soon acquire, an institution-wide perspective that is essential in overcoming the narrow interests of others. Campus citizens like professors Jan Bowman and Pamela Jolicoeur, who chaired the faculty Educational Policies and Planning Committee and General Education Subcommittee, respectively, at California Lutheran University, and John Paden, who chaired the curriculum review committee at George Mason University, exemplify the kind of dedication that secures lasting faculty commitment to general education. Although curriculum review committees typically are disbanded after their proposals are adopted, key individuals often continue to remain involved to sustain the fledgling programs, sometimes serving as administrators of the programs or members of college-wide committees on general education. The close collaboration of faculty leaders and academic administrators is critical to effective reform, and it needs to be sustained at the highest institutional levels, because they represent shared authority at its best.

A third element, one missing in most curriculum reforms, is the board of trustees, the seat of legal authority for academic organizations. In practice, shared authority has meant that boards concern themselves largely with policies about management, finances, physical plant, and fund raising. They have tended to adopt a laissez-faire attitude toward academic programs, have delegated responsibility to the president, and through that office to the deans, and, ultimately, to the faculty. Of course, boards should not infringe on academic freedom, be involved with faculty hiring, or dictate texts. But boards do have a responsibility to provide oversight for the instructional program. They can and should inquire about the quality of the academic program, whether students are acquiring the marks of educated people, how faculty are responding to the public debate about quality, what the administration and faculty are doing to strengthen the instructional program (especially general education), and what evidence exists that students are achieving the desired outcomes. As we have seen in Chapter

Three, strong general education programs can have important benefits for admissions, retention, fund raising, and public relations — all areas of significant trustee responsibility. I would argue that trustees are not keeping their trust unless they press the administration and faculty to provide strong leadership for the heart of the undergraduate course of study. More institutions should follow the example of Roanoke College, which held a board retreat to discuss, among other topics, general education — its importance, national trends, and steps being taken at the college to strengthen its own curriculum.

We might close this discussion by observing that the fragmentation in governance parallels the fragmentation in the curriculum. To put it in its simplest terms, the administration has responsibility for the curriculum but not the academic authority to act strongly. The faculty has the authority but its fragmentation does not allow it to exercise responsibility. Trustees have legal responsibility but, lacking knowledge, they have no academic standing to act. For general education to achieve its goals, for reforms to be undertaken when called for, and for changes to remain vital after the initial excitement of reform diminishes, each of these constituencies must assume its responsibility for the general education curriculum. They must work together to nurture general education and assure that it is not orphaned.

***Embedding General Education into Departments.*** The academic department is the basic organizational unit in most colleges and universities. As legions of would-be reformers have learned, departments have the ability to scuttle institution-wide initiatives that do not fit in with their priorities, staffing patterns, or resource levels. Put positively, successful reform occurs when the purposes are incorporated into the values and day-to-day operations of the departments. In terms of curriculum, the key is to forge essential interconnections between general education and the major.

General education is sometimes seen as being in opposition to the major, and it is presumed that, in a zero-sum game, what helps one must harm the other. Yet that is another example of the destructive "either-or" thinking that is so common in today's educational debate, a view that feeds competition and drives wedges between people; "both-and" thinking, on the other hand, creates alliances and brings people together. Boyer (1987, p. 290) says, "Rather than divide the undergraduate experience into separate camps—general versus specialized education—the curriculum of a college of quality will bring the two together." Better ways must be found to do this, ideally establishing a symbiotic relationship. I suggest three courses of action: the enriched major, the enriched introductory course, and connected learning.

An *enriched major* rests on the proposition that students in any specialization should learn more than technical knowledge and skills. Boyer (1987) suggests an enriched major that would have students grapple with three questions that put their specialization into perspective: "What is the history and tradition of the field to be examined? What are the social and economic implications to be pursued? What are the ethical and moral issues within the specialty that need to be confronted?" (p. 290). These are exciting questions that can captivate faculty and students alike in any major. Indeed, they are precisely the kinds of questions that ought to be addressed—not just by undergraduate students but by graduate students in doctoral programs, who are preparing to become our future college teachers. These questions could be dealt with in newly designed courses, in revisions of existing courses, or by extracurricular means of presentations by scholars or practitioners, for example.

I want to suggest also an *enriched introductory course*, the course that is the staple of both academic majors and general education. Most such courses aim to introduce students, whether majors or nonmajors, to the central bodies of knowledge within the discipline. But they could do more. For one thing, they should engage students and cultivate their curiosity and interest in further learning. (Often, however, such courses not only fail to stimulate interest but they actually turn off what motivation students do bring [Tobias, 1990].) Another benefit is that some introductory courses in revised curricula meet specific criteria for general education courses. While such criteria vary from college to college, they include—in addition to subject matter knowledge—such things as teaching the ways of thinking within the field, active methods of learning, or multicultural perspectives. Another possibility is also found in some reformed curricula; that is, incorporating writing, critical thinking, or global studies as part of a college-wide across-the-curriculum emphasis. These various kinds of courses all provide an introduction to the discipline, but they do more: They provide a more enriching experience for students unfamiliar with a field.

A third approach, termed *connected learning*, is suggested by a new report on the academic major by the Association of American Colleges (1991). The report argues that academic major programs, no less than general education, should be coherent; they should have a beginning (usually an introductory course), a middle, and an end (often a culminating senior seminar or research project). The middle-level courses, it says, often function as "miniature distribution requirements," where learning is not cumulative and does not provide a "common basis for discourse." Further, the report calls for generalizing from the major, engaging in connected learning by relating ideas with other domains. "Connected learning calls for actively making relationships between fields, applying knowledge from one context to another, and taking seriously students' interests in relating academic learning to the wider world of public issues as well as individual experiences and goals" (p. 19).

These are varying ways to merge the interests of general education and specialization and to bring them together into the operations of departments. If departments recognize that strong general education is in their own self-interest as well as in that of both their major and nonmajor students, important long-term support will almost certainly follow.

### Conclusion

When a college or university becomes aware that it needs to devise a stronger general education program, that in itself is a powerful signal that something more than the curriculum is amiss. A college is a system, and problems in the most central instructional program are an indication that something else-where is causing those problems. Any change in the general education curriculum, however outstanding it is, will almost certainly erode and the curriculum will revert to the old ways— unless it is supported by a number of related changes elsewhere in the institution. If an institution expects to sustain and main-tain a revised general education curriculum, therefore, it needs to make fundamental changes in related academic policies and structures.

The modern university, even a small college, is not uni-dimensional. It has multiple missions and serves many goals. It is simply not possible to take any one function, even one as central as general education, and make it a sun around which all the academic planets rotate. On the other hand, if the other missions and activities undermine the single largest academic program at the very heart of the whole undergraduate educa-tion, then the institution has a problem. Structural adjustments need to be made in order to keep the center strong. Creating a professoriate that values general education, taking teaching seriously, developing communities of learners, making shared authority work, and incorporating general education within the departments are valuable ways to sustain curriculum reforms.

*Chapter Seven*

# Focusing on Student Learning and Development

Since the general education movement began, we have gained a good deal of experience with the problems and issues that fueled the reforms. We have learned about the obstacles to curricular change, and we have learned much from the curriculum changes that colleges have adopted. This learning should inform future change and make it both easier and more effective than in the past. Perhaps the most important thing we have learned is that by keeping students' educational needs paramount, college faculties can overcome the substantial inertia and the natural resistance to change, including their own parochial concerns about turf and workload, and design coherent and high-quality general education programs. It takes a great deal of time, often involves some setbacks, and everyone who has gone through it has an ample supply of "war stories." But many institutions representing all types, sizes, and missions have succeeded in devising more purposeful and coherent general education curricula suited to all of their students.

Johnston and his associates (forthcoming, p. 2) observe that the campus initiatives have been one-sided. "They have addressed the 'supply side' of general education. But they have largely ignored the 'demand side'—the understandings, concerns, and attitudes students bring to this coursework. These factors have much to do with the readiness and disposition of students to engage with general education on the terms that real learning requires. They help determine a student's ability to achieve a general education as much as do the content and architecture of our programs, or the conviction, expertise, and energy with which we teach them." Students and their experiences need to be better understood, and that understanding must be used to improve their general education.

We have also learned that students are seldom full partners in the process of revising general education. Neglecting students is a mistake. Some curriculum task forces often include students, but many do not; student members of task forces tend to speak less frequently, and their contributions often are not acknowledged or taken seriously. Faculty members sometimes complain that student members do not attend meetings regularly or make constructive contributions. Some task forces do not study the actual experiences of students with the current curriculum, and even after a revision is adopted, students are sometimes presented the new requirements with little rationale. For example, recently I had a lengthy conversation with the capable chair of a general education task force who described the many and various things it had done to involve faculty members and administrators. Not once did he mention students—not as members of the group, not as individuals to be consulted, not even the leaders of the student government or editors of the student newspaper whose support might be considered important. We need to involve students more deeply in thinking about general education and "let them in on the secrets," as a colleague once put it.

There is little reliable evidence on the matter, but I suspect that students are less affected than they might be by changes in the general education curriculum. This is so for several reasons. Although many colleges and universities are making changes to strengthen general education, the changes often are modest or even cosmetic. Too, many institutions make optional their freshman seminars, writing programs, or multicultural courses, for example, thereby missing many students, especially those who are most in need of such instruction. Further, although many faculty members have faithfully revised some courses to carry out the purposes of the curriculum, large numbers of courses remain unaffected by the changes. This is a simple matter of arithmetic, not necessarily the good will of the faculty. For instance, if every faculty member teaching under-graduates at a given college alters one course (an ambitious assumption), and the teaching load is six courses, then five-sixths of all courses remain largely unaffected. Although 100 percent of the faculty members have been involved, the actual changes experienced by the average student are in one-sixth of his or her course work, which does not seem to be a very powerful intervention. Of course, if the changes are concen-trated in required courses, their potential is greater.

Finally, curriculum reform does not lead in a straight line to student learning and development. Rather, there is a chain of somewhat discrete steps, and some educational power may be lost in the transition from one to another. Curriculum change typically starts with agreement on educational goals, about the qualities desired for students. Next, that vision must be incorpo-rated into a curriculum structure and a set of graduation re-quirements to cultivate those qualities. Then both the purposes and the curriculum need to be understood and affirmed by individual faculty members in their own instructional roles. Next, professors must review and possibly revise their courses to assure that they contribute in the desired ways to the education of students. At the end of this process, students must enroll in the courses, understand what is expected of them, learn the material, and experience the desired benefits. Because students are the last link in this chain of curriculum reform, some of the power of the change may have dissipated by the time it reaches them. Special efforts are needed to make sure that the intentions behind the curriculum actually carry over each of these crucial transitions if students are to benefit fully from them.

To assure that curriculum change produces a positive impact on students, we need to develop a larger, more holistic view of students and a more complete understanding of their experience in the curriculum. Such a view has been a missing ingredient in the debate, and it has too often been neglected in the process of fashioning curriculum improvements. An expanded view of students should lead to their more effective classroom learning of general education.

The evidence presented in Chapter Five is that several separate practices contribute to the improvement of students' education. These include

- Comprehensive curriculum revision
- Curricular requirements rather than options for such items as interdisciplinary core courses, advanced courses, courses using original sources, freshman and senior seminars, and several across-the-curriculum emphases
- A policy of active learning in at least certain curriculum components
- A major program of faculty development pointed specifically toward general education
- Linking general education with student services, including admissions, orientation, and advising

These are all avenues that should continue to be pursued if a college wants to enhance the general education of students, and plenty of work remains to be done with each.

In regard to the last item, for example, Johnston and associates (forthcoming, p. 16) declare in their article summarizing the research literature that in admissions, "Early communication with students centers around videos and viewbooks designed to catch the jaded student eye... — not around the purposes of an education or their connection to students' emerging goals or plans."

In respect to orientation: "Orientation programs tend to focus on the social and personal aspects of adjustment to college, neglecting intellectual and academic matters. . . . Orientations can introduce students to the curriculum, helping them through direct, repeated, and thoughtful explanations to understand the potential value to them of general education especially" (pp. 17–18).

Advising, they say, is "too infrequent to make much of a difference" and "too perfunctory and concerned with logistical detail." Further, it is separated from career advising, which is ironic when career preparation is the top goal of students. "[Students] report problems *linking* their academic planning with career opportunities. And they do not understand the separation enforced by college and university administrative structures, of academic and career planning" (p. 21). More effective admissions, orientation, and advising activities—ones that include a healthy respect for general education—are part of the future agenda.

Viewing general education through the eyes of students, one is led directly to the issues of teaching and learning, a topic that has received little attention in the public debate and campus reforms. Students care not just about the content of the curriculum but also about how well they are taught. For example, a student leader criticized a comprehensive curriculum change proposal: "I don't think it's any great leap forward if we don't address issues of pedagogy."

Even though the quality of teaching in general education courses sometimes reaches memorable heights, it often is less than inspiring. Too often, teaching in general education lacks status, and it is consigned to low-ranking faculty members and, where they are available, teaching assistants. The dominant image of a general education course is a large class in which the professor lectures to passive students who memorize the material to pass the tests. This image is a caricature, because not all classes are large, not all professors are inexperienced, not all lectures are dull, not all learning is passive. But it does capture the inert quality of teaching and learning that pervades traditional general education courses. That is why many institutions with new curricula recruit their best teachers for general education; stress active learning; keep classes small in freshman seminars, writing courses, and interdisciplinary core courses; and take other steps to create a more engaging climate for learning.

An effective pedagogy of general education needs to go further. It should draw from what is known about teaching and learning in general and apply it to the specific setting of general education courses. It would involve four agendas: (1) attending to the personal-emotional aspects of learning, (2) developing the values of students, (3) recognizing the diversity of students, and (4) extending learning beyond the classroom.

## Attending to Personal-Emotional Aspects of Learning

"Learning is an intensely emotional experience," Joseph Katz and Mildred Henry (1988, p. 7) taught us. Although college education quite rightly centers on the mind — the acquisition of knowledge and the capacities for thought — it is a mistake to regard students, as some critics seem to do, as mere vases into which must be poured history, literature, science, and other subjects. Faculty members seldom talk about the emotional aspects of learning, but the good teacher knows about them, and she or he uses the students' interests, experiences, and perspectives to make the subject matter come to life. A student puts her self-esteem on the line whenever she ventures an answer to a question, makes an analysis, assesses the adequacy of a theory, critiques a book, or states her own opinions. If the overture is met with empathy and understanding from the teacher and fellow students — even if constructive criticism is offered — it can result in increased confidence, trust, and self-esteem. With repeated practice and positive feedback, the student becomes more skilled in thinking critically, expressing her views, and defending her ideas.

On the other hand, if her comments are ignored, met with derision, or rejected out-of-hand, self-esteem suffers, confidence is eroded, and learning slowly becomes an anxiety-producing, even a frightening experience. For such students, learning can become abusive; students can suffer emotionally in relation to learning just as surely as if they were the victims of family or sexual abuse. The victims of what I call "learning abuse" find that their emotional life in the classroom or in reading and writing becomes constricted: They restrain their curiosity, read only what is assigned, answer teachers' questions only when they cannot be avoided, study only what is on the examination, parrot answers memorized from a text or lecture, and keep instructors at a distance. These are classic ways for victims of abuse to try to control authorities and events that are personally threatening. If these measures to cope within the situation are not successful, the student may take the extreme measure of leaving a course or even dropping out of school. The fact of the matter is that emotion is a powerful factor in what students learn and why they do not learn.

The role of emotion in learning has relevance for pedagogy everywhere, but it has particular implications for general education. General education curricula often require courses in fields that engender anxiety in certain students. Some students have anxieties about mathematics or science, often traceable to early abusive learning experiences and even cultural expectations. Certain other students may possess a constricted emotional life that hinders the development of imagination, creative expression, or appreciation of verbal nuance called for in courses dealing with such diverse topics as literature, public policy, scientific theory, or the fine arts. Students with test anxiety may be stymied when faced with mandated tests dealing with reading, writing, and mathematics or with classroom assessments where it is difficult for them to demonstrate what they actually know. Special sensitivity to these matters in core courses can help many of these students overcome their fears, experience success, and build confidence in areas they might otherwise have avoided. For further discussion about resistance to learning and practical suggestions for overcoming it, see Stephen Brookfield (1990), especially Chapter Eleven.

On the other hand, certain courses such as freshman seminars, writing-intensive courses, and advanced seminars are designed precisely to engage students in the learning process, invite them to participate in class activities, connect their ideas with their lives, and express ideas orally and in writing. These classes succeed only if teachers are sensitive to the wide range of personal concerns of students, draw them out, and give them positive feedback—even as they encourage students to stretch their minds and master the substance of the course. Such courses can be personally demanding for students and teachers alike, because they may be emotionally charged, but precisely this kind of education can have a genuinely transforming effect on students.

The old pedagogical saw holds: "Telling is not teaching, and listening is not learning." It calls attention to the fact that a teacher must go beyond the presentation of ideas and facts, no matter how brilliant; more essential is to know how the ideas are received, how they fit into the minds of students. Psychologists know that the mind is not an empty vessel into which knowledge is deposited for recall when needed but is a dynamic system that is organized in ways particular to the life of an individual. The same idea learned by two different individuals takes on somewhat different meanings because it connects with the repository of their prior ideas and experiences. Unless teachers know their students reasonably well, it is impossible for them to know whether or how any given idea will be understood, integrated into the mind, or used by the student. Several techniques have been suggested to enlighten a teacher about how students understand the main ideas of a course: frequent use of quizzes (Light, Singer, and Willett, 1990); "one-minute papers" at the beginning or end of a class for students to indicate the most important thing learned and the question(s) that remain unanswered (Cross and Angelo, 1988, pp. 148–150); examination of students' class notes; and reading of journals kept by students.

*Motivation.* A related issue is the matter of motivation. Faculty members at most colleges today cannot assume that students have a high level of motivation for learning the subject matter in the general education courses they teach. Perhaps they never could assume this; good teachers have always gone out of their way to make their courses interesting. It is simply not clear to some students why curriculum requirements exist; those in business and other career-related majors, in particular, do not understand why they should have to take courses in the liberal arts that seem to have little relationship to their intended careers. The college and the teacher need to provide a clear and strong rationale about the practical value of general education courses to the students. Even if not fully accepted by the students, clarity about the goals of general education and the individual courses will at least help minimize misunderstanding and student resentment toward their studies.

Moreover, the teacher needs to deliver the goods in the course by linking the subject matter with the interests of students. Educators have known for decades that it is easier to learn things that are personally significant than those with no relationship with the person. Good teachers like Jaime Escalante, the celebrated mathematics teacher and subject of the movie *Stand and Deliver*, have always tried to understand their students and to use examples and metaphors from their daily lives as an enticement to master difficult ideas. Whether at an introductory or advanced level, a college and a teacher take on an added burden of responsibility to make a course stimulating and valuable whenever students are required to take it. Particularly for these courses, the teacher needs to find ways to link the content with the students and to stimulate student interest in the substance.

Let me illustrate this principle with a personal anecdote. My wife and I recently took ballroom dance instruction, and in the first session the instructor — a veteran of such classes — spent about 80 percent of the time trying to overcome resistance, embarrassment, anxiety, and fear among the students, primarily the men. He made our anxieties and fears explicit, helped us to laugh about them, and taught us some simple dance steps to practice over and over as we slowly built competence and confidence. We all learned the basics, even in that first session. It occurred to me that it would be a good strategy for any teacher, but particularly of a required course, to devote a certain portion of each class, perhaps 10 to 20 percent, specifically to generating or sustaining student interest in the subject matter, allaying fear of failure, and seeing that students succeed with at least the basic steps.

*Developmental Stages.* While evaluating an interdisciplinary core course on the Western tradition, I asked a group of teachers how the students seemed to be doing. The professors expressed a familiar litany of concerns: Students were passive and waited to be told what to do, they hesitated to participate in discussions of key texts, and they avoided drawing their own conclusions. I recognized these concerns as signs of a stage of student development, and when I asked whether they were familiar with the literature in that area, all said no. After I sketched the theory of William Perry, they saw these concerns in a very different way.

Perry (1970) posits that students develop intellectual and moral sophistication through a series of progressive stages. The lowest stage of development is *dualism*, in which the student assumes that there is either truth or falsehood. Truth is thought to be contained in the text and dispensed by the teacher, the primary authorities; the task for the student is simply to master the "objective" knowledge that is presented. Such students who are dualists want to be told by the authorities what is correct, think talking with their peers is a waste of time, and hesitate to think independently or express their own views.

Eventually the student may discover that interpretations of phenomena are in conflict, alternative theories account for the same set of facts, and disagreements exist among authorities. This presents an epistemological crisis that leads the students to a second stage that Perry calls *multiplicity*, in which she or he decides that knowledge, rather than being fixed and certain, is simply a matter of opinion. At this time the student believes every opinion is as good as every other one. Eventually, students may learn that some opinions are better than others; they are supported by stronger reasons and empirical evidence, or they are based on a more appropriate set of specified assumptions. This third stage is called *relativism*, because knowledge is relative to an intellectual framework. The final stage is labeled *commitment in relativism*, which means that a student develops his or her own personal views about how to understand a phenomenon and is able to act on that understanding in the absence of objective truth.

The implication is that students with a dualist frame of reference, which is typical of traditional-age freshmen, are not able to perform sophisticated mental functions, such as analyzing alternative interpretations of Plato's *Republic* or comparing and contrasting different explanations for the rise and fall of the Roman Empire. This is because many students have not yet developed the intellectual abilities for grappling with conflicting interpretations that may both have some explanatory power. Aspirations for higher-quality general education programs sometimes outstrip student abilities. For example, one liberal arts college introduced a series of interdisciplinary core courses. A complex freshman eight-semester credit course was intended to provide historical and literary foundations of the Western world from Rome to the Renaissance and to include special additional instruction in writing. At the end of the first year, one of the teachers concluded, "The course is too sophisticated in design and too complicated in execution to serve as a required first semester freshman course in history, literature, and writing." The dean (1988) wrote, not entirely tongue in cheek, "In the final analysis we concluded that not only was it too cumbersome for freshmen, it also was too sophisticated and demanding for faculty."

Another implication has to do with the general pedagogical prescription of stage theorists, namely that students should be *challenged* by being given learning tasks that stretch their capabilities and, at the same time, *supported* to reduce the threat of failure and to cope with the insecurity of not knowing with certainty. The dual use of challenge and support stimulates more sophisticated mental functioning. New general education programs have raised standards, but they have not been strong in developing pedagogical strategies for supporting the different developmental stages of student learning.

*Learning Styles.* Scholars have identified a number of learning styles used by students (Claxton and Murrell, 1987; Kolb, 1984) Teachers would be well advised to employ various pedagogical strategies that are responsive to students with different learning styles; they might even offer alternative ways for students to demonstrate their learning. For example, Belenky, Clinchy, Goldberger, and Tarule (1986) studied "women's ways of knowing." They discovered that women students tended to react negatively to the pervasive epistemology in the academy, that of the dispassionate, detached pursuit of "objective truth." Women were likely to rely on "connected knowing," that is, to get into ideas of an individual by understanding them in relationship to the person and to the circumstances in which they are embedded. Intellectual development of women appears to take place in the context of personal relationships—not detached from them. Clinchy (1991) says that teachers need to connect with women students so that these students can, in turn, connect with the ideas and substance of the course. Clinchy's evidence shows that women are able to master complex and abstract ideas but prefer to learn them in relation to the individual person and the particular context from which they are derived. The study of learning styles and developmental stages is relatively new and still developing (Kurfiss, 1988), but the results are sufficiently rich to contribute to a more effective pedagogy of general education.

*Connecting Learning with Students' Lives.* The point is not that teachers should become psychiatrists or perform amateur psychoanalysis on their students. Rather, it is that for learning to be most effective, students' lives, not just their minds, need to be actively engaged in the learning process. I have illustrated the point by stressing the personal-emotional aspects of learning, but the same logic applies to students' careers, interests, talents, values, obligations to family and community, and other aspects of life as they relate to learning. Opportunities can and should be provided in general education courses for students to connect their learning with their lives.

A practical way for faculty members to gain insight into their students was suggested by Katz and Henry (1988) and field-tested by faculty members in institutions of higher learning throughout the state of New Jersey. It involves two faculty members pairing off, visiting each other's classes, and providing feedback to each other. Most important, each teacher interviews three or so students in his or her class every week or two. Students are asked why they are in the course, what they are most interested in, how they view ideas of the course, how items discussed connect—or fail to connect—with other aspects of their lives, and the like. Professor Steve Golin of Bloomfield College, who directed the project, reported that this simple technique used by over 200 faculty members has the power to transform teaching. He writes (Golin, 1990, p. 10): "Collaborating with a peer is itself transforming. We see that our frustrations and our hopes are not unique. The isolation of teaching is subverted. . . . For many faculty, the student interviews are an even more powerful agent of our self-transformation. As students reflect on their experience, or explain how they construct meaning, we listen, or ask questions. The roles are reversed: They teach, we take notes. . . . Enjoying their active participation and excited by the view from below, we look for ways to bring some of that excitement and enjoyment into the classroom."

### Developing Student Values

The curriculum reform movement is an attempt to improve the quality of education by addressing the knowledge and skills that are learned by students. This is essential, and important gains are being made, but the goal will not be achieved unless the dominant values of students are also engaged. The observation of Gene Maeroff (1990, p. A12) about public schools applies equally well to colleges: "School reform will barely matter if the values shaping the school culture remain untouched. Self-discipline and inner controls must be cultivated in young people if they are to be engaged in learning of intellectual consequence."

The Carnegie Foundation for the Advancement of Teaching (1990, pp. 9–10) had compiled some troubling data that indicate that the values at the heart of undergraduate education are being undermined. Large numbers of students invest little time in study—less than a quarter report studying as much as sixteen hours a week—and much time in gainful employment. Half of full-time students work, and they average twenty hours per week; for part-timers it is thirty-six hours. Students should not be blamed for working many hours, since the cost of attending college has escalated, financial aid has not kept pace, and the burden has shifted increasingly to students as financial aid has tilted from grants to loans. Nonetheless, quality education requires an investment of time beyond what most students make. The same report says that the majority of college faculty believe that most undergraduates at their institutions only study enough to get by, they are less willing to work hard on their studies, and their institutions spend too much time and money teaching what should have been learned in high school. If the values reflected in these practices and views are not checked, they will have corrosive effects on the integrity of the educational process. If students do not study much, the content of the curriculum is inconsequential.

But more: Students should understand the values that are manifest in public and private affairs—in relations among nations, in social and economic policies, in relationships among family and friends, and in personal ambitions and behaviors. As students see and analyze the expressions of values and the clash of competing ideals, they have an opportunity to confront their own ethics and beliefs, explore the implications of their own values, test them in an open academic interchange, and develop more principled views.

The general education curriculum, having always been associated with deeply moral issues, is one of the places where this can and should happen. Consider a few of the influential titles in the literature of general education. *General Education in a Free Society* (1945), the famous Harvard "Redbook," was a recipe for preserving democracy through education after the horrors of World War II. Earl McGrath (n.d.), former U.S. commissioner of education, wrote *General Education and the Plight of Modern Man*, arguing that it can give meaning and significance to life. In *Educating for Survival* (1977), Boyer and Kaplan asserted the need to strengthen social bonds by stressing commonalities among all peoples. Humankind's most basic values over the centuries and across cultures have historically been identified as the province of general education.

Further, the substance of campus general education programs and courses lends itself well to the analysis and discussion of values. The rise and fall of civilizations; the insights of enduring literature; great drama portraying the psychic heights and depths of individuals; the study of motives, both grand and base, of people in all walks of life; the analysis of concepts such as peace, freedom, responsibility, and justice; the design of the state and social institutions to serve human ends; the ethical issues in science and technology: It is difficult to imagine how any of these topics could be adequately taught without an explicit focus on the values that infuse them.

But higher education has, for the most part, abandoned values education. It gave up trying to shape the morals of students through the curriculum earlier this century, spurred on by the ideal of the research university, the professionalization of faculty, and the rise of new professionals in student affairs who became responsible for students outside of class. The in loco parentis doctrine was jettisoned in the 1960s, so that institutions abandoned virtually all responsibility for students outside of class, too.

As Warren Bryan Martin declared, it is time for colleges and universities to once again get into the business of values education. In his words (1982, p. 146): "education capable of meeting contemporary needs is moral education. It is education for character." Further, he says it must be a part of the core curriculum. "Advanced general education has an objective to work through a set of practices — historical, social, whatever — in order to get at motivations and purposes; wherein facts are important but no more so than the meanings attached to the facts; wherein the question of 'how' is always followed by 'why' and 'so what'; wherein the particular is important insofar as it illuminates the ideal; wherein intentions no less than behavior are a focal point of concern" (p. 146).

Although it should never impose a set of beliefs, a college or university can and should, I believe, confront through its general education program the values held by students, raise their sights by encouraging them to alternatives, and expect them to defend their own positions with reasoned arguments. That is a formula for cultivating the development of the conscience and giving students practice thinking through controversial issues and making reasonable choices among competing goods. For example, the importance of communal needs and the responsibility of individuals to the common good should be stressed to counter the individualism of students—which, after all, mirrors the American citizenry itself with its tendency to look out for number one, narrow interest-group politics, and demand for government services without paying taxes to support them. Students should be encouraged to serve others and to celebrate common achievements to counter self-centeredness. Rather than cave in to their fascination for the rich and famous, the college should take steps to help students understand the plight of the poor, sick, and oppressed, whether in this country or throughout the world. It should emphasize the values of equal justice, human rights, mercy, and caring. Rather than allowing students to put down those who differ, which leads in some cases to harassment or even physical attacks on minorities, women, gays, and foreigners, we should help students to understand, tolerate, and celebrate differences of race, gender, nationality, age, and culture. Students should be aware of their privileged opportunity to receive higher education, and they should be encouraged to return some of that largess in the form of service to others. Although students—and others—should be free to make up their own minds, they should be presented with contrasting values, expected to think through the alternatives, and develop their own views.

One of the reasons higher education abandoned value instruction was the rise of the philosophy of logical positivism during the early part of this century. Positivism attempted to distinguish between statements of fact and statements of value, and it held that since value propositions could not be proven true or false, they were essentially matters of taste and hence had no place in the academy. But as David H. Smith (n.d.), director of Indiana University's Poynter Center for the Study of Ethics and American Institutions, pointed out: "the intellectual spell of positivism has been broken. Persons aware of the Holocaust, observers of the economic disparities between the developed and developing world, individuals experiencing discrimination on racial, religious, or gender grounds—all may find it difficult to agree that morality is simply a matter of taste."

Recent scholarship on literary criticism and the interpretation of texts—deconstructionism, psychoanalysis, Marxism, and feminism, among others—call into question the basic fact–value dichotomy. Many intellectual leaders now believe that knowledge cannot be value-free and that it is far more dangerous for values to slip into academic work unconsciously than for us to be aware of them and their role in our scholarship, teaching, and lives.

In the words of Robert Sandin (1989), it is possible to teach "values without indoctrination." Indeed, Richard Morrill (1980) has articulated a number of ways to teach values to students that are consistent with the standards of modern scholarship. These include describing and analyzing the values in the larger world; identifying the values in the subjects students study; articulating students' own values; and assessing the adequacy of values in terms of criteria such as consistency, coherence, comprehensiveness, authenticity, and adequacy to the situation.

Doctrinaire approaches that seek conformity to a particular belief system or code of conduct (apart from the integrity of the intellectual and educational processes) are contrary to an open process of inquiry. Whether from the left or the right, such efforts threaten the very nature of the academic enterprise. But it is possible to reclaim the broad center of moral discourse—from the far right and left with their political agendas, on the one hand, and from the value-free scientists and scholars, on the other hand. In their general education programs and beyond, colleges and universities should be helping students to engage in ethical reflection, participate in moral discourse, think through value-laden topics, and choose among alternatives in a reasoned way.

In short, it is doubtful that we can achieve our goal of improving the quality of education unless we include a specific agenda to address the values of students. What would it avail us to produce an educated mind without helping to put that mind to good use, without developing an "educated heart" to guide it?

## Responding to Diversity

Much of the debate about general education tends to assume a traditional student body: eighteen-to-twenty-two-year-old, full-time students, mostly residential. Although this is an accurate characterization of the student body in many institutions, the fact of the matter is that most student bodies include large numbers of students who are older, part-time, and commuters. Typically, they have families, are gainfully employed for substantial periods of time, and have social relationships throughout the community (Levine, 1989). Women outnumber men among American undergraduates, and they are disproportionately represented among adult learners; often they are going through a major transition that prepares them to secure a better job. People of color, too—Asian Americans, blacks, Hispanics, Native Americans—are growing in numbers on college campuses. Indeed, Thomas Ehrlich (1991) has labeled these groups of students the "new majority," and as president of Indiana University launched a massive initiative to develop better ways of educating these students throughout each of the system's campuses.

As important as it is for institutions to respond to the diversity of their own students, the challenge of dealing with cultural diversity is greater than that. The ability to understand and deal with culturally diverse people is an important goal for everyone, simply because American culture is growing more diverse. Consider race, for example. The 1990 census (Barringer, 1991) found that in one decade the number of Asians in the population increased 108 percent, Hispanics 53 percent, Native Americans 38 percent, blacks 13 percent, and Caucasians six percent. Also, the country is increasingly more closely intertwined with other cultures and nations. All of us are affected by this new reality, and we must think through our own beliefs and values concerning such issues as race. Further, we need to engage in public dialogue in order to create conditions to prepare for students to live and work effectively in a multicultural world.

Dealing with diversity, especially in general education, is

one of the toughest jobs on today's college campuses. Discussions about diversity have been called "difficult dialogues" and used as the theme of the 1991 National Conference of the American Association for Higher Education. According to its brochure (1990), the dialogues are difficult "because basic issues are being reexamined, and because deeply (and often unconsciously) held beliefs are at stake."

The dialogues are difficult for another reason: The basic strategy for dealing with cultural diversity has changed. For decades we tried the "melting pot" approach. Immigrants were expected to abandon the ways of the old culture, learn English, and adopt American patterns. Ethnic and racial minorities that would not—or could not—adopt the ways of the dominant majority were marginalized and kept from receiving the full benefits of the culture. General education programs tended to mirror this societal pattern by featuring Western civilization courses that stressed the history, philosophy, literature, and art of the dominant culture. The melting pot image is being superseded by the image of the handmade quilt, which keeps the distinctive qualities of each piece of fabric and joins them together into a holistic new item. Today, the strategy is to respect the integrity of various cultures and to fashion ways for different peoples to study, work, and live together, while preserving their essential differences. The task facing general education today is to develop an inclusive multicultural curriculum by incorporating different cultural perspectives in our curricula and teaching the legacies of various ethnic groups. In the words of Johnetta Cole (1991), president of Spelman College and American Association for Higher Education (AAHE) conference keynoter, "We are for difference. For respecting difference. For allowing difference. Until difference doesn't make any more difference."

A great similarity exists between racial and ethnic differences and differences in terms of gender. Attitudes about men and women, sex roles, and expectations about gender are deepseated cultural constructs and ingrained from an early age. Traditional views of men and women are being challenged everywhere today, and demands for equality, fairness, and educational opportunity must be heeded, in education as well as elsewhere in society. The law mandates these changes, even if the culture is slow to catch up with the new realities. Gender issues, no less than those of race, are difficult—and necessary—for students to talk about, analyze, and understand.

What is called for is a four-fold strategy to address this task: sensitizing and educating faculty and students about gender and cultural differences; developing more inclusive general education curricula and courses; devising a pedagogy that is more effective for minority groups; and providing special support to groups of students when it is needed.

Sensitizing individuals to the importance of cultural differences and helping them understand why it is important is perhaps the first place to begin. Without this step, nothing else can be accomplished. Perhaps the most persuasive argument for a more inclusive approach within the academy is offered by Elizabeth Minnich (1990). She argues that without including perspectives of various cultural groups, one is left with "partial knowledge" about history, literature, or philosophy, for example. Failing to pursue all avenues to truth and settling for partial knowledge is anathema to the academic. Lectures, seminars, brown bag lunches, and retreats have been used by various colleges and universities to foster discussion about gender and ethnic issues and to introduce some of the new scholarship on these topics.

Various activities have been used to get individuals engaged with the subject, including movies such as Spike Lee's *Do the Right Thing* or Christine Choy's *Who Killed Vincent Chin?* Role playing of critical incidents in racial relationships highlights issues and can serve as a good way to start a conversation. Robert Barry at Loyola University Chicago (1987) developed a useful exercise for students, or, with variations, for faculty, to explore multicultural issues. It involves individuals from two different cultures or subcultures following a set of prepared questions about such topics as why they came to college, the nature of their families, what they do for fun, where they get their money, and their early experience with cultural differences. Each individual must listen to the other person, each has an opportunity to say something of importance to the other, and both talk in a personal and specific way about their differences. It can be a profound learning experience and lead to constructive suggestions for improving interpersonal relations on the campus.

After individuals acquire a certain level of sensitivity and knowledge and they feel comfortable discussing multicultural issues, then it is possible to address the curriculum issues. One complicating factor is that even if individuals agree that change should take place, they disagree about what kind it should be. Zelda Gamson (1989) has differentiated between the "restorationists," who want to restore something they think has been missing, such as the history and literature of the West, and the "expansionists," who want to include something they believe has never been in the curriculum, such as the voices of women and minorities. These alternative views typically come to bear on discussions of the humanities, social sciences, and fine arts. Of course, as we have seen, it is possible to have both — more emphasis on history and culture of the West but with a more inclusive point of view. Nonetheless, this is an issue often faced by curriculum reformers.

Various curriculum patterns have been devised to deal with multicultural education. These include a single course required of all students, a menu of courses from which students may choose, a minicourse with partial credit, and efforts to infuse multicultural content throughout the curriculum. However they decide to structure the curriculum, many institutions operate faculty development activities — seminars, institutes, and workshops — to encourage faculty to learn new material and incorporate new scholarship into courses. This is a vital step, because a critical problem of implementing a new curriculum, however it is configured, is to find enough faculty members who are qualified to teach the course(s). Typically, colleges and universities must develop the expertise of their own faculty to implement whatever curriculum they decide is appropriate. Although it is necessary, an inclusive curriculum is not sufficient; an effective pedagogy also is needed.

A great similarity exists between problems of multiculturalism and those of women's issues. Public dialogue has been sponsored in many colleges and universities to discuss gender issues. Role playing can also highlight critical incidents of gender relationships. General education curricula are perfect for incorporating the voices of women that so many feel have been missing. A near-classic paper issued by the Project on the Status and Education of Women (Association of American Colleges, 1982), *The Classroom Climate: A Chilly One for Women*, makes the point well. It points out many ways women students have been slighted, ranging from the explicit (for example, disparaging of women's intellectual ability and using of sexist humor) to the subtle (for example, interrupting women students more and responding to comments by women less than those made by men). In the words of a woman studying business administration at Berkeley who was cited in the paper (p. 1): "Have I been overtly discriminated against? Possibly no. Have I been encouraged, helped, congratulated, received recognition, gotten a friendly hello, a solicitous 'can I help you out?' The answer is no."

This analysis, I believe, is pertinent to the treatment of students of racial and ethnic minorities, too. Teachers convey their attitudes in a myriad of ways, some explicit and some subtle, and they need to be conscious of the impact of their classroom behavior on students of all cultures. Cultural differences in interpreting verbal and nonverbal cues compound the problem. The point is this: All students deserve a classroom environment that is warm, that values them and their ideas and gives them every opportunity to learn and develop.

And we must keep in mind that the benefits are not simply for individuals from the less dominant cultures. For example, if men students see limited or negative views of women communicated by their professors, it may reinforce their own limited views, which may interfere with their ability to accept women students as full peers, to work collaboratively with them, and to learn from them. It may also develop habits that eventually hinder their ability to relate to women as equals in the workplace, family, and community. Being able to work and live effectively in a multicultural world is important regardless of one's gender, race, or cultural heritage.

Finally, special support mechanisms may need to be created to ensure the success of certain groups of students. The mathematics workshop designed by Uri Treisman at the University of California, Berkeley, is an example. He discovered that most of the black students at Berkeley did poorly in entry-level mathematics courses, which prevented them from majoring in the sciences and technological fields. While interviewing minority students, he discovered an important cultural phenomenon. Asian students tended to study together in groups, but blacks, even with high ability and a history of success in high school, tended to study in isolation and not benefit from the intellectual assistance and interpersonal support of peers. Treisman (1985, pp. 30–31) established a workshop with special features: "(1) the focus on helping minority students to *excel* at the University, rather than merely to avoid failure; (2) the emphasis on collaborative learning and the use of small group teaching methods; and (3) faculty sponsorship, which has both nourished the program and enabled it to survive."

This voluntary program entails about two hours a day for four or five days a week in which students work together doing mathematics assignments with informal consultation by teachers. The students know that they are expected to do well in their courses, and they are responsible not only for their own success but for that of their peers, too. Evidence documents its success in both the performance and persistence of student participants.

I am aware that some thinkers (D'Souza, 1991) are critical of this emphasis on multiculturalism, seeing it as motivated by a political rather than educational agenda, leading to an insipid "political correctness," and even infringing on the freedom of speech that has racist or sexist overtones. These are worrisome matters. But we must realize that maintaining the status quo is every bit as much of a political agenda, being insensitive to the experiences and knowledge of individuals lacking power is unacceptable, and expressions of hatred are anathema to education. Indeed, these matters pale compared to the alternative of neglecting the obvious cultural factors that affect knowledge, education, and modern life. The very best way for colleges and universities to deal with them, I believe, is to bring the issues into the classroom and examine all cultures and orthodoxies critically. What better way is there than by having students read about cultural perspectives, by expecting them to analyze controversial issues and to subject them to the rules of evidence under the tutelage of scholars, and by giving them the experience of discussing issues of difference and sameness with a wider variety of individuals and viewpoints than they are used to? It is not easy business and mistakes will be made, but from my point of view, it is the right agenda.

In sum, we might recall the aphorism of Clyde Kluckhohn, an early American anthropologist: Every man (in the idiom of the day) is like all other men, some other men, and no other man. A quality general education program should affirm each of these three truths. It should help students understand how they are like everyone in the human race, understand and develop their own unique qualities, and learn about their own cultural tradition as well as that of others.

### Extending Learning Beyond the Classroom

With our expanded view of students, we also need to broaden our view of where learning takes place. To accomplish all of the educational purposes of a college, we must look beyond the formal curriculum, especially the 30 to 50 percent of the total that is typically accorded to general education. Some things are more easily learned in the informal give and take of social interaction outside of class, such as learning about a different culture by making a friend from a foreign country or developing communication abilities by providing leadership for a campus group. The full curriculum of a college should consist of both the formal curriculum and the co-curricular experiences students have beyond it that have educational significance.

Unfortunately, this is not the typical state of affairs. A proposal from a leading liberal arts college summed up the usual situation:

Students tend to regard the classroom as the sphere of the faculty or of academics. At the same time, they regard time outside of class as wholly other, as unrelated to the College. This bifurcation pro- duces many curious affects [sic]. Students think of residence halls as hotels rather than as places where learning occurs. Time after 4:00 P.M. becomes "my" time; course assignments become "homework"; stu- dents who wish to speak up in class may be ridiculed; evening presentations by visiting schol- ars are poorly attended. Despite often heroic efforts, faculty find it increasingly difficult to as- sume that students will pursue extracurricular ac- tivities of value to their education unless such ac- tivities are "required" [anonymous, 1989].

Another leading college acknowledged that its policy of "benign neglect" about student life beyond the classroom was no longer viable. It concluded that this policy conveyed to students a sense that college did not care for them; the policy also was related to the college's comparatively high student attrition rate.

The educational importance of informal student-faculty interaction outside of class has been well documented. Ernest Pascarella and Patrick Terenzini (1991, p. 620), in their massive summary of the research on how college affects students, put it this way.

The educational impact of a college's faculty is enhanced when their contacts with students extend beyond the formal classroom to informal non- classroom settings. . . . [The] extent of informal contact with faculty is positively linked with a wide range of outcomes. These include perceptions of intellectual growth during college, increases in in- tellectual orientation, liberalization of social and political values, growth in autonomy and indepen- dence, increases in interpersonal skills, gains in maturity and personal development, educational aspirations and attainment, orientation to scholarly careers, and women's interest in and choice of sex-atypical (male dominated) careers.

The most influential aspects of student-faculty interactions appear to be intellectual discussions that extend the range of the curriculum.

What is not so well known is that student interaction with their peers is also related to most of these same outcomes. In the words of Pascarella and Terenzini (1991, p. 604): "The environmental factors that maximize persistence and educational attainment include a peer culture in which students develop close on-campus friendships, participate frequently in college-sponsored activities, and perceive their college to be highly concerned about the individual student and to place a strong emphasis on supportive services (including advising, orientation, and individualized general education courses that develop academic survival skills)."

The key factor identified by these scholars as well as others (Astin, 1985a; Pace, 1990) is the *amount of involvement* by individual students in both academic and nonacademic activities. This implies that much of the responsibility for obtaining a quality education rests with each student, but there are steps that institutions can take to elicit student involvement.

One of the most thorough efforts to extend the learning of general education beyond the classroom has been made at Southeast Missouri State University (Zeller, Hinni, and Eison, 1989). Following the faculty's adoption of a forty-eight-semester-hour liberal education program, a task force was created to develop comprehensive co-curricular initiatives that were linked to the educational goals and the new curriculum. Included are the following:

- University studies resource manual listing student affairs programs, stating the mission of each department, and describing the educational skills and learning opportunities served by each program
- Co-curricular bulletin providing concise information about activities, organizations, clubs, and leadership positions

- Student activities calendar of events distributed weekly to students, faculty, and staff
- Independent studies and practicum opportunities informing junior and senior students about possibilities in student affairs departments
- Paraprofessional/peer adviser positions with training for resident advisers, peer advisers, career-planning advisers, orientation co-leaders, and academic tutors;
- Assessment of outcomes of co-curricular involvements on such variables as skills in communications, management, problem solving, organization, and citizenship
- Cross-cultural residence hall providing specialized housing for domestic and international students interested in increasing cross-cultural awareness and communications, aided by workshops throughout the year

Like faculty elsewhere, some at Southeast Missouri are reported to be interested in and supportive of these co-curricular efforts while others are indifferent. From the student perspective, however, these efforts must further the purposes of general education more than when the curriculum is disconnected from the rest of student life.

George Kuh and his associates (Kuh, Lyons, Schuh, and Whitt, 1990, pp. 4–5) have studied what they call "involving colleges"—colleges that engage students in learning activities beyond the classroom—and identified five qualities that distinguish them:

> a) A clear, coherent mission and philosophy that communicate high but reasonable challenges presented to students buttressed by an ethic of care. Involving Colleges deliberately accentuate, or minimize, interpersonal distinctions to attain the institution's mission and purposes...;
> b) Campus environments that use the physical setting... to educational advantage and that create a human scale organization in which anonymity is discouraged and numerous opportunities are pro-

vided for meaningful involvement in out-of-class
activities;

c) A complicated web of cultural artifacts (history,
myths, sagas, heroes/heroines, etc.) that promotes
involvement through a theory of membership (i. e.,
everyone is considered and expected to be a full
member of the community) and communicates to
students "how the institution works";

d) Policies and practices that hold students responsible for their own behavior and learning, blur the
artificial boundaries between in-class and out-of-
class learning opportunities, distribute resources
consistent with the institution's educational purposes, and enable sub-communities of students to
flourish . . .; and

(e) institutional agents who promote student participation in educationally purposeful out-of-class
learning activities.

The establishment of multiple communities, each linked with
the educational mission of the institution, is recommended, as
the authors liken an involving college to "one house with many
rooms." For more information about this work, see Kuh, Schuh,
Whitt, and Associates (1991).

Lacking an inviting community of learners, students can
and do find a sense of belonging in groups that are unhelpful, if
not downright antithetical, to educational purposes. The media
carry stories about abuses in athletics, fraternities, and so-
rorities where some students try to impress their friends with
dangerous or threatening activities. More chilling are under-
ground hate groups that lead to racial or sexual violence. These
aberrations are symptoms of fissures among members of an
academic community. To some extent, they also are desperate
attempts to find a sense of belonging in the absence of a genuine
community.

Several institutions are taking steps to make the whole of
the campus a learning environment for the benefit of the general education of students.

- *Our Learning Environment* is the report of the faculty's plan to achieve the ten desired learning outcomes that they derived from Goshen College's strategic plan. It details steps that the small Mennonite school hopes to take to strengthen the overall campus climate for learning.
- The College of Holy Cross and Reed College created new positions responsible for integrating curricular and extra-curricular activities for freshmen.
- Students at Berea College are required to attend ten events in the Convocation Program each semester; part-time students must attend four per course.
- Miami University (Ohio) provides grants for student or other groups for co-curricular projects that support liberal education purposes. Their co-curricular programs have traditionally been strong, but until now they have not been directed toward specifically liberal education purposes.

If the curriculum and co-curricular aspects of college life were joined more closely, the college experience would be more coherent and students would have a better and more holistic education. Because so much more can be done on this front at most institutions, this represents another agenda for the future.

## Conclusion

Once a campus agrees on what students should learn, the formal curriculum can be made more purposeful by focusing instruction on those goals that are specifically valued. If faculty members had a better understanding of students, they would have greater sensitivity to the personal and emotional aspects of learning, prevent learner abuse, and help overcome the anxieties and fears that are residues of past difficulties. They would be better able to enhance student motivation to learn by linking the subjects of study with aspects of students' lives. A genuine education has moral dimensions, and teachers should confront students' values which are sometimes at cross-purposes with learning, and examine the value-laden issues that pervade their subjects. A better understanding of students would recognize

their diversity and incorporate academic substance that connects to various cultures and histories. And finally, the college
would broaden its view of the curriculum and embrace a range
of learning activities beyond the classroom.

What these proposals amount to is a plea to get beyond
the question of *what* students should know and to refocus attention on the question of *who* our students are and might become.
It shifts attention from the curriculum that the college offers or
that the faculty teach to the curriculum that the students learn.
The recommendations in this chapter are designed to promote
an effective pedagogy of general education. By looking at the
"demand side" rather than the "supply side" of general education, these recommendations provide greater assurance that the
benefits of the curriculum actually reach their intended beneficiaries, our students.

It is easy to say that faculty should consider the personal
aspects of learning, curricula should cultivate the values of
students, colleges should establish inclusive curricula, and the
co-curriculum should be linked closely to the curriculum, but it
is admittedly difficult to accomplish any one of these objectives.
That is why they are so seldom attempted in a coordinated,
institutional way, let alone accomplished. It is much easier, for
example, for faculty and student affairs staffs to operate with an
invisible wall between them than it is to abandon comfortable, if
dysfunctional, stereotypes and to genuinely work together for
the education of students. Like curriculum reform itself, the
reason for contemplating these recommendations is not the
ease of life for campus staff but the betterment of education for
students—an end that is reason enough to take up the challenge.

# Chapter Eight

# An Institutional Agenda
# for Strengthening General Education

A great deal has been accomplished and much has been learned since the curriculum reform movement began over a decade ago. Here is a brief summary.

1.  Education zoomed to the top of the national agenda and stayed there. Everyone agrees that college education can, and should, be better, despite very different conceptions about what constitutes quality and how to improve it.
2.  College faculties have discussed what students need to learn if they are to live and work productively in the twenty-first century. In many institutions, they have reached agreement about the knowledge, skills, and personal qualities their institutions should cultivate in students, regardless of academic specialization or intended career.
3.  Special task forces have been assembled to study issues and make recommendations for improvements in the undergraduate curriculum, and new forums—retreats, open hearings, workshops—have been created for faculty members to discuss basic ideas and consider proposals.
4.  Hundreds of institutions—nobody knows exactly how many—have revised general education curricula to purposefully direct student learning toward the most valued goals.

5. Despite the fact that each campus must devise its own curriculum, several prominent trends are evident: a greater emphasis on the liberal arts and sciences, more attention to fundamental skills, higher standards, greater structure, among others discussed in Chapter Two.

6. Important barriers to meaningful reform exist on college campuses. In addition to the complex substantive intellectual issues involved, the most prominent are the protectiveness of academic departments and professors' specialties, the added work required to change a curriculum, concerns about sufficient resources, and the difficulty of fashioning broad areas of agreement across the entire campus.

7. Valuable benefits accrue to institutions able to surmount these barriers and to make their curricula more purposeful. Students receive higher-quality education and experience greater curricular coherence; faculty members derive benefits of professional growth and renewal; and institutions gain a greater sense of community, sharper identity, and often larger enrollment.

8. The greatest benefits are reaped by the undergraduate colleges that make the largest changes, which presumably involve the most comprehensive and boldest thinking about the central part of each student's education.

9. Systematic faculty development programs — where teachers are given time and assistance to learn new material, develop engaging pedagogical practices, and incorporate them into their courses — are crucial to successful curriculum change.

10. Students benefit most from certain kinds of general education curricula, such as required interdisciplinary core courses and courses using original sources, as well as mandated study across the curriculum of such subjects as writing, critical thinking, and ethics or values.

11. New organizational supports have been created to implement and to sustain reforms, such as an administrator with sole responsibility for general education and a campus-wide faculty committee to oversee the core curriculum.

This adds up to an impressive list of accomplishments. But the history of general education during this century is one of ebbs and flows, periods of reform followed by eventual erosion of the changes made — leading to calls for another wave of reform. This history teaches us that all of the gains that have been made by literally hundreds of colleges in the last decade are in danger of being washed away: If "reformed campuses" go back to "business as usual," today's hard-earned reforms will be threatened, too. The reforms need to be institutionalized and to continue to receive attention from faculty and administrative leaders who must continuously help "the faculty as a whole to take responsibility for the curriculum as a whole," in the words of *Integrity in the College Curriculum* (Association of American Colleges, 1985).

## Five Stages of the Curriculum Revision Process

Although much has been accomplished, much more remains to be done, regardless of where an institution is in terms of its general education program. Colleges are at five different stages in the curriculum revision process, each of which is associated with different dynamics and challenges.

Too many colleges and universities have not yet been affected by the debate or reform movement, despite the vocal and visible activity taking place all about them. Many of them operate fragmented curricula held together by political alliances. They lack an educational rationale that is known and shared by students and faculty, leading to a low regard for this portion of the curriculum. Leaders of these colleges need motivation to review their programs and perhaps to start a modest revision in at least some component. They need information about what is happening on other campuses: the issues in the debate; current curricular trends; and the benefits that students, faculty members, and institutions are deriving from a strong general education program. More important, they need to grasp that a high-quality general education might give them a competitive edge, or at least keep them from falling behind many of their competitors. As a member of one board of trustees told me, "If you're not moving ahead, you're falling behind."

Where does the impetus for change come from? The sources are many and varied. Internally, the most common one is leadership from an academic administrator, one of the few people on a campus with knowledge and responsibility for the curriculum as a whole. New deans, in particular, have been effective sources for change, because such a person sees the instructional program in a fresh way, has little vested in the existing curriculum, and is eager to set a constructive agenda. Some presidents have pointed to problems with the curriculum and pressed the institution to focus on general education. And occasionally a faculty member with an institution-wide perspective, often by virtue of a leadership position on a committee or in a department or division, will provide the spark. Typically, one of these individuals learns about what other similar institutions are doing through attending a conference, reading the literature, or talking with his or her counterpart at another institution. In the last few months, I have been contacted for information about improving the quality of general education by such diverse individuals as a faculty member at the Community College of Florida, the dean of DeVry Institute in Columbus, a librarian at the University of Minnesota, Crookston, and the chancellor of the Minnesota State University system. The impetus for improvement can come from anyone.

As important as internal sources are, external forces also elicit change. Regional accrediting bodies routinely review the general education curriculum, and in recent years they have not been hesitant about praising or criticizing the quality of offerings. Assessment instigated by a state often causes an institution to reconsider its goals and to assess whether students are mastering them. Foundations use the carrot rather than the stick, and often their initiatives elicit interest and catalyze action where none has existed.

Some colleges are at a second stage and are conducting a review of their instructional programs. Although I opined a few years ago that the curriculum reform movement was peaking, I was wrong, because I regularly learn of more institutions that are just embarking on comprehensive curriculum reviews. Many more are working on portions of their instructional program, such as writing, multicultural education, or a values project. For institutions at this point, individuals who provide leadership must decide on the organization and procedures of the curriculum review; decide which publications and model programs to study; conduct studies of their own students and curriculum; and hold conversations with students, faculty members, and administrators to hear about their concerns and solicit their ideas. For example, North Dakota State University, Wilmington College, Bunker Hill Community College, and the University of St. Thomas recently have established curriculum review groups that are hard at work on these tasks.

Curriculum task forces usually learn that they must not only reach agreement among themselves but they must bring their colleagues along with them. There are strategies that help bring the review to a successful conclusion (Gaff, 1980; Wee, 1981; Gamson, forthcoming). They include establishing a stance of openness and responsiveness, learning about issues in the curriculum debate, finding out what other institutions are doing, conveying knowledge about new ways to think and better ways to organize the curriculum to colleagues, structuring opportunities for colleagues to discuss the issues in a nonthreatening and constructive fashion, taking straw polls, being sensitive to the concerns that are expressed, seeking feedback on draft proposals and making revisions in light of it, and making certain that everyone who votes is at least knowledgeable about what the proposal contains.

A third group of colleges has made small or piecemeal changes that are helpful but not sufficient. Some of these institutions are now exploring bolder and more comprehensive changes. Johnson C. Smith and Pacific Lutheran Universities and Trenton State College are working to extend gains made in selected components, such as writing, freshman-year seminars, integrated studies, science, and new scholarship on gender and cultural pluralism, to more comprehensive programs. Leaders of these efforts typically become part of a network of knowledgeable colleagues, both on- and off-campus; build on the positive experiences and goodwill generated from small-scale efforts; and develop the vision, courage, and strategies to effect larger-scale reforms. The political pressures almost inevitably press toward modest change. Doing little appears to be less threatening, cheaper, a lot easier, and involving less risk—at least in the short term. But continuing with a mediocre general education curriculum in the long term may prove more threatening, expensive, harder, and riskier. Malcom Huckabee, provost of Averett College, put it bluntly: "We have come about as far as we can with piecemeal approaches." He is now working with the faculty toward a more comprehensive revision of the college's general education curriculum.

At a fourth stage, colleges and universities have approved curricular changes and are working on their implementation: Hiram College is implementing its interdisciplinary collegiums; the University of Nevada, Reno, is in the first year of its three-course Western and American Civilization sequence; and Ohio University is implementing the third tier (consisting of interdisciplinary seminars) of its general education curriculum. Implementation is a notoriously difficult stage of the curriculum change process; some proposed changes have not made it past this stage. Several agendas emerge here. One of the most important is faculty development—time, energy, and resources for the faculty to learn new material, acquire new pedagogical approaches, and develop new or revised courses. It is also important to explain the rationale of the changes to students, secure their understanding and support, and help those affected to deal with all of the practical details of making the transition from the old curriculum. New directors of general education and campus-wide committees need to define their roles, establish their authority, and develop criteria and guidelines for reviewing and approving courses.

At this stage it is vital to assess the experience of students and faculty—sometimes including a pilot test prior to full implementation—to identify strengths and weaknesses, to work out the bugs, and to make the curriculum progressively a more positive experience for everyone involved. Assessment allows problems to be identified and dealt with in an open and formal way rather than festering below the surface and being aggravated by rumor and inaccurate information. It also allows successes to become visible and to reinforce those who labored to bring them about.

A fifth stage is that of institutionalization. Some colleges and universities have made significant curriculum changes that seem to be working well. Newly implemented changes, however, usually are fragile, and they need time to become rooted deeply in the life of the institution. Any of a number of techniques are used. The preparation of an accreditation review is an opportunity to focus attention on the educational purposes and consequences of the curriculum. The Evergreen State College, for example, hosted a nontraditional site visit in conjunction with its reaccreditation, involving a number of national general education experts as well as individuals with specialized expertise. It functioned as a kind of high-level seminar and provided useful feedback about Evergreen's distinctive educational program, which involves learning communities and a great deal of student responsibility for learning. Bethel College (Minnesota) adopted a new curriculum in 1985 and has conducted faculty development projects that focused on curricular aspects dealing with writing, ethics, internationalism, student development, computer literacy, and science and technology. Whereas the early effort focused on helping the faculty teach to the knowledge and skill goals embodied in the curriculum, another project called "Teaching Beyond Content" assists faculty in cultivating "personal capacities" of students, such as empathy, creativity, integration, and learning to learn. The Western College program at Miami University continues to assess its students and interdisciplinary program; it received its second academic excellence award from the Ohio Board of Regents for demonstrated achievements. Celebrations and other symbolic events help a community to recall its basic commitments to general education. Austin College celebrated the thirtieth anniversary of its distinctive interdisciplinary program in 1988 with a conference and reunion. As Professor Jack Carlson commented, "I think . . . such programs, if they've survived that long, deserve to be celebrated!"

It should be apparent that attending to the quality of education at the center of baccalaureate education should not be viewed as a fad, something that will soon go out of fashion. Rather, committed academics will make a vocation out of constantly considering, as Trilling (1980) expressed it, "what a liberal and humane education consists in." Nor should improvements in general education be seen as a one-time fix, as implied by the faculty member who said, "We will be done with the curriculum revision next year, and then we can concentrate on other things." On the contrary, as soon as academics start to neglect general education, they are sowing the seeds for its destruction and creating conditions for a subsequent call for its overhaul. In the words of one wag, strengthening general education "is like crossing the Sahara. It just goes on and on."

## Continuing the Spirit of Reform

The spirit of reform needs to be kept alive because, although much has been accomplished, much more remains to be done. The public debate about quality education continues and fans the fires of reform, and indeed, the parade of crisis-oriented literature shows no sign of letting up. In his review of several books, John Searle (1990, p. 34) observes,

Bloom demonstrated to publishers and potential authors one thesis beyond doubt: it is possible to write an alarmist book about the state of higher education with a long-winded title and make a great deal of money. This consequence appears to provide at least part of the inspiration for a number of other books, equally alarmist and with almost equally heavy-duty titles, for example *The Moral Collapse of the University: Professionalism, Purity and Alienation* by Bruce Wilshire; *Killing the Spirit: Higher Education in America* by Page Smith; *Tenured Radicals: How Politics Has Corrupted Our Higher Education* by Roger Kimball; and *The Moral and Spiritual*

*Crisis in Education: A Curriculum for Justice and Compassion* by David Purpel.

As with movie sequels, each successive volume deploring the state of higher education packs less punch and loses some shock value. But as long as the debate continues, it fosters a climate conducive to further improvements on college campuses.

As we have seen, quiet and constructive curriculum change most often occurs on campuses out of the glare of television cameras and print media; that pattern will continue to be the order of the day. Indeed, the colleges and universities in my survey, at whatever stage they may be, are continuing to work on improvements in general education.

I asked the campus leaders about the most important *current initiative* to improve general education, and specific items were mentioned at no less than 217 of the 226 institutions responding. This is a remarkably high number, especially since respondents had to write in their answers and not simply make a check mark.

The particular nature of the initiatives varied widely, as might be expected, given the diversity of institutions, the varying nature of their programs, and the various lengths of time they have been working on general education. Below are some representative comments from leaders of different types of institutions.

*Comprehensive colleges and universities*
- Foreign language requirement
- Adding international/multicultural perspective
- Setting up three general education task forces to prepare interdisciplinary sequences in the humanities, social sciences, and natural sciences
- A university-wide core curriculum committee reviewing the entire general education program
- Implementing new program, with enormous faculty development

*Doctoral and research universities*
- A complete overhaul of the curriculum

- Implementing the new curriculum in autumn 1990, review of all majors to make them consistent with the new curriculum
- An American cultures requirement
- Four separate curriculums; attempting to consolidate to one common model
- Integrating perspectives in gender, race, and class into every course

*Liberal arts colleges*
- College-wide quantitative reasoning requirement
- General education task force, using a newly approved purpose statement; has been charged to review general education, looking at outcomes, interdisciplinary options, and reduced total credit hours; has a general education coordinator working closely with the task force
- The development of strategies to provide greater evidence of student academic achievement
- The continued implementation of the Common Learning course for first-year students, and the development of a senior thesis requirement for most, if not all, students

*Community colleges*
- A college-wide review of the entire general education program
- Inclusion of a humanities requirement in all vocational degree programs
- A high-technology communication program; a two-semester History of Civilization program through the vision of interdisciplinary primary sources; an Ethics and Values program
- Portfolio system in writing and general education learning assessment

None of these are trivial matters; each is a serious effort to enhance the education of students at the various colleges. Despite the progress they have already made, these colleges are continuing to actively pursue important ongoing agendas to enhance their general education programs.

The deans also gave us a glimpse of the future. They were

asked, "What trends or issues do you think will influence curriculum change at your institution during the 1990s?" The top two
agenda items were multicultural and global perspectives. The
future, it seems, is already here, since these are very powerful
current trends; the respondents are saying that they can only
become more important. Austin Doherty from Alverno College
put it well: "Students being developed for the 21st century will
need to develop their global awareness and understanding of
effective citizenship to a very sophisticated degree. This will
require knowledge on a broader scale than is part of our current
design, more comprehensive understanding of value systems
and issues, and ability to communicate in all its forms."

The next two categories of expected future pressures are
what might be called general demand for better or broader
education and the changing nature of students. In regard to the
former, deans cited the centrality of the liberal arts with special
mention of such topics as the humanities, sciences, writing,
values, and connected learning. In regard to students, one person wrote, "The changing character of the student body which
differs greatly from the academy many faculty knew as students.
The need to include rather than to exclude the diverse student
body through transformation of higher education's purpose."
Other items mentioned by numerous individuals include
shrinking financial resources, student outcomes assessment,
and the need to hire new faculty, who are sympathetic to general
education. All of these issues are ones with which we are already
familiar.

### The New Motivation for Further Improvement

The spirit of educational reform in the future may be
propelled not simply by altruistic or idealistic motivations. It
may tap the most potent motivator known to humankind—self-
interest. For students, acquiring a strong general education
is essential and in their long-term, enlightened self-interest.
Of course, a broad general education can enrich their inner
lives and give them more control over the external world; it can
open opportunities that are simply unavailable to the poorly

educated; it can give them the capacity for democratic self-government and the ability to contribute to the civic good.

These traditional values of education, general or otherwise, are well and good, but today's students, as a group, are most concerned with career preparation or enhancement. What many do not know is that general education is valuable for their careers, too. Today's jobs require more intellectual sophistication, higher-level skills, better communication ability, and greater sensitivity to other people—all staple objectives of general education. Given the rapid changes in careers, individuals who have wide-ranging intellectual resources, sophistication to think through complex issues, personal qualities to see a task through to completion, and communication and interpersonal skills to present their ideas will be most likely to surmount the challenges of changes in tomorrow's work life. Norman Cousins (1978, p. 15) expressed it well.

> The irony of the emphasis being placed on careers is that nothing is more valuable for anyone who has had a professional or vocational education than to be able to deal with abstractions or complexities, or to feel comfortable with subtleties of thought or language, or to think sequentially. The doctor who knows only disease is at a disadvantage alongside the doctor who knows at least as much about people as about pathological organisms. The lawyer who argues in court from a narrow legal base is no match for the lawyer who can connect legal precedent to historical experience and who employs wide-ranging intellectual resources. The business executive whose competence in general management is bolstered by an artistic ability to deal with people is of prime value to his company. For the technologist, the engineering of consent can be just as important as the engineering of moving parts. In all these respects, the liberal arts have much to offer.

For faculty, participating in comprehensive thinking about general education with colleagues from across the campus and working to implement a program offers them intellectual stimulation and fosters their professional growth. Ann Ferren (1990, p. 31), commenting on the personal dimension of revising the general education curriculum at American University, observed: "the reform process has helped faculty members reset their expectations, strengthen their commitments, establish bonds with each other, and express their generativity just at the stage of life — middle age, for that is demographic composition of our faculties — when they can be expected to do so."

Not all professors are equally interested in general education, of course, and some rightly concentrate their energies on research or teaching their academic specialties to their major or graduate students. But even in such specialized pursuits, general education is present in the background, if not the foreground. In the first national report devoted to the academic major, the Association of American Colleges (1991, p. 5) defined the goal of specialized study as more than learning a specialty.

> The work of the major is only partly done when students gain facility in its culture, when they learn the nuances of its special language to such a degree that they can take an active part in its conversation. To fulfill its role in liberal learning, the major must also structure conversations with other cultures [disciplines] represented in the academy, conversations that more nearly reflect the diversities within our world and require patient labors of translation. Ultimately, the goal of the major should be the development of students' capacities for making connections and for generating their own translations and syntheses. Fostering such capacities is an intrinsic, not an elective, responsibility of each major program.

Of course, practice often falls short of this goal, but if one accepts the premise of this definition, then work in a specialty is not conducted apart from other fields and general education but in dynamic relationships with them. The major, properly seen, may be in the foreground or the background vis-à-vis general education, but it is not separate from it. All should recognize the centrality of general education as an integral part of higher and specialized learning and support such a vital function.

For institutions, a strong general education program brings both educational and institutional benefits. When presidents and trustees learn that revisions in general education can lead to larger enrollments, more visibility, and better fund raising, they recognize it as a hard-headed approach to institutional advancement. General education is too important a matter to be treated in the laissez-faire fashion of the past. It is vital for administrations and faculties to work together to craft a common curriculum that serves both educational and institutional interests. More than one president has pressed the faculty to develop a comprehensive and distinctive curriculum so that he or she can get on with the business of marketing it. This, of course, puts the cart before the horse; a curriculum should be shaped primarily by educational, not marketing, reasons. But today good education constitutes good marketing. As knowledge of these consequences becomes more widely known, we can expect the interest in strengthening the center of the instructional program to intensify. Then, caring for general education will no longer be an obligation or a service done out of idealism or a sense of duty; it will be what institutions must do for their own interests.

Self-interest also characterizes many stakeholders in higher education beyond the campuses. Business leaders want a well-educated workforce; politicians seek an educated citizenry to drive their economies; citizens hope that education will improve not just the life chances of students but the quality of life of the society that supports it. Although these groups may have very different ideas about education and how to improve it, at some level they tend to coalesce around the dominant trends in the general education reform movement described in Chapter Two. That is one reason why Montgomery Community College has organized a citizens advisory council on general education that brings together a wide range of citizens to speak on behalf of general education. Such community councils are common-place in vocational areas, but there may be value in using their ideas and influence to enhance general education, too.

## Future Agendas

The redoubled effort I am calling for should build on what has been done and learned about curriculum change to date. For one thing, academics must periodically revisit the overarching learning goals of the institution and review curric-ula and courses to see that they address the goals in explicit ways. The single biggest factor leading to curriculum reform has been the realization of college faculties that their students were not adequately learning what they should be. As more and more faculties confront this issue and collectively discuss their views of what constitutes an educated person, they may be expected to adopt more purposeful and structured curricula.

Yet these collective goals, even if they have been developed with widescale participation and adopted by large majorities, soon lose their power to guide instruction. The tendency is for an institution to publish the goals in official documents and simply assume that they guide the work of teachers and students. The sad fact is that without periodic review, courses tend to take on a life of their own and to depart from the faculty's collective judgment about the most important educational objectives. Pro-fessors retire or go on leave; replacements with little under-standing of the institutional goals are hired; new courses are introduced and older ones are modified to reflect new interests or knowledge of professors. All of these are natural events in the life of an institution, but they allow discrepancies in the curricu-lum—the curriculum offered by the institution, that taught by the faculty, and that learned by the students—to widen. Continu-ous efforts to close these gaps are required.

Second, a larger number of colleges should undertake a serious review of the curriculum. Many have thus far neglected or only flirted with reform, and more should become more

serious about the matter, especially as the benefits of a comprehensive revision coupled with a systematic faculty development
program become better known. From my travels I am amazed to
learn of college faculties that have not discussed in any organized way the serious and repeated charges leveled at higher
education. The executive vice president at a leading private
research university said its faculty had not even discussed the
issues, let alone made any programmatic change. A faculty
committee at a land grant university looked bewildered when I
asked if their colleagues had discussed the early criticisms by
Bennett and Bloom, read about the more recent ones, or considered the recommendations of the national reports. When I told
an academic vice president of a university system in a medium-
size state that I was writing about the curriculum reform movement, she asked, "What movement?" It seems that general education has not made it onto the agenda of the several colleges in
the system. It is as though the debate about quality education—
although it has been featured in best-selling books, the print and
electronic media, and political campaigns—has no relevance to
them. Perhaps they expect the problem to go away if they ignore
it long enough. Or perhaps they do not perceive that any consequence of the outcry over better education will threaten them.

My sense is that they are wrong. The need to raise the level
of education is so central to the nation and such a long-term task
that it will not just go away. The societal expectation of higher
quality in education has great relevance to academics, and the
consequences of tackling or ignoring the demand to improve
the curriculum eventually will become all too apparent. Political
and business leaders, alumni, donors, students and their families—all of these stakeholders may be expected to convey their
feelings about the effectiveness of the instructional program in
tangible ways. Although an individual college may ignore the
issue for a time, it will face progressively tougher times as its
competitors take steps to strengthen their offerings and build
constituent support for their efforts.

A third change we should see in the future is a broadening
of the terms of the debate, much of which has been dominated
by the question of content: What should students learn? This

question has been pursued by many individuals. But as I have
pointed out earlier in this book, the subject matter is only one
element, albeit a crucial one, in the educational equation. We
have to move beyond content and its place in the formal curriculum, as important as that is, to consider other critical elements,
including the students, the teachers, and the environment
within which education takes place. Who are the students, what
experiences have shaped their lives, what interests them, how do
they learn, and how can they be enticed to become actively
involved in learning? What are the motivations of the teachers,
what constraints keep them from excelling, and how can their
effectiveness be enhanced? How can the social and physical
circumstances for learning be improved? What are the most
supportive environments for learning, and what do we need to
do to create them? By broadening the debate to include such
questions, a fuller understanding of the complexities of effective
education is possible, and fresh strategies for improvement
come into view.

A fourth agenda item related to the broadening of the
debate is a wider range of reforms, extending from the formal
curriculum to the whole of the college environment. A great
deal of research (Astin, 1977; Chickering, 1969, 1981; Feldman
and Newcomb, 1969; Pascarella and Terenzini, 1991) has demonstrated the powerful impact that peer groups, informal
student-faculty relationships, student subcultures, and extracurricular activities have on students. Although the classroom is
properly the focus of the effort to improve education, colleges
and universities go to great trouble and expense to provide
other loci of activity: the library, science laboratory, computer
center, playing field, chapel, dormitory, Greek system, cafeteria,
student center, women's center, commuter student lounge, special houses for ethnic minority students, international student
center, and many more. Each and every one of these settings
should be seen as an adjunct to the classroom. Each of the
activities that takes place in these settings should have an explicit educational agenda, and they should attempt to further
the educational purposes that undergird the curriculum and
the classroom. As North Central College's Gerald Berberet as-

serted, "everything that happens on a campus has curricular implications."

Fifth, this agenda should attract new individuals to the movement, and they may be expected to devise new strategies for improvement. Faculty members and academic administrators have been the dominant actors, which is natural for a debate driven by concerns about subject matter. But as the terms of the debate are broadened, and as student life beyond the classroom comes to play a larger role, the way opens for contributions from student affairs professionals and other administrative staff. The professional literature of student affairs administrators is filled with pleas for strengthening ties to academic affairs (Brown, 1990). Large numbers of these individuals are found on college campuses, and they have much to contribute to the overall education of students. They can help set high expectations, establish an intellectual tone in the student culture, articulate the values of general education, and advance the learning of students beyond the formal curriculum.

Finally, several more years of assessment and research should yield a body of empirical findings about general education curricula and their effects. The public debate and the curriculum reform movement have been fueled by rhetoric and reason — analyses of deficiencies, calls for change, arguments for and against various proposals, and impassioned pleas and diatribes of various sorts. A notable absence of empirical evidence and knowledge of probable outcomes of various curricular practices characterize these efforts. We do know that students perform comparatively poorly on test scores, but we do not know with any certainty how to reverse that situation. For example, research does not tell us if reading a traditional list of Western classics is better than one featuring important works by people of color, women, and Third World authors. This lack of knowledge is one of the reasons why passion and conviction so dominate the debate.

With the large number of new curricular approaches and the increase in the assessment of educational outcomes, we should be able progressively to build a body of empirical knowledge about various curricula and their consequences at different kinds of colleges and universities. Several national research projects are in process, many with funding from the Exxon Education Foundation. For example, Astin is studying student outcomes associated with different types of college curricula; Gamson is examining the process of curricular change in comprehensive universities; Aubrey Forrest is exploring the portfolio method of assessing student achievement; and Virginia Smith is analyzing principles of good practice in general education. The institutional assessments and multi-institutional research projects will allow us to learn more about the actual conduct of general education programs, their consequences, and strategies for strengthening them.

### Developing a Supportive Academic Culture

My call for continued reform, then, is nothing less than an appeal that academics keep the ideal and practice of general education at the center of their attention. Organizational supports are needed to maintain and sustain a vigorous general education curriculum. This means policies, structures, and practices that keep the attention of the faculty members and administrators focused on the core of the baccalaureate. A college or university must institutionalize the continuing dialogue and shared conceptions that help general education programs sustain their intellectual and pedagogical vitality and their capacity for renewal. Such mechanisms as cross-disciplinary seminars, ongoing faculty development, assignment of administrative responsibility, and assessment of results are not only examples of good practice in general education — they also are essential foundations for lasting reform. Simply put, undergraduate general education must become central to the culture of the institution — its way of conducting business — and not be undercut by other priorities.

How to do it? The notion of an academic culture sounds vague, and it is hard for some to see how it can be manipulated to work for change. Here is a five-part plan: (1) Become familiar with the concept of organizational culture; (2) develop a vision about general education, its role in the education of students and in the institution; (3) develop a strategic plan for the curriculum and institution; (4) implement the plan throughout the entire institution; and (5) assess the results.

*The Concept of Organizational Culture.* Colleges and universities are bureaucracies in the classic sense of that term: They divide responsibilities into manageable units, hire individuals with specialized expertise to work in each office, and organize offices hierarchically in reporting relationships. Like all bureaucracies, different offices in colleges often are not well coordinated, individuals in one office sometimes pursue their own narrow interests at the expense of larger ones, and breakdowns in communications are commonplace. Although the curriculum is regarded as the special province of the faculty, certain of its committees, such as personnel and budget, may work at cross purposes with the goals and philosophy of general education. Administrative officers often fail to give general education the kind of support that they might. The concept of organizational culture provides a way of correcting these problems and getting different offices, programs, and individuals to pull together toward common highly valued ends.

The concept developed initially in corporate America, in the context of the body of "excellence literature" (Ouchi, 1981; Peters and Waterman, 1982; Gagliardi, 1986; Lorsch, 1986; Walton, 1988). Effective business organizations, such as International Business Machines, McDonalds, Disney, and Delta Airlines, were found to affirm a common set of values and expectations and then consistently work to manifest them in all of their affairs. General Electric, one of the world's largest corporations, now talks of seeking to become a "boundaryless company." An awkward term, it means that externally suppliers and customers are drawn closer to the business, becoming functional partners; internally responsibilities between different offices are blurred. GE's *1990 Annual Report* (1991, p. 2) states: "Engineering doesn't create a product and then 'hand it off' to manufacturing. They form a team, along with marketing and sales, finance and the rest. Customer service? It's not somebody's job. It's everybody's job. Environmental protection in plants? It's not the concern of some manager or department. Everybody's an environmentalist." GE is striving to create a common culture so that it is internationally competitive and not weighed down by its own bureaucracy. Although it confesses to "pulling dandelions in its own bureaucracy" for years, it needs to keep doing it or individuals backslide.

*A Vision.* Although colleges and universities are not businesses, the concept of organizational culture has relevance to higher education; indeed, it has gained increased attention there (Cameron and Ettington, 1988). Scholars have suggested that the academic culture can be managed specifically to improve the functioning of institutions and to further the ends of education. A vision of the centrality of general education, both its role in the education of students and its role in the institution, could be devised. Some curriculum task forces have articulated its role in education, but few have taken the further step of articulating what it means institutionally. Often enormous energy has gone into the development of a new general education curriculum only to be undermined by faculty personnel policies that reward research over teaching, budget formulas that systematically starve lower-division course offerings, or departmental decisions that assign the best teachers to teach courses for major students. The whole of the academic culture needs to be directed to further the most central educational values and commitments of the institution through institutional policies, structures, and complementary actions of individuals throughout. The vision, to borrow from GE, is that everybody would become a general educationalist.

A large university obviously serves several missions, as does even a small college. But general education should be recognized as central to every specialized, professional, or vocational program. Even research and graduate education can be carried on without sacrificing undergraduate education (as often happens), and this complementarity can well become part of the vision of an institution.

*Strategic Planning.* Strategic planning gives the vision practicality. It is typically the responsibility of the administration or board of trustees, and it usually is driven by concerns about the institution's market niche, enrollment, finances, or fund raising. But effective strategic planning starts with the educational program; educational excellence is pivotal to success in the marketplace, in recruitment, in fund raising, and elsewhere.

General education reforms are integrally related to strategic planning at several institutions. One of the touchstones of a curriculum review is the college's mission, history, and character, so that the general education program reflects core values and builds on important strategic strengths. Sometimes a college will develop a strategic plan calling for initiatives specifically in general education. Bethany College (Kansas), for example, developed a plan with sixteen priorities, seven of them in the area of the curriculum; this planning gave impetus and direction for a new general education program. Marietta College worked on a new mission statement simultaneously with its curriculum revision. It affirmed its historic role as a liberal arts college and checked its gradual shift to career preparation, as it made a comprehensive revision in its core curriculum. At Wright State, an urban comprehensive university, the liberal arts had been overshadowed by professional units as five out of six majors were concentrated in business, mathematics and science, engineering, education, and nursing. After approving what was described as a "common curriculum which provides focus, structure, and coherence where none had been, and which thus assures a broader, deeper and more meaningful general education than had been available for our students in the past" (Wright State University, n.d., p. 10), the faculty broke into spontaneous applause lasting for several minutes. Subsequently, a strategic plan was adopted that prominently emphasizes general education, teaching, faculty development, cultural and racial diversity, and assessment—all of which reinforce the common curriculum.

The University of Minnesota is currently embarked on a

major initiative to improve quality, especially in undergraduate education. For several years, it has worked toward a plan to focus attention and resources on quality. President Nils Hasselmo proposed a bold initiative for excellence in undergraduate education to correct several problems most apparent at the flagship Twin Cities campus: low graduation rates, insufficient sections of general education courses to meet student demand, inadequate advising. Because prospects for additional funding from the state are dim, he has devised a plan for the reallocation of university resources to fund quality improvements. The plan is to reallocate within and between every unit a total of $60 million over a five-year period, 10 percent of the entire base budget. The major beneficiaries are intended to be the Twin Cities College of Liberal Arts and Institute of Technology, the coordinate campuses of Duluth and Morris, and other programs enrolling 84 percent of the undergraduates. Difficult and politically controversial decisions have been made by the university: the campus at Waseca will be closed; large reductions will be made in central administration; certain colleges will lose funds; several academic and support units will be consolidated; and certain non-academic activities will be curtailed. But undergraduate education will be stronger. Although the fiscal difficulties of the state threaten to undercut this scheme, the university intends to stick to its plans.

Paralleling the university's undergraduate initiative and reallocation plan, the Twin Cities Campus Task Force on Liberal Education (1991) provided leadership for a recently approved university-wide curriculum for all undergraduates. The general education program will be guided by "clearly stated objectives" and consist of a "limited number of courses developed specifically to serve those objectives." This all-university curriculum will replace separate curricula established by separate colleges. It will do away with what the report calls a "crazy quilt of collegiate systems that defies explanation, confuses students, and inhibits cross-college transfers" (p. 31). The program includes a required seminar for new students; a minimum of three courses in each of three major divisions (physical and biological sciences, history and social science, and the humanities and

arts); required study of cultural diversity, citizenship and public
ethics, international perspectives, and environmental education; and an intensive writing program including a composition
course and four writing intensive courses. New courses will be
developed as the program is phased in. Although it is too early
to know the final result, this is an illuminating case of strategic
planning (complete with hard-hitting resource allocation decisions) being used to strengthen undergraduate general education at a large research university.

*Implementation.* This is the point where the vision and
plan are expressed in the life of the institution, calling for
serious commitment and strong leadership to make the hard
decisions between competing priorities and to insist that general education is fully supported throughout the institution. It
has implications for all academic functioning.

- The educational vision and plan need to become a conscious part of the identity of the institution, which must
  project a clear image to internal and external audiences of
  what the college or university stands for.
- The president, top administrators, and faculty leaders must
  articulate the importance of a broad general education for
  all students and illustrate with specific examples commitment of the institution to this function.
- The formal general education curriculum should contain
  the quality, content, and coherence that would be expected
  of the central feature of the institution.
- The faculty need to understand their responsibilities for general education, and these should be clearly used in hiring
  professors, evaluating their suitability for advancement, determining salary levels, and recognizing accomplishments.
- Students should understand the importance of general education, see it dovetail with their majors, and know the rationale behind each of their required courses. They should
  feel responsible for their own learning, actively engaged in
  their coursework, and both challenged and supported by
  their teachers.

- Student affairs and the co-curriculum should be carefully coordinated with the curriculum and serve explicit educational purposes.
- All administrative staff should be aware of their educational role, and their offices should support curricular goals.
- Members of the community should be brought together — often in small natural communities — to think, analyze, argue, and dream about issues and themes that pervade general education: multicultural diversity, global studies, and ethics and values.

In short, fostering a coherent academic culture entails a persistent series of related efforts to keep everybody's attention focused on the thing that is the center of the entire enterprise — a broad general education for all.

*Assessment.* The effectiveness of these several efforts should be assessed, scrutinized, and publicly discussed to find better ways of achieving the institution's avowed goals. Assessment, in this sense, would not be pursued because it is mandated by some outside agency but because it sheds light about how well the college or university is achieving its own most valued goals of learning. Assessment is an instrument to achieve self-consciousness and to assure integrity of the instructional program.

The reality discovered by educational researchers is that the measured impact of any single educational program on students tends to be slight. Demonstrable institution-wide changes in students, the sorts that are sought by educational reformers and assessors, most often are the result of cumulative rather than one-shot treatments. Pascarella and Terenzini (1991, p. 655) sum up the evidence this way, saying that "the enhancement of the educational impact of college is most likely if policy and programmatic efforts are broadly conceived and diverse. It also implies, however, that they should be consistent and integrated." They urge educational leaders not to be misguided by searching for a single large lever of change but to concentrate on pulling many small levers more often. The implication is that general education programs will have greater impact on students if their purposes are addressed across the curriculum, indeed, across the institution. In the words of these scholars, "For significant changes to occur, a collective act of institutional will is needed" (p. 656), which is precisely why a coherent academic culture is necessary. It entails a series of persistent, related efforts to keep everybody's attention focused on the one thing that is the center of the entire enterprise—a broad general education for all.

Robert Stevens, director of the Classic Learning Core at the University of North Texas, wrote to me after I spoke on creating an academic culture that is thoroughly supportive of general education purposes. "I understand your notion of 'college culture' to imply that in the struggle to enlarge and ennoble the soul of the student, none of our dealings with him are 'innocent.' From recruitment through financial aid and advising to curriculum and graduation requirements, I suppose we send messages to students, and for years, perhaps, the messages have been mixed" (personal communication, Jan. 16, 1989).

Unless the academic culture becomes more favorable to undergraduate general education, today's curriculum reforms are in serious jeopardy. We will see more poignant personal memoirs from curriculum reformers like Joseph Tussman. Tussman (1969) provided the leadership to re-create the Meiklejohn two-year Experimental College for freshmen and sophomores at Berkeley during the 1960s. The communal program had a coherent common curriculum that concentrated on central issues in four pivotal historical periods: ancient Greece, seventeenth-century England, early America, and contemporary America. After being encouraged to develop the program by institutional leaders, he ran into several problems. Most of the faculty Tussman contacted were either not interested or unavailable. He was able to attract only two who committed to the full two years, two more who agreed to one year, and a few graduate teaching assistants. During the second two-year phase, he relied on friends on leave from other universities to complete the staffing. Despite their encouragement, top administrators denied the request for six permanent tenure slots for this non-departmental program. Tussman (p. 26) was very clear that "the whole point of the Program was its commitment to a special kind of common intellectual life that by its very commonality nourished a deeper individuality," but the program was buffeted by pressures for autonomy among professors and the desire of students to "do their own thing," in the parlance of the time.

Despite the enormous difficulties of launching and operating this small enterprise, Tussman (1988, p. 41) recalled that it was enormously fulfilling. "I remember the second run seminar as the most exciting, the most significant intellectual and moral experience of my whole life, unmatched, unapproached by anything I experienced in four decades of interesting University life, mostly at Berkeley. . . ."

Although it had significant educational successes, the program was terminated after four years, the result of, in Tussman's poignant words, "the interplay of intelligence, habit, power, of self-interest, ignorance, and irresponsibility in the conduct of affairs in a great institution" (p. 61). Reflecting two decades later on his experience of trying to create a coherent intellectual community in a setting that prizes individual professors in separate departments offering discrete courses to isolated students, Tussman (p. 59) concludes: "The fundamental delusion may have been to suppose that it was possible for a great organism like the University to nourish or sustain for long an enterprise at odds with its essential nature. . . . the University, simply by being what it is, has killed the College."

### Toward a College of Integrity

If general education is to be genuinely reformed, we need not just "integrity in the curriculum," in the terms of the Association of American Colleges report, but integrity throughout the entire college culture. Virtually every college and university emphasizes a broad general education for students in its mission statement, its catalogue, and its recruitment materials; the rhetoric is often flowery, occasionally even eloquent. But the rhetoric often becomes disconnected with daily life on the campus. General education becomes problematic, not because people openly oppose the ideal, but because individuals do not practice what the institution preaches. The reality needs to be brought closer to the rhetoric.

What is needed is to develop a college of integrity in regard to general education. A college of integrity says what it does and does what it says, not just in the curriculum but in *all* of its activities. It backs up the official rhetoric about general education with a strong, comprehensive, and coherent curriculum and with an organization that solidly supports it. It embeds the curriculum within a coherent academic culture to make general education permanent and central to the education of students and to the operations of the institution itself.

It would be naive to think that one could remake academic culture and turn traditional values upside down so that the least of them, general education, would become the first. That simply will not happen. But every campus has many individuals—throughout the faculty, administration, and student body—who actually believe in the idealism of the philosophy and practice of general education. In addition, in many areas undergraduate students—nonmajors as well as majors—*are* being well educated: in certain courses, departments, programs, and offices. What is needed is to identify these areas, discover the people who are doing exceptional teaching and learning and give them recognition and rewards, elevate them and their achievements to a more prominent position in the prevailing culture, and provide encouragement for others to do similar things. Bringing groups of these individuals together can be a catalyst for institutional improvements.

Leaders on campus after campus have been pleasantly surprised to learn of the large amount of residual goodwill that exists toward general education. There is no need, therefore, to change basic values but merely to expand this awareness of the richness of the existing culture. The institution can build on the strengths that are already within its culture and thus can create a more supportive environment for general education. In this environment, a college of integrity can indeed be achieved.

# Resource:

## General Education Questionnaire

We use the term general education in its broadest sense for the purposes of this questionnaire. When we say general education, we include the formal curriculum required of all students, often referred to as the "breadth component," "core curriculum," or "distribution requirements." We also include faculty development, course revisions, and even extracurricular programs to the extent that they enrich general education.

Name of your institution_____

1. What is the **most notable** feature of the general education curriculum?


2. What is the most important **current initiative** regarding general education you are working on (if any)?


3. How many **credit hours** are required for graduation from your college with a B.A. degree (A.A. degree in 2-year col-

leges) and for general education? Are these less, the same, or more credits than a decade ago?

| | CREDIT HOURS | | AMOUNT | | |
|---|---|---|---|---|---|
| | **Quarter** | **Semester** | **Less** | **Same** | **More** |
| A. For graduation | ☐ | ☐ | ☐ | ☐ | ☐ |
| B. For general education | ☐ | ☐ | ☐ | ☐ | ☐ |

4. During the **last decade** which of the following steps has your institution taken to strengthen the general education program? Please answer with reference to the **most recent change** in each category and indicate the year(s) implemented. (**Check all that apply.**)

| | YES | YEAR |
|---|---|---|
| A. Changed requirements for: | | |
| 1) Admission | ☐ | 198__ |
| 2) Grading | ☐ | 198__ |
| 3) Graduation | ☐ | 198__ |
| B. Changed curriculum structure: | | |
| 1) Changed distribution system | ☐ | 198__ |
| 2) Added new types of courses (e.g., freshman seminars) | ☐ | 198__ |
| 3) Increased interdisciplinary "core" courses | ☐ | 198__ |
| C. Stressed improvement of individual courses: | | |
| 1) Revised introductory or other courses | ☐ | 198__ |
| 2) Increased attention to "the canon," traditions of the academic disciplines | ☐ | 198__ |
| 3) Incorporated "new scholarship" (e.g., gender or global studies) | ☐ | 198__ |
| 4) Stressed certain skills "across the curriculum" (e.g., writing) | ☐ | 198__ |
| D. Engaged in faculty development for: | | |
| 1) Subject matter knowledge | ☐ | 198__ |

    2) Effective pedagogy, enhanced
        learning        ☐    198___

  E. Other, specify:_____    ☐    198___

5. For each of the following **areas**, indicate the number of credits **required** (either quarter or semester) and whether these are less, the same, or more than a decade ago.

| | # OF CREDITS | | AMOUNT | | |
|---|---|---|---|---|---|
| | Quarter | Semester | Less | Same | More |
| A. Writing | ☐ | ☐ | ☐ | ☐ | ☐ |
| B. Speaking | ☐ | ☐ | ☐ | ☐ | ☐ |
| C. Mathematics | ☐ | ☐ | ☐ | ☐ | ☐ |
| D. Computer literacy | ☐ | ☐ | ☐ | ☐ | ☐ |
| E. Foreign language | ☐ | ☐ | ☐ | ☐ | ☐ |
| F. Humanities | ☐ | ☐ | ☐ | ☐ | ☐ |
| G. Fine arts | ☐ | ☐ | ☐ | ☐ | ☐ |
| H. Natural sciences | ☐ | ☐ | ☐ | ☐ | ☐ |
| I. Social sciences | ☐ | ☐ | ☐ | ☐ | ☐ |
| J. Other, specify: | ☐ | ☐ | ☐ | ☐ | ☐ |

6. Does your current general education program include any of the following **special features**? (**Check all that apply.**)

| | YES, OPTIONAL | YES, REQUIRED |
|---|---|---|
| A. Freshman seminar | ☐ | ☐ |
| B. Senior seminar, project | ☐ | ☐ |
| C. Advanced or upper-division courses | ☐ | ☐ |
| D. Interdisciplinary "core" courses | ☐ | ☐ |
| E. Courses using original sources | ☐ | ☐ |
| F. Honors courses | ☐ | ☐ |

G. Courses for under-
   prepared students          ☐                    ☐
H. Service learning           ☐                    ☐
I.  Independent study         ☐                    ☐
J.  Internships, work         ☐                    ☐
K. Other, specify:            ☐                    ☐

---

7. Some colleges give special emphasis to certain instructional themes **across the curriculum**, whether or not they change graduation requirements or curriculum structures. Please indicate whether your general education program gives special emphasis across the curriculum for the following components. (**Check all that apply.**)

|  | YES, OPTIONAL | YES, REQUIRED |
|---|---|---|
| A. Writing | ☐ | ☐ |
| B. Global studies | ☐ | ☐ |
| C. Gender issues | ☐ | ☐ |
| D. Cultural pluralism | ☐ | ☐ |
| E. Science and technology | ☐ | ☐ |
| F. Computer literacy | ☐ | ☐ |
| G. Ethics or values | ☐ | ☐ |
| H. Critical thinking | ☐ | ☐ |
| I. Other, specify: | ☐ | ☐ |

---

8. If your general education program includes an "across-the-curriculum" emphasis, what **mechanisms** are used to implement it? (**Check all that apply.**)
   ☐  A. Assisting faculty to develop new knowledge or skills
   ☐  B. Supporting faculty to develop new courses
   ☐  C. Identifying courses with special emphasis which students may take if they choose
   ☐  D. Requiring students to take special emphasis course(s)
   ☐  E. Making the emphasis a criterion for general education courses

☐ F. Charging a committee to approve such special courses

☐ G. Initiating a writing, speaking, or other resource center to support student learning

☐ H. Appointing an administrator to lead the program

☐ I. Other, specify:_____

9. Is it **faculty policy** that the curriculum is to involve more active learning or other engaging pedagogical practices?

☐ A. No formal policy

☐ B. Yes, in some curriculum components

☐ C. Yes, in all curriculum components

If yes, how is this policy implemented?

10. Has there been a **systematic program** to develop faculty knowledge or skills to strengthen general education?

☐ A. No systematic program

☐ B. Yes, a modest one

☐ C. Yes, a major one

If yes, what is the most **notable feature** of this faculty development program?

11. How many faculty members **teaching general education** courses would you say were involved in this development program?

☐ A. None

☐ B. Fewer than 10 percent

☐ C. 10–29 percent

☐ D. 30–49 percent

☐ E. 50 percent or more

12. In general, how do you rate the **effectiveness** of this faculty development program?

☐ A. Not very effective

☐ B. Moderately effective

☐   C. Very effective
    Reason(s) for your answer:

13. Ideally the relation between general education and the programs of departmental **majors** is complementary, but in practice they may conflict. How would you assess that relationship on your campus?
    ☐   A. General education tends to weaken the majors
    ☐   B. The majors tend to weaken general education
    ☐   C. There is a healthy balance between them
    Reason(s) for your answer:

14. In terms of **governance**, does your institution have: (**Check all that apply.**)

|  | NO | YES |
|---|---|---|
| A. A chief academic officer, responsible for general education as well as all other academic matters | ☐ | ☐ |
| B. An administrator with primary responsibility for general education? | ☐ | ☐ |
| C. An institution-wide faculty committee specifically for general education? | ☐ | ☐ |
| D. Directors of program components, e.g., writing | ☐ | ☐ |

15. Some colleges attempt to **coordinate student affairs and other support services** with the general education program. Indicate the extent to which the purposes and values of general education are furthered by each of the following:

|  | NOT VERY MUCH | SOMEWHAT | QUITE A LOT | VERY MUCH |
|---|---|---|---|---|
| A. Admissions | ☐ | ☐ | ☐ | ☐ |
| B. Orientation of students | ☐ | ☐ | ☐ | ☐ |

|  |  |  |  |  |
|---|---|---|---|---|
| C. Academic advising | ☐ | ☐ | ☐ | ☐ |
| D. Campus convocations | ☐ | ☐ | ☐ | ☐ |
| E. Study skills, tutoring | ☐ | ☐ | ☐ | ☐ |
| F. Residence hall programs | ☐ | ☐ | ☐ | ☐ |
| G. Library | ☐ | ☐ | ☐ | ☐ |
| H. Other, specify: | ☐ | ☐ | ☐ | ☐ |

16. In general, how **effective** do you think these student affairs and support activities, as a group, are in promoting the purposes of general education?
    ☐ A. Not very effective
    ☐ B. Moderately effective
    ☐ C. Very effective
    Reason(s) for your answer:

17. Have the changes in your current general education program been **formally evaluated?**
    ☐ A. We haven't made final decisions about evaluation yet.
    ☐ B. We intend to evaluate it but haven't started.
    ☐ C. We are in the process of evaluating it.
    ☐ D. We have completed an evaluation.

18. Whether you have completed an evaluation or not, how important do you think the following **purposes** are to address in an evaluation?

|  | NOT VERY | FAIRLY | QUITE | VERY |
|---|---|---|---|---|
| A. Student learning of content | ☐ | ☐ | ☐ | ☐ |
| B. Student mastery of skills | ☐ | ☐ | ☐ | ☐ |
| C. Student satisfaction | ☐ | ☐ | ☐ | ☐ |

D. Demonstration of
changes in students,
"value added"            ☐        ☐        ☐        ☐
E. Faculty effectiveness  ☐        ☐        ☐        ☐
F. Faculty satisfaction   ☐        ☐        ☐        ☐
G. Efficiency of
instruction              ☐        ☐        ☐        ☐
H. Program management     ☐        ☐        ☐        ☐
I. Institutional vitality ☐        ☐        ☐        ☐

19. The remainder of the questionnaire seeks your opinions
and perceptions about any changes in general education
that have been made at your institution. Overall, **how much
change** did you plan and how much did you achieve in the
current general education program compared with the previous one?

|  | AMOUNT PLANNED | AMOUNT ACHIEVED |
|---|---|---|
| A. A small change | ☐ | ☐ |
| B. A moderate change | ☐ | ☐ |
| C. A large change | ☐ | ☐ |

20. How would you say **attitudes** toward general education have
changed for each of the following since the current program
was established?

|  | LESS FAVORABLE | NOT MUCH CHANGE | MORE FAVORABLE |
|---|---|---|---|
| A. Students | ☐ | ☐ | ☐ |
| B. Faculty | ☐ | ☐ | ☐ |
| C. Administration | ☐ | ☐ | ☐ |

21. What was the major **impetus** behind the current general
education program?

22. What major **barriers** did you encounter? What **strategies**
did you use to overcome them?

23. Often a change in one part leads to changes in other parts of an institution. What kind of **impact** would you say your current general education program has had on each of the following areas?

| | NEGATIVE IMPACT | NO IMPACT | POSITIVE IMPACT |
|---|---|---|---|
| A. Student admissions | ☐ | ☐ | ☐ |
| B. Student retention | ☐ | ☐ | ☐ |
| C. Faculty renewal | ☐ | ☐ | ☐ |
| D. Faculty reward structure | ☐ | ☐ | ☐ |
| E. Efficient utilization of faculty | ☐ | ☐ | ☐ |
| F. Institutional identity | ☐ | ☐ | ☐ |
| G. Sense of community | ☐ | ☐ | ☐ |
| H. Public relations, visibility | ☐ | ☐ | ☐ |
| I. General education budget | ☐ | ☐ | ☐ |
| J. Institutional fund raising | ☐ | ☐ | ☐ |
| K. Other, specify: | ☐ | ☐ | ☐ |

_____

24. To what extent would you say the change in your current general education program has resulted in the following **consequences**?

| | NOT VERY MUCH | SOMEWHAT | QUITE A LOT | VERY MUCH |
|---|---|---|---|---|
| A. Higher-quality education | ☐ | ☐ | ☐ | ☐ |
| B. Greater curricular coherence | ☐ | ☐ | ☐ | ☐ |
| C. More active learning | ☐ | ☐ | ☐ | ☐ |

D. Faculty renewal     ☐          ☐          ☐          ☐
E. Greater
   appreciation for
   racial and
   cultural
   diversity           ☐          ☐          ☐          ☐
F. Revitalized
   institution         ☐          ☐          ☐          ☐

25. Some argue that attempts to raise quality works against
    **access**, particularly against minorities and disadvantaged
    students. Has your general education change:
    ☐   A. Decreased access?
    ☐   B. Had little or no impact on access?
    ☐   C. Increased access?

26. How close is your general education program to **your own
    ideal** one for your students, faculty, and institution?
    ☐   A. Not very close
    ☐   B. Somewhat close
    ☐   C. Quite close
    ☐   D. Very close
        Reason(s) for your answer:

27. What is your greatest **concern or disappointment** with your
    current general education program?

28. What **trends or issues** do you think will influence curricu-
    lum change at your institution during the 1990s?

29. What **advice** would you give to others embarking on a similar endeavor?

Thank you very much for you assistance. May I use your name and identify your institution if appropriate in my publication?

☐ No  ☐ Yes   Name and title:_____

# References

Advisory Council on General Education. *Academy, Economy, and Society: Extending and Supporting General Education.* Trenton, N.J.: New Jersey Department of Higher Education, 1990.

"America's Best Colleges." *U.S. News and World Report,* Oct. 16, 1989, pp. 53–84.

American Association for the Advancement of Science. *The Liberal Art of Science: Agenda for Action.* Washington, D.C.: American Association for the Advancement of Science, 1990.

American Association for Higher Education. *Preliminary Program for 1991 National Conference.* Washington, D.C.: American Association for Higher Education, 1990.

Association of American Colleges. *The Classroom Climate: A Chilly One for Women.* Project on the Status and Education of Women. Washington, D.C.: Association of American Colleges, 1982.

Association of American Colleges. *Integrity in the College Curriculum.* Washington, D.C.: Association of American Colleges, 1985.

Association of American Colleges. *Engaging Cultural Legacies: Shaping Core Curricula in the Humanities.* A proposal to the National Endowment for the Humanities, Washington, D.C.: 1989.

Association of American Colleges. *Liberal Learning and the Arts and Sciences Major.* Vol. 1: *The Challenge of Connecting Learning.* Washington, D.C.: Association of American Colleges, 1991.

Astin, A. W. *Four Critical Years: Effects of College on Beliefs, Attitudes, and Knowledge.* San Francisco: Jossey-Bass, 1977.

Astin, A. W. "Involvement: The Cornerstone of Excellence." *Change,* July/Aug. 1985a, pp. 35–39.

Astin, A. W. *Achieving Educational Excellence: A Critical Assessment of Priorities and Practices in Higher Education.* San Francisco: Jossey-Bass, 1985b.

Barringer, F. "Census Shows Profound Change in Racial Makeup of Nation." *New York Times,* Mar. 11, 1991, p. A1.

Barrows, T. S., Clark, J. L., and Klein, S. F. "What Students Know About Their World." *Change,* May/June, 1980, pp. 10–17.

Barry, R. "Gonzaga Workshop." Unpublished paper, Department of Philosophy, Loyola University Chicago, 1987.

Bass, R. "The Role of the Student on a Committee for Academic Reform." *Liberal Education,* summer 1981, pp. 124–128.

Belenky, M. F., Clinchy, B. M., Goldberger, N. R., and Tarule, J. M. *Women's Ways of Knowing.* New York: Basic Books, 1986.

Bennett, W. J. *To Reclaim a Legacy.* Washington, D.C.: National Endowment for the Humanities, 1984.

Bergquist, W. H., Phillips, S. R., and Quehl, G. A. *A Handbook for Faculty Development.* Vol. 1. Washington, D.C.: Council of Independent Colleges, 1975.

Bergquist, W. H., Phillips, S. R., and Quehl, G. A. *A Handbook for Faculty Development.* Vol. 2. Washington, D.C.: Council of Independent Colleges, 1977.

Blackburn, R. T., and others. *Changing Practices in Undergraduate Education.* Berkeley, Calif.: Carnegie Council on Policy Studies, 1976.

Bloom, A. *Closing of the American Mind.* New York: Simon and Schuster, 1987.

Booth, W. C. "Cultural Literacy and Liberal Learning: An Open Letter to E. D. Hirsch, Jr." *Change,* July/Aug. 1988, pp. 11–21.

Bowen, H. R., and Schuster, J. H. *American Professors: A National Resource Imperiled.* New York: Oxford University Press, 1986.

Bowen, W. G., and Sosa, J. A. *Prospects for Faculty in the Arts and Sciences.* Princeton, N.J.: Princeton University Press, 1989.

Boyer, C. M., and Algren, A. "Visceral Priorities: Roots of Confusion in Liberal Education." *Journal of Higher Education,* Mar./Apr., 1981, pp. 173–181.

Boyer, E. L. *College: The Undergraduate Experience in America.* New York: Harper & Row, 1987.

Boyer, E. L., and Kaplan, M. *Educating for Survival*. New Rochelle, N.Y.: Change Magazine Press, 1977.

Boyer, E. L., and Levine, A. *A Quest for Common Learning*. Washington, D.C.: Carnegie Foundation for the Improvement of Teaching, 1981.

Breneman, D. W. "Are We Losing Our Liberal Arts Colleges?" *AAHE Bulletin*, American Association for Higher Education, Oct. 1990, pp. 3–6.

Brookfield, S. D. *The Skillful Teacher*. San Francisco: Jossey-Bass, 1990.

Brown, J. W. *Innovation for Excellence: The Paracollege Model*. Lanham, MD.: University Press of America, 1989.

Brown, S. S. "Strengthening Ties to Academic Affairs." *New Futures for Student Affairs*. San Francisco: Jossey-Bass, 1990.

Brubacher, J. S. *On the Philosophy of Higher Education*. San Francisco: Jossey-Bass, 1977.

Cameron, K. S., and Ettington, D. R. "The Conceptual Foundations of Organizational Culture." In J. C. Smart (ed.), *Higher Education: Handbook of Theory and Research*. New York: Agathon, 1988.

Carnegie Forum on Education and the Economy. *A Nation Prepared: Teachers for the Twenty-First Century*. Washington, D.C.: Carnegie Forum on Education and the Economy, 1986.

Carnegie Foundation for the Advancement of Teaching. *Missions of the College Curriculum: A Contemporary Review with Suggestions*. San Francisco: Jossey-Bass, 1977.

Carnegie Foundation for the Advancement of Teaching. *A Classification of Institutions of Higher Education*. Princeton, N.J.: Carnegie Foundation for the Advancement of Teaching, 1987.

Carnegie Foundation for the Advancement of Teaching. *Campus Life: In Search of Community*. Princeton, N.J.: Princeton University Press, 1990.

Carter, L. K. "Charting a New Course of Study." *Currents*, Council for the Advancement and Support of Education, June 1989, pp. 6–13.

Cheney, L. V. *50 Hours: A Core Curriculum for College Students*. Washington, D.C.: National Endowment for the Humanities, 1989.

Cheney, L. V. *Tyrannical Machines*. Washington, D.C.: National Endowment for the Humanities, 1990.

Chickering, A. W. *Education and Identity*. San Francisco: Jossey-Bass, 1969.

Chickering, A. W., and Associates. *The Modern American College*. San Francisco: Jossey-Bass, 1981.

Claxton, C. S., and Murrell, P. H. *Learning Styles: Implications for Improving Educational Practice*. ASHE-ERIC higher education report no. 4. Washington, D.C.: Association for the Study of Higher Education, 1987.

Clinchy, B. Speech broadcast on Minnesota Public Radio, Jan. 3, 1991.

Cohen, M. D., and March, J. G. *Leadership and Ambiguity: The American College President*. New York: McGraw-Hill, 1974.

Cole, J. Excerpt of speech on cover of program of the National Conference of the American Association for Higher Education, Washington, D.C., 1991.

Commission on the Core Curriculum. *Report of the Commission on the Core Curriculum*. New York: Columbia College, 1988.

Cousins, N. "Editorial: How to Make People Smaller Than They Are." *Saturday Review*, Dec. 1978, p. 15.

Cross, K. P. "A Proposal to Improve College Teaching — or — What 'Taking Teaching Seriously' Should Mean." *AAHE Bulletin*, American Association for Higher Education, 1986, pp. 9–14.

Cross, K. P., and Angelo, T. A. *Classroom Assessment Techniques*. Ann Arbor: National Center for Research to Improve Postsecondary Education, University of Michigan, 1988.

"CUNY Officials Propose New Academic Standards." *Chronicle of Higher Education*, Jan. 30, 1991, p. A2.

Diamond, R. M., Gray, P. J., and Roberts, A. O. *The Syracuse University Focus on Teaching Project. Progress Report: The First Two Years*. Syracuse, N.Y.: Center for Instructional Development, Syracuse University, Jan. 1991.

Dickinson College. Grant proposal to the Knight Foundation, 1990.

Dressel, P. L., and De Lisle, F. *Undergraduate Curriculum Trends*. Washington, D.C.: American Council on Education, 1969.

D'Souza, D. *Illiberal Education: The Politics of Race and Sex on Campus.* New York: Free Press/Macmillan, 1991.

Eble, K. E., and McKeachie, W. J. *Improving Undergraduate Education Through Faculty Development: An Analysis of Effective Programs and Practices.* San Francisco: Jossey-Bass, 1985.

"Education." *Wall Street Journal Reports.* Feb. 9, 1990.

"Education: Bossy Businessmen." *Economist*, Aug. 26, 1989, pp. 21 –22.

Ehrlich, T. *Our University in the State: Educating the New Majority.* Bloomington: Indiana University President's Office, 1991.

Feldman, K. A., and Newcomb, T. M. *The Impact of College on Students.* San Francisco: Jossey-Bass, 1969.

Ferren, A. "Curriculum Reform: The Personal Dimensions." *Liberal Education*, May/June, 1990, pp. 24–31.

Fidler, P. P., and Hunter, M. S. "How Seminars Enhance Student Success." In M. L. Upcraft and J. N. Gardner (eds.), *The Freshman Year Experience: Helping Students Survive and Succeed in College.* San Francisco: Jossey-Bass, 1989.

Franklin, P. "The Prospects for General Education in American Higher Education." In I. Westbury and A. C. Purves (eds.), *Cultural Literacy and the Idea of General Education.* Chicago: National Society for the Study of Education, 1988.

"Further Debate on the Core Curriculum." *Chronicle of Higher Education*, Jan. 24, 1990, p. A17.

Gabelnick, F., MacGregor, J., Matthews, R. S., and Smith, B. L. *Learning Communities: Creating Connections Among Students, Faculty, and Disciplines.* New Directions for Teaching and Learning, no. 41. San Francisco: Jossey-Bass, 1990.

Gaff, J. G. *Toward Faculty Renewal.* San Francisco: Jossey-Bass, 1975.

Gaff, J. G. "Avoiding the Potholes: Strategies for Reforming General Education." *Educational Record*, Fall 1980, pp. 50–59.

Gaff, J. G. *General Education Today: A Critical Analysis of Controversies, Practices, and Reforms.* San Francisco: Jossey-Bass, 1983.

Gaff, J. G., and Davis, M. L. "Student Views of General Education." *Liberal Education*, Summer 1981, pp. 112–123.

Gaff, J. G., and Morstain, B. R. "Evaluating the Outcomes." *Institutional Renewal Through the Improvement of Teaching.* New Directions for Higher Education, no. 24. Jossey-Bass, 1978.

Gagliardi, P. "The Creation and Change of Organizational Cultures: A Conceptual Framework." *Organizational Studies,* 1986, 7 (2), 117–134.

Gamson, Z. F. "Changing the Meaning of Liberal Education." *Liberal Education,* Nov./Dec. 1989, pp. 10–11.

Gamson, Z. F. Proposal to the Exxon Education Foundation, University of Massachusetts-Boston, project in process.

General Electric Company. *1990 Annual Report.* Fairfield, Conn.: General Electric, 1991.

Golin, S. "Peer Collaboration and Student Interviewing." *AAHE Bulletin,* Dec. 1990, pp. 9–10.

Goodwin, G. L. Opening remarks at a faculty meeting, College of St. Scholastica, Duluth, Minn., Sept. 1989.

Gordon, J. "Freshman Seminar: Theory and Practice." *A Pamphlet for Instructors.* Southwest Texas State University, San Marcos, Tex., n.d.

Group for Human Development in Higher Education. *Faculty Development in a Time of Retrenchment.* New Rochelle, N.Y.: Change Magazine Press, 1974.

Harvard Committee. *General Education in a Free Society.* Cambridge, Mass.: Harvard University Press, 1945.

Harvard Committee. *Report on the Core Curriculum.* Cambridge, Mass.: Office of the Dean, Faculty of Arts and Sciences, Harvard University, 1978.

Hefferlin, JB. *Dynamics of Academic Reform.* San Francisco: Jossey-Bass, 1969.

Hirsch, E. D., Jr. *Cultural Literacy.* Boston: Houghton-Mifflin, 1987.

Holmes Group. *Tomorrow's Teachers: A Report of the Holmes Group.* East Lansing, Mich.: Holmes Group, 1986.

Hutchings, P., and Marchese, T. "Watching Assessment: Questions, Stories, Prospects." *Change,* Sept./Oct. 1990, pp. 12–38.

Johnston, J. S., Jr., and others. "The Demand Side of General Education: Attending to Student Attitudes and Understandings." *Journal of General Education,* forthcoming.

Katz, J., and Henry, M. *Turning Professors into Teachers.* New York: Macmillan, 1988.

Kennedy, D. Text of address to the Academic Council and the general campus community. Reprinted in *Campus Report*, Apr. 11, 1990, Stanford University, Palo Alto, California, 1990.

Kerr, C. "Foreword." In F. Rudolph, *Curriculum: A History of the American Undergraduate Course of Study Since 1636*. San Francisco: Jossey-Bass, 1977.

Kimball, B.A. "The Historical and Cultured Dimensions of the Recent Reports." *American Journal of Education*, 1988, *98*, 293–322.

Kimball, R. *Tenured Radicals*. New York: Harper & Row, 1990.

Kirby, D. J. *Ambitious Dreams: The Values Program at LeMoyne College*. Kansas City, Mo.: Sheen and Ward, 1990.

Kolb, D. A. *Experiential Learning*. Englewood Cliffs, N.J.: Prentice-Hall, 1984.

Kuh, G. D., Lyons, J. W., Schuh, J. H., and Whitt, E. J. "Campus: One or Many Communities?" Paper presented at American Council on Education, Washington, D.C., Jan. 1990.

Kuh, G. D., Schuh, J. H., Whitt, E. J., and Associates. *Involving Colleges: Successful Approaches to Fostering Student Learning and Development Outside the Classroom*. San Francisco: Jossey-Bass, 1991.

Kurfiss, J. G. *Critical Thinking: Theory, Research, Practice, and Possibilities*. ASHE-ERIC higher education report no. 2. Washington, D.C.: Association for the Study of Higher Education, 1988.

Lacey, P. A. "Let's Not Perpetuate Our Mistakes of the Past as We Prepare a New Professorial Generation." *Chronicle of Higher Education*, Apr. 18, 1990, pp. B1–B3.

Lambert, R. D. *International Studies and the Undergraduate*. Washington, D.C.: American Council on Education, 1989.

Levine, A., and Associates. *Shaping Higher Education's Future: Demographic Realities and Opportunities, 1990–2000*. San Francisco: Jossey-Bass, 1989.

Light, R. J., Singer, J. D., and Willett, J. B. *By Design: Planning Research in Higher Education*. Cambridge, Mass.: Harvard University Press, 1990.

Lorsch, J. W. "Managing Culture: The Invisible Barrier to Organizational Change." *California Management Review*, 1986, *28* (2), 95–109.

McGrath, E. *General Education and the Plight of Modern Man.* Indianapolis, Ind.: Lilly Endowment, n.d.

Maeroff, G. I. "Three Missing Keys to Public School Reform." *Wall Street Journal*, May 21, 1990, p. A12.

Martin, W. B. *A College of Character: Renewing the Purpose and Content of College Education.* San Francisco: Jossey-Bass, 1982.

Matthews, J. T. "Decline in Education." *Washington Post*, Oct. 13, 1981, p. A23.

Matthews, R. S. "Learning Communities in the Community College." *Community, Technical, and Junior College Journal*, Oct./Nov. 1986, pp. 44–47.

Minnich, E. K. *Transforming Knowledge.* Philadelphia: Temple University Press, 1990.

Mohrman, K. "Liberal Learning Is a Sound Human Capital Investment." *Educational Record*, Fall 1983, pp. 56–61.

Mooney, C. J. "Stanford Unveils Plan Designed to Elevate Status of Teaching." *Chronicle of Higher Education*, Mar. 13, 1991, p. A15.

Morrill, R. *Teaching Values in College.* San Francisco: Jossey-Bass, 1980.

National Institute of Education. *Involvement in Learning.* Report of study group on the conditions of excellence in American higher education. Washington, D.C.: National Institute of Education, 1984.

Nelsen, W. C. *Renewal of the Teacher Scholar.* Washington, D.C.: Association of American Colleges, 1981.

Nelsen, W. C., and Siegel, M. E. *Effective Approaches to Faculty Development.* Washington, D.C.: Association of American Colleges, 1980.

O'Keefe, M. "A New Look at College Costs: Where Does the Money Really Go?" *Change*, Nov./Dec. 1987, pp. 12–34.

Ouchi, W. G. *Theory Z: How American Business Can Meet the Japanese Challenge.* Reading, Mass.: Addison-Wesley, 1981.

Pace, C. R. *The Undergraduates.* Los Angeles: Center for the Study of Evaluation, University of California, Los Angeles, 1990.

Palmer, P. J. "Good Teaching: A Matter of Living the Mystery." *Change*, Jan./Feb. 1990, pp. 11–16.

Panel on the General Professional Education of the Physician. *Physicians for the Twenty-First Century*. Washington, D.C.: Association of American Medical Colleges, 1984.

Pascarella, E. T., and Terenzini, P. T. *How College Affects Students*. San Francisco: Jossey-Bass, 1991.

Perry, W. G. *Forms of Intellectual and Ethical Development in the College Years*. New York: Holt, Rinehart & Winston, 1970.

Peters, T. J., and Waterman, R. H. *In Search of Excellence*. New York: Harper & Row, 1982.

Pollack, R. "Science as a Creative Process." *Liberal Education*, Mar./Apr. 1988, pp. 11–15.

Ravitch, D. "Multiculturalism: E Pluribus Plures." *American Scholar*, 1990, pp. 337–354.

"Report Says Skills Not Keeping Pace with Job Demands," Minneapolis *Star Tribune*, Sept. 8, 1989, p. A6.

Rivlin, A. M., Jones, D. C., and Meyer, E. C. *Beyond Alliances: Global Security Through Focused Partnerships*. Washington, D.C.: Brookings Institution, 1990.

Rudolph, F. *Curriculum: A History of the American Undergraduate Course of Study Since 1636*. San Francisco: Jossey-Bass, 1977.

Sandin, R. T. *Values and Collegiate Study*. Atlanta, Ga.: Mercer University, 1989.

Schaefer, W. D. *Education Without Compromise: From Chaos to Coherence in Higher Education*. San Francisco: Jossey-Bass, 1990.

Schlesinger, A., Jr. "The Opening of the American Mind." *New York Review of Books*, 1989, p. 1.

Schuster, J. H., Wheeler, D. W., and Associates. *Enhancing Faculty Careers*. San Francisco: Jossey-Bass, 1990.

Searle, J. "The Storm over the University." *New York Review of Books*, Dec. 6, 1990, pp. 34–42.

Seldin, P., and Associates. *How Administrators Can Improve Teaching*. San Francisco: Jossey-Bass, 1990.

Siegel, M. E. "Empirical Findings on Faculty Development Programs." In W. C. Nelsen and M. E. Siegel, *Effective Approaches to*

*Faculty Development.* Washington, D.C.: Association of American Colleges, 1980.

Smith, D. H. "Ethics and the Educated Person: A Proposal." Bloomington: Poynter Center, Indiana University, n.d.

Smith, P. *Killing the Spirit: Higher Education in America.* New York: Viking, 1990.

Smith, V. Speech at Council of Independent Colleges Deans Institute, San Francisco, Nov. 1989.

Snyder, B. R. *The Hidden Curriculum.* New York: Knopf, 1971.

"State Notes." *Chronicle of Higher Education,* Mar. 7, 1990.

Steinman, E. "A New Age of General Education." *Panorama,* California State University, San Bernardino, Spring 1988, p. 1.

Sykes, C. J. *ProfScam.* New York: St. Martin's Press, 1988.

Task Force on the Core Curriculum. *Report on the Core Curriculum.* Cambridge, Mass.: Harvard University, 1977.

Task Force on the Future of Journalism and Mass Communication Education. *Challenges and Opportunities in Journalism and Mass Communication Education. Journalism Educator,* Spring 1989.

Task Force on the Undergraduate Experience. *Report.* Evanston, Ill.: Northwestern University, 1988.

Task Group on General Education. *A New Vitality in General Education.* Washington, D.C.: Association of American Colleges, 1988.

Tobias, S. "They're Not Dumb. They're Different." *Change,* July/Aug. 1990, pp. 11–30.

Toombs, W., Fairweather, J., Chen, A., and Amey, M. *Open to View: Practice and Purpose in General Education 1988.* University Park, Pa.: Center for the Study of Higher Education, Pennsylvania State University, 1989.

Treisman, P. U. "A Study of the Mathematics Performance of Black Students at the University of California, Berkeley." Berkeley: Mathematics Department, University of California, Berkeley, 1985.

Trilling, L. "The Uncertain Future of the Humanistic Educational Ideal." In M. Kaplan (ed.), *What Is An Educated Person?* New York: Praeger, 1980.

Tussman, J. *Experiment at Berkeley*. New York: Oxford University Press, 1969.

Tussman, J. "A Venture in Educational Reform: A Partial View." Occasional paper no. 67. Berkeley: Center for Studies in Higher Education, University of California, Berkeley, 1988.

Twin Cities Campus Task Force on Liberal Education. *A Liberal Education Agenda for the 1990s and Beyond on the Twin Cities Campus of the University of Minnesota*. University of Minnesota, Minneapolis, 1991.

Walton, M. *The Demming Management Method*. New York: Putnam, 1988.

Wee, D. *On General Education: Guidelines for Reform*. New Haven, Conn.: Society for Values in Higher Education, 1981.

Wegner, C. *Liberal Education and the Modern University*. Chicago: University of Chicago, 1978.

Wheaton College. Grant proposal to the Consortium for the Advancement of Private Higher Education, Norton, Mass., 1985.

Wilson, R. C., and others. *College Professors and Their Impact on Students*. New York: Wiley, 1975.

Wright State University. *The Humanities at the Center of the Core Curriculum and the College of Liberal Arts*. Grant proposal to the National Endowment for the Humanities, Dayton, Oh.: n.d.

Zeller, W., Hinni, J., and Eison, J. "Creating Educational Partnerships Between Academic and Student Affairs." In D. C. Roberts (ed.), *Designing Campus Activities to Foster a Sense of Community*. New Directions for Student Services, no. 48. San Francisco: Jossey-Bass, 1989.

Zemsky, R. *Structure and Coherence*. Washington, D.C.: Association of American Colleges, 1989.

Zuckerman, M. B. "Brother, Can You Spare a Dime?" *U.S. News and World Report*, Aug. 22, 1988, p. 68.

# *Index*

**A**

Abusive learning experiences, 181–182

Academic advising, impact of, 128, 129, 179–180

Academic culture, support from, 224–232

Academic majors, general education in relation to, 85–87

Academic staff, and student affairs staff, 128–129, 131–133, 139, 179, 205, 222–223

Across-the-curriculum approaches: educational benefits of, 135–137; and faculty development, 111–112, 136–137; impact of, 73–74, 91, 92

Active learning: and curriculum reform, 56–57; as educational benefit, 125–127, 138–139; and faculty development, 112; impact of, 85, 91

Admissions, impact of, 128, 130–131, 179

Advising, academic, impact of, 128, 129, 179–180

Advisory Council on General Education, 9

Africa: disputes in, 6; and reformed curriculum, 45

Albion College, Center for Ethics at, 56

Algren, A., 67

Alverno College: and future trends, 216; moral reflection at, 56

American Association for the Advancement of Science, 37

American Association for Higher Education, 194

American Association of University Professors, 167

American University: comprehensive change at, 61; faculty experiences at, 218; leadership at, 170

Amey, M., 71, 92

Angelo, T. A., 183

Antioch College, comprehensive change at, 61, 151–152

Arizona, University of, active learning at, 57

Arnold, M., 23

Asia, and reformed curriculum, 45

Assessment, and curriculum reform, 58–60, 65–146, 211–212, 223–224, 230–232

Association of American Colleges: and academic support, 170, 174; and curricular issues, 14, 18, 21–22, 24; Engaging Cultural Legacies project of, 52, 69; and institutional agenda, 208, 218, 232; Project on the Status and Education of Women of, 197

Astin, A. W., 11–12, 125, 127, 201, 222, 223

Austin College, institutionalization at, 212

Authority, shared, 167–172

Averett College, and piecemeal change, 211

**B**

Bacon, F., 3
Bankhead, T., 64
Barringer, F., 193
Barrows, T. S., 49
Barry, R., 195
Bass, R., 130
Beethoven, L. von, 3
Belenky, M. F., 186–187
Bemidji State University,
    distribution requirements at, 45
Bennett, W. J., 15, 27, 221
Bennington College,
    individualization at, 152
Berberet, G., 222
Berea College, convocations at, 204
Bergquist, W. H., 104
Berra, Y., 162
Bethany College (Kansas), strategic
    planning at, 227
Bethel College (Minnesota),
    institutionalization at, 212
Blackburn, R. T., 71
Bloom, A., 15, 23, 24, 213, 221
Bloomfield College, and learning
    connected with lives, 188
Bohr, N., 38
Booth, W. C., 18–19
Bowen, H. R., 157
Bowen, W. G., 157
Bowman, J., 109, 170–171
Boyer, C. M., 67
Boyer, E. L., 14, 15, 23, 87, 166–167,
    172–173, 189
Breneman, D. W., 35
Brookfield, S. D., 182
Brooklyn College: core courses at,
    44–45; leadership at, 170
Broome County (Community)
    College: comprehensive change
    at, 61; freshman seminar at, 47
Brown, J. W., 55
Brown, S. S., 223
Brown University: and
    commonality, 24; writing at, 40
Brubacher, J. S., 67

Bunker Hill Community College,
    curriculum review at, 210
Bush Foundation, 69, 105, 113

**C**

California at Berkeley, University of:
    and cultural diversity, 51;
    Experimental College at, 231–
    232; mathematics workshop at,
    198; teaching at, 163; women
    students at, 197
California at Los Angeles,
    University of (UCLA), and
    shared authority, 168
California at Santa Cruz, University
    of, cluster colleges at, 152
California Lutheran College:
    faculty development at, 109;
    integration of knonwledge at,
    53; leadership at, 171
California State Polytechnic
    University, integration of
    knowledge at, 55
California State University at San
    Bernardino, impact of change
    at, 75
California State University system,
    general education through all
    years at, 58
Cameron, K. S., 226
Carlson, A., 7
Carlson, J., 212
Carnegie Forum on Education and
    the Economy, 35
Carnegie Foundation for the
    Advancement of Teaching, 14,
    23, 69, 166–167, 188
Carnegie Mellon University,
    teaching at, 163
Case, C., 89, 109
Catonsville Community College:
    comprehensive change at, 61;
    distribution requirements at, 45;
    faculty support at, 159
Central America: disputes in, 6;
    and reformed curriculum, 45,
    49, 50

Change. *See* Reform of general education

Chemical Bank, employees for, 9

Chen, A., 71, 92

Cheney, L. V., 15–16, 18, 72, 75

Chicago, University of: core curriculum at, 18; and integration of knowledge, 52; subcollege at, 153

Chickering, A. W., 127, 222

China, ancient, and reformed curriculum, 52

China, People's Republic of: competition by, 6; and reformed curriculum, 49–50, 52

China, Republic of, competition by, 6

Choy, C., 195

City University of New York, and standards, 43

Clark, J. L., 49

Claxton, C. S., 186

Clayton State College, moral reflection at, 56

Cleveland, H., 52

Clinchy, B. M., 186–187

Cohen, M. D., 25, 165

Coherence: as educational benefit, 125–127; improvement in, 83–84; issues of, 21–23

Cole, J., 194

Colleges and universities: academic values in, 158–159; agenda for, 206–233; assessment of reform by, 58–60, 65–146, 211–212, 223–224, 230–232; and competition, 7–8; conclusion on, 174–175; current initiatives by, 214–215; differences in, and reforms, 96–98; and educational benefits, 141; environment at, 222; experimental, for general education, 151–153; and faculty development, 117–118; implementation stage at, 211–212; institutionalization stage at, 212–213; of integrity, 232–233; involving, characteristics of, 202–203; learning environment at, 203–204; piecemeal change at, 210–211; review stage at, 209–210; self-interest of, 145, 218–219; shared authority in, 167–172; structures in, 156–174; subcolleges in, 153–154; support from, 149–175, 224–232; trends and innovations in, 32–64; at unaffected stage, 208–209

Columbia College, science courses at, 37–38

Columbia University, core courses at, 102–103, 150, 157–158

Commission on the Core Curriculum, 157–158

Commission on Workforce Quality and Labor Market Efficiency, 8

Commonality, issues of, 23–24

Community College of Florida, impetus for change at, 209

Community of learners: developing, 165–167; and integration of knowledge, 53–54

Competition, and curriculum debate, 6–8

Comprehensiveness, issues of, 24–27

Concordia College at Moorhead, global studies at, 50

Confucius, 3, 4

Connected learning, 174

Connecticut, University of, assessment at, 59–60

Consortium for the Advancement of Private Higher Education, 39, 49, 69, 105

Content, issue of, 15–21

Convocations, impact of, 128, 130–131

Copernicus, N., 3

Core curriculum, issues of, 17–18

Cousins, N., 217

Crick, F. H. C., 38

Cross, K. P., 163, 183

Cultural diversity: and curriculum reform, 51–52; impact of, 73, 85, 92; sensitivity to, 195–196; and student diversity, 193

Cultural literacy: impact of, 79;
 issue of, 15, 18–19
Culture: academic, support from,
 224–232; organizational, 224–
 225; strategic planning for, 226–
 228; vision for, 225–226
Curie, M., 37
Curie, P., 37
Curriculum: and active learning,
 56–57; analysis of, 3–31;
 approaches to debate on, 5–12;
 assessment of reform in, 58–60;
 background on, 3–5, 67–68;
 benefits of debate on, 30–31;
 and co-curriculum, 199–204;
 coherence of, 21–23, 83–84,
 125–127; commonality in, 23–
 24; components and supports
 for, 13, 90–93; and
 comprehensiveness, 24–27;
 content of, 15–21; critique of
 debate on, 27–31; and cultural
 diversity, 51–52; estimated
 educational value of, 124–133;
 extension of general education
 through all years, 57–58; faculty
 development and types of, 109–
 112; focus of, 12–14; for
 freshman year, 45–47; in global
 studies, 48–51; and integration
 of knowledge, 52–55; issues of,
 14–27; in liberal arts and
 sciences, 34–38; methodology
 for studying, 68–70, 235–245; on
 moral reflection, 55–56;
 multicultural, 19–21; review of,
 220–221; scope and nature of
 change in, 67–99; for senior
 year, 47–48; skills development
 in, 38–41; and social trends, 12–
 13; stages in revising, 208–213;
 standards and requirements for,
 41–43; and student diversity,
 196–197; tighter structure for,
 43–45; trends in, 33–60; in
 typical general education, 70–75

D

Dante, A., 3
Darwin, C., 3, 38

Davidson College, teacher-scholars
 at, 162
Davis, M. L., 123–124
deBary, T., 157–158
Defiance College, leadership at,
 169
deGaulle, F., 168
De Lisle, F., 71
Delta Airlines, 225
Departments, general education
 embedded into, 172–174
DePauw University, standards at, 42
Descartes, R., 3
DeVry Institute, impetus for
 change at, 209
Dewey, J., 152
Diamond, R. M., 163
Dickinson College, active learning
 at, 57
Dillard University, writing at, 40
Disney Corporation, 225
Diversity, cultural, 51–52, 73, 85,
 92, 193, 195–196
Doherty, A., 216
Dole, E., 8–9
Dorosz, L, 51
Dressel, P. L., 71
D'Souza, D., 27, 198

E

Earlham College: moral reflection
 at, 56; teaching at, 161–162
Eble, K. E., 107, 113, 137–138
Eckerd College: comprehensive
 change at, 61; faculty support at,
 159
Educational benefits: analysis of,
 121–146; correlates of gains in,
 133–141; estimated, 124–133;
 function of, 10–11; and general
 education aspects, 134–137; for
 human capital, 8–9; and
 institutional impacts, 140–141;
 for national security, 9–10; and
 student services, 128–133;
 support mechanisms for,
 137–139
Educational Testing Service, 49

Ehrlich, T., 193
Einstein, A., 3
Eison, J., 201
Emerson, R. W., 3, 4
Empire State College, learning contracts at, 152
Enriched introductory course, 173–174
Enriched major, 173
Enrollment, general education impact on, 80–81
Escalante, J., 184
Ethics, in reformed curriculum, 55–56. *See also* Moral reflection
Ettington, D. R., 226
Europe: changes in, 6; competition by, 6; national curricula in, 13; and reformed curriculum, 36, 44, 153; and traditional curriculum, 4, 15
European Economic Community, competition by, 6
Evergreen State College: institutionalization at, 212; learning communities at, 53, 54, 152; mathematics at, 40; Washington Center at, 54
Exxon Education Foundation, 223

**F**

Faculty: and academic values, 158–159; and across-the-curriculum themes, 111–112, 136–137; commitment of, 157–160; and comprehensiveness of change, 25–26; experiences of, 159–160, 218; leadership by, 170–171; self-interest of, 145, 217–218; student interactions with, 200; training of, 157–158, 160–162
Faculty development: aspects of, 100–120; background on, 100–101; conclusion on, 119–120; and educational benefits, 137–138; features of, 104–105; goals of, 104; history of, 101–103; impact of, 108–109, 111; and institutional type, 117–118;

outcomes of, 112–119; principles of, 107–108; program types in, 103–109; and reform purposes, 115–117; and renewal, 79–80, 116; and scope of change, 74, 79–80, 91, 92–93; and sensitivity to individual needs, 118–119; for teaching, 161, 164; and type of curricula, 109–112
Fairweather, J., 71, 92
Faraday, M., 37
Feldman, K. A., 127, 222
Ferren, A., 170, 217–218
Fidler, P. P., 47
Florida, standards in, 42
Florida, Community College of, impetus for change at, 209
Foreign language, curriculum reform in, 40–41
Forrest, A., 223
France, authority in, 168
Franklin, B., 3, 4
Franklin, P., 22
Freshman year, curriculum for, 45–47
Freud, S., 3
Frick, F., 56
Fund for the Improvement of Postsecondary Education, 105
Fund raising, general education impact on, 81

**G**

Gabelnick, F., 54
Gaff, J. G., 102, 107, 113, 123–124, 210
Gagliardi, P., 225
Galileo, G., 3
Gamson, Z. F., 22, 196, 210, 223
Gardner, J., 45
Gender differences, and student diversity, 194–195. *See also* Women
General education: agenda for, 206–233; attitudes toward, 82–82, 94, 97, 114–115, 123–124, 139–140; concepts of, 13–14, 23;

deans' ideals of, 87–89; demand side of, 176–177, 205; and educational benefits, 134–137; embedded into departments, 172–174; experimental institutions for, 151–153; extended through all years, 57–58; future agendas for, 219–224; history of, 149–156; impact of, 77–78; as organizational orphan, 26; questionnaire on, 235–245; restructuring programs for, 150–151; and sensitivity to individual needs, 167; significance of changes in, 83–89; structures for, 156–174; support for, 149–175; typical curriculum in, 70–75; and values education, 189–192. *See also* Reform of general education

General Electric (GE), 225, 226

George Mason University: alternative structure at, 154; integration of knowledge at, 55; leadership at, 171

Gibson, G., 80

Global studies: and curriculum reform, 48–51; impact of, 73, 91

Goethe, J., 3

Goldberger, N. R., 186–187

Golin, S., 188

Gonzalez, J., 170

Goodwin, G. L., 119–120

Gorbachev, M., 27

Gordon, J., 46

Goshen College: learning environment at, 202; travel requirement at, 49

Governance supports, and size of change, 91, 93

Gray, P. J., 163

Greece, ancient: and reformed curriculum, 36, 52, 153, 231; and traditional curriculum, 4

Gregorian, V., 24

Grinnell College, and commonality, 24

Group for Human Development in Higher Education, 102

Gustavus Adolphus College: alternative structure at, 154; integration of knowledge at, 55

**H**

Hall, P., 170

Hamline University, admissions at, 131

Harvard University: core curriculum at, 14, 17, 44; "Redbook" from, 189

Hasselmo, N., 227

Hefferlin, JB, 25–26

Henry, M., 181, 187

Herodotus, 3

Hess, R., 170

Hetrick, B., 45

Higher education. *See* Colleges and universities

Hill, P., 53

Hinni, J. 201

Hiram College: implementation stage at, 211; integration of knowledge at, 53

Hirsch, E. D., Jr., 15, 18, 79

Hobart and William Smith Colleges, comprehensive change at, 61

Hofstra University, subcollege at, 154

Holmes Group, 35

Holy Cross, College of: and China, 49–50; learning environment at, 203

Homer, 3

Hong Kong, competition by, 6

Hood College, core courses at, 45

Hope College, senior year at, 48

Hovde, P., 50

Huckabee, M., 211

Humboldt, K. W., 3

Hunter, M. S., 47

Hunter College, science course at, 38

Hutchings, P., 59

Hutchins, R. M., 153

## I

Ictinus, 3
Illinois Wesleyan University, language teaching at, 41
Implementation: and institutional culture, 228–230; stage of, 211–212
Indiana University: and minority students, 193; Poynter Center for the Study of Ethics and American Institutions at, 191
Individual needs, sensitivity to, 118–119, 167, 195–196
Indonesia, competition by, 6
Institutional type: and educational benefits, 141; and faculty development, 117–118; and reform, 96–98
Institutionalization, stage of, 212–213
Integration of knowledge, and curriculum, 52–55
Integrity, colleges of, 232–233
Inter American University, leadership at, 170
Interdisciplinary courses, educational benefits of, 135
International Business Machines, 225
Iraq, and Gulf War, 6, 10
Isaiah, 3, 4

## J

Jackson State University, critical thinking at, 40
Japan: competition by, 6, 49; and global studies, 50
Johnson C. Smith University, and piecemeal change, 210
Johnston, J. S., Jr., 123, 176–177, 179–180
Jolicouer, P., 170–171
Jones, D. C., 9–10

## K

Kaplan, M., 14, 189
Katz, J., 181, 187

Kennedy, D., 162–163
Kerr, C., 12
Kimball, R., 19, 20, 213
King's College, assessment at, 59
Klein, S. F., 49
Kluckhohn, C., 199
Knight Foundation, 57
Knowledge: and content issues, 15–16; integration of, 52–55
Kolb, D. A., 186
Korea, Republic of, competition by, 6
Kuh, G. D., 202–203
Kurfiss, J. G., 187

## L

Lacey, P. A., 161–162
LaGuardia Community College: integration of knowledge at, 53–54; writing at, 40
Lambert, R. D., 50
Latin America: disputes in, 6; and reformed curriculum, 45, 49, 50
Leadership, and shared authority, 169–172
Learning: abuse in, 181–182; active, 56–57, 85, 91, 112, 125–127, 138–139; aspects of, 176–205; beyond the classroom, 199–204; conclusion on, 204–205; connected, 174; connected with students' lives, 187–188; environment for, 203–204; goals of, 220; personal-emotional aspects of, 181–188; resistance to, 182; styles of, 186–187
Learning communities: developing, 165–167; and integration of knowledge, 53–54
Lederberg, J., 38
Lee, S., 195
Levine, A., 15, 23, 193
Liberal arts, curriculum reforms in, 34–36
Library, impact of, 128, 130
Light, R. J., 183
Lilly Endowment, 105; Workshop on the Liberal Arts of, 69

Literacy, cultural, 15, 18–19, 79
Lorsch, J. W., 225
Los Medanos College:
comprehensive change at, 61;
and faculty development, 109;
impact of change at, 89; moral
reflection at, 56
Louisiana College, moral reflection
at, 56
Loyola University of Chicago, and
student diversity, 195–196
Lyons, J. W., 202–203

**M**

Macalester College, standards at, 42
McCabe, R., 43
McDonalds, 225
McGrath, E., 189
MacGregor, J., 54
McKeachie, W. J., 107, 113, 137–138
Madonna College, writing at, 40
Maeroff, G. I., 188
Majors, academic: enriched, 173;
general education in relation to,
85–87
Malaysia, competition by, 6
March, J. G., 25, 165
Marchese, T., 59
Marietta College: freshman seminar
at, 47; strategic planning at, 227
Martin, W. B., 190
Marx, G., 64
Marx, K., 3
Mary Washington College:
leadership at, 170; standards
at, 42
Massachusetts, University of,
teaching at, 163
Matthews, J. T., 10
Matthews, R. S., 54
Meiklejohn, A., 153, 231
Mellon Foundation, 105
Memphis State University,
comprehensive change at, 61
Mendel, G., 38
Metropolitan State University
(Denver), faculty committees at,
169

Mexico, and global studies, 50
Meyer, E. C., 9–10
Miami-Dade Community College:
comprehensive change at, 61;
and standards, 43
Miami University: co-curriculum at,
204; institutionalization stage at,
212; integration of knowledge
at, 55
Michigan, University of; subcollege
of, 153; teaching at, 163
Middle East, disputes in, 6, 10, 49
Milton, J., 3
Minnesota, governors of, 7
Minnesota, University of: Burton
Hall at, 3–4; College of Liberal
Arts at, 41; language teaching at,
41; liberal arts in business at, 35;
strategic planning by, 227–228
Minnesota at Crookston, University
of, impetus for change at, 209
Minnesota at Duluth, University of,
and strategic planning, 228
Minnesota at Morris, University of:
comprehensive change at, 61–
63; and strategic planning, 228
Minnesota at Twin Cities, University
of, and strategic planning,
227–228
Minnesota at Waseca, University of,
and strategic planning, 228
Minnesota State University system,
impetus for change in, 209
Minnich, E. K., 195
Minority students: and higher
standards, 42–43; learning styles
of, 198; as new majority, 193
Modern Language Association, 168
Mohrman, K., 11
Montgomery Community College,
citizens advisory council at, 219
Mooney, C. J., 162
Moral reflection: curriculum on,
55–56; impact of, 73, 91
Morraine Valley Community
College, faculty committees at,
169
Morrill, R., 192
Morstain, B. R., 113

Motivation: for further reform, 216–219; issue of, 183–184
Mount St. Mary's College: comprehensive change at, 61; core courses at, 45
Muhlenburg College, freshman and senior seminars at, 48
Murrell, P. H., 186

**N**

National Endowment for the Humanities, 27, 69, 105, 109
National Institute of Education, 58
Nelson, W. C., 102, 113, 116, 162
Nevada at Reno, University of: core courses at, 36; faculty development at, 115; implementation stage at, 211
New College (Florida), accelerated curriculum at, 152
New Jersey, learning connections in, 187–188
New Jersey Department of Higher Education, Advisory Council on General Education of, 9
New York Telephone, employees for, 9
Newcomb, T. M., 127, 222
Newton, I., 3
North Carolina at Asheville, University of, humanities core at, 36
North Central College: environment at, 222; leadership at, 169
North Dakota State University, curriculum review at, 210
North Texas, University of: alternative structure at, 154; Classic Learning Core at, 54–55, 230
Northeast Missouri State University: assessment at, 60; standards at, 42
Northwestern University: senior year at, 48; teaching at, 163

**O**

Ohio Board of Regents, awards from, 212
Ohio State University, teaching at, 163
Ohio University: comprehensive change at, 61; implementation stage at, 211; senior year at, 48
O'Keefe, M., 8
Orientation, impact of, 128, 130, 179
Ouchi, W. G., 225
Outcomes: of faculty development, 112–119; improvement in 83–85; and size of change, 93–95

**P**

Pace, C. R., 201
Pacific, University of the: and orientation, 130; School of International Studies at, 50
Pacific Lutheran University, and piecemeal change, 210
Pacific Rim, and reformed curriculum, 50
Paden, J., 171
Paine College, speaking at, 40
Palmer, P. J., 163
Panel on the General Professional Education of the Physician, 35
Pascarella, E. T., 200–201, 222, 230
Pedagogy. See Teaching
Perpich, R., 7
Perry, W. G., 185
Personal qualities, and content issues, 17
Peters, T. J., 225
Phidias, 3
Phillips, S. R., 104
Planning, strategic, 226–228
Plato, 3, 185
Pluralism. See Cultural diversity
Political correctness: issues of, 20; and student diversity, 198–199
Pollack, R., 37–38
Positivism, logical, decline of, 191

Professional studies, liberal arts in, 35–36
Project on the Status and Education of Women, 197
Purpel, D., 213

**Q**

Quality: concepts of, 11–12; as educational benefit, 125–127
Quehl, G. A., 104

**R**

Raphael, 3
Ravitch, D., 20
Reagan administration, 27
Reed College: leadership at, 169; learning environment at, 203
Reform of general education: and administrative bias, 142–144; analysis of trends in, 32–64; aspects of, 1–64; assessing impacts of, 58–60, 65–146, 211–212, 223–224, 230–232; background on, 32–33; comprehensive, 60–63; comprehensive or piecemeal, 89–95; conclusions on, 63–64, 98–99; consequences of, 75–83; continuing spirit of, 213–216; and curricular issues, 3–31; of curriculum, 33–60; educational benefits of, 121–146; and faculty development, 100–120; future trends in, 215–216; human face of, 118–119; impetus for, 209; institutional differences in, 96–98; motivation for further, 216–219; negative impact of, 81–82; scope and nature of, 67–99; and self-interest, 144–146, 216–219; significance of, 83–89; steps in, 178, 208–213; for student learning and development, 176–205; and student values, 188–192; summary of, 206–208; sustaining, 147–233

Requirements: curricular, 41–43; educational benefits of, 136
Residence halls, impact of, 128, 130–131
Rivlin, A. M., 9–10
Roanoke College: core courses at, 36; faculty development at, 80; trustee leadership at, 171–172
Roberts, A. O., 163
Rudolph, F., 12, 155
Rutherford, E., 37

**S**

St. Andrews Presbyterian College, moral reflection at, 56
St. Benedict, College of, faculty training at, 159
St. John's College, great books at, 152
St. Joseph's College, core course on Mexico at, 50
St. Mary's College of Maryland, standards at, 42
St. Michael's College, focus on Japan at, 50
St. Olaf College, Paracollege at, 55
St. Scholastica College, faculty development at, 119–120
St. Thomas, University of, curriculum review at, 210
San Diego, University of, global studies at, 50
San Jose State University: and cultural diversity, 51; faculty committees at, 169
Sandin, R. T., 192
Sarah Lawrence College, student-centered program at, 152
Schaefer, W. D., 168
Schlesinger, A., Jr., 24
Schuh, J. H., 202–203
Schuster, J. H., 107, 157
Sciences, curriculum reform in, 36–38
Searle, J., 213
Seldin, P., 170
Senior year, curriculum for, 47–48

Seton Hill College: comprehensive change at, 61; freshman year at, 47

Shakespeare, W., 3

Siegel, M. E., 102, 113

Singapore, competition by, 6

Singer, J. D., 183

Skills: across-the-curriculum approaches for, 73; and active learning, 85; and content issues, 16–17; curriculum reform for, 38–41

Smith, B. L., 54

Smith, D. H., 191

Smith, J., 52

Smith, P., 213

Smith, V., 26, 223

Snyder, B. R., 67

Socrates, 3

Sonoma State University, subcollege at, 154

Sosa, J. A., 154

South Carolina, University of, freshman seminars at, 45–46

Southeast Asia, disputes in, 6

Southeast Missouri State University, co-curriculum at, 201–202

Southern Illinois University at Edwardsville, general education through all years at, 58

Southwest Texas State University, freshman seminars at, 46

Spelman college, and student diversity, 194

Staff, academic and student affairs, 128–129, 131–133, 139, 179, 205, 222–223

Standards, and curriculum reform, 41–43

Stanford University: teacher-scholars at, 162–163; Western civilization course at, 21

States: assessment by, 58; and competition, 7; curriculum change across, 41; standards in, 42–43

Steinman, E., 75

Stevens, R., 54, 230–231

Strategic planning, for supportive academic culture, 226–228

Student services: and educational benefits, 128–133; and size of change, 91, 93; staff for, and academic staff, 128–129, 131–133, 139, 179, 205, 222–223

Students: aspects of educational benefits for, 121–146; aspects of learning and development by, 176–205; attitudes of, 123–124, 139–140; background on, 121–124; challenge and support for, 186; co-curriculum for, 199–204; conclusions on, 141–142, 144, 204–205; correlates of gains for, 133–141; developmental stages of, 184–186; diversity of, 193–199; educational needs of, 176–181; estimated educational value to, 124–133; faculty interactions with, 200; future agenda for, 221–222; involvement of, 122–123, 177, 201; learning connected with lives of, 187–188; learning styles of, 186–187; minority, 42–43, 193, 198; motivation of, 183–184; and personal-emotional aspects, 181–188; self-interest of, 144–145, 216–217; support mechanisms for, 197–198; values of, 188–192

Study skills and tutoring, impact of, 128, 129

Susquehanna College, freshman and senior seminars at, 48

Swarthmore College, honors program at, 152

Syracuse University: comprehensive change at, 61; science courses at, 38; teaching at, 163

**T**

Tarule, J. M., 186–187

Task Force on the Core Curriculum, 14

Task Force on the Future of
Journalism and Mass
Communication Education, 35
Task Force on the Undergraduate
Experience, 48
Task Group on General Education,
13–14, 17
Teaching: as intellectual challenge,
163; personal-emotional aspects
of, 181–188; quality of, 180–181;
and scholarship, 162–163; and
student diversity, 197; valuing,
160–165
Tennessee at Knoxville, University
of: assessment at, 60; and
cultural diversity, 51
Terenzini, P. T., 200–201, 222, 230
Texas, standards in, 42
Texas Lutheran College, faculty
committees at, 169
Thailand, competition by, 6
Title III grant, 61, 105
Title VI grant, 105
Tobias, S., 173
Toombs, W., 71, 92
Treisman, P. U., 198
Trenton State College, and
piecemeal change, 210
Trilling, L., 102–103, 213
Trustees, leadership by, 171–172
Tussman, J., 231–232
Twin Cities Campus Task Force on
Liberal Education, 228

**U**

Union of Soviet Socialist Republics:
change in, 27, 49; relations with,
5–6
United Kingdom: and reformed
curriculum, 231; and traditional
curriculum, 4, 15
U.S. Department of Education, 61
Universities. *See* Colleges and
universities
Utah Valley Community College,
integration of knowledge at, 53

**V**

Values, academic, 158–159;
education in, 190–192;
institutional, and general
education, 78–79; and integrity,
233; student, 188–192. *See also*
Moral reflection
Vision, for supportive academic
culture, 225–226
Voltaire, 3

**W**

Wabash College, integration of
knowledge at, 52–53
Walton, M., 225
Wasescha, A., 160
Washington College, computing at,
40
Waterman, R. H., 225
Watson, J. D., 38
Wee, D., 210
Wegner, C., 18
Weingartner, R., 18
Western Civilization courses, issues
of, 19–21
Western Maryland College, global
studies at, 49
Western Washington State
University, subcollege at,
153–154
Wheaton College, Center for Work
and Learning at, 48
Wheeler, D. W., 107
Whitt, E. J., 202–203
Whittier College: integration of
knowledge at, 53; writing at, 39
Whitworth College, writing at, 39
Willett, J. B., 183
William Jewell College, writing at,
39
Wilmington College, curriculum
review at, 210
Wilshire, B., 213
Wisconsin, University of,
Experimental College of, 153
Women: learning styles of, 186–

187; and student diversity, 193,
194–195, 196–197
Wright State University, strategic
planning at, 227
Writing: across the curriculum, 73;
skill development in, 38–40

**Z**

Zeller, W., 201
Zemsky, R., 22
Zuckerman, M. B., 6–7